ASHU DUTT holds an M.B.A. from Bernard M. Baruch College, City University of New York, New York and has held several key positions at top tier investment and corporate firms around the world. It was his international exposure that sparked the realization about the universal applicability of Indian wisdom for modern business and governance practices.

Ashu is the author of numerous best selling finance books and has anchored some of India's marquee programs on financial markets, including for CNBC TV 18, NDTV and Bloomberg. He can be reached at ashu@ ashudutt.com

ANAV DUTT is the recipient of the Asian Institute of Finance 2015 Award for the "Best Original Paper on Finance" for his paper on "The Psychological Impact of Losses on the Future Performance of Futures & Options Traders." He is also the recipient of the School Alumni Network's 2016 Citation for Excellence in English Literature.

Anav has worked on two books as a co-author with Ashu Dutt and is completing his first novel.

Other Financial Books
by Ashu Dutt

~

14 Wealth-Building Secrets of Value Investing

~

15 Easy Steps to Mastering Technical Charts

~

22 Stock Market Trading Secrets

~

36 Strategies for Striking it Rich in Commodity Trading

~

How to Make a Fortune in Futures and Options

~

Trading the Markets for a Living

~

Niti: Timeless Indian Wisdom on Business Success, Wealth and Power

The Beanstalk Does Grow to the SKY

How to Make a Fortune through Multibaggers

ASHU DUTT
~
ANAV DUTT

www.visionbooksindia.com

www.visionbooksindia.com

Disclaimer

The author and the publisher disclaim all legal or other responsibilities for any losses which investors may suffer by investing or trading using the methods described in this book. Readers are advised to seek professional guidance before making any specific investments.

A Vision Books Original

ISBN 10: 93-86268-07-8
ISBN 13: 978-93-86268-07-5

First Published in 2017 by
Vision Books Pvt. Ltd.
(Incorporating Orient Paperbacks and CARING imprints)
24 Feroze Gandhi Road, Lajpat Nagar 3
New Delhi 110024, India.
Phone: (+91-11) 2984 0821 / 22
email: visionbooks@gmail.com

Printed at
Anand Sons
C-88 Ganesh Nagar, Pandav Nagar Complex
Delhi 110092, India.

Dedication

~

To my dear daughter,
Arshiya Dutt.

Contents

~

Introduction: Decoding the Secret World of Multibaggers 17

- Multibagger investing is different in Asia 20
- Why reading US books and authors on investing does not work in Asia 21

1. Multibagger Axioms 23

- The timing of your buying and selling is critical 24
- Re-rating of the market reduces investing risk 25
- Anticipate the flow of money 26
- You must limit your losses 26
- Multibagger fundamentals are not what you think they are 27
- Stock prices may drop, rise, or rise exponentially on the same fundamentals 28
- Time of least interest in the market is the best time to buy 29
- Defy consensus at the extremes 30
- Expertise in fundamentals plus psychology plus technicals is a pre-requisite for picking multibaggers 31
- Big money comes in short bursts 32
- Uncertainty takes over if you think too far ahead 33
- Don't rely on past data 34
- If you feel comfortable, you are not trying hard enough 34
- Value is what the market attaches to a stock 35
- Don't diversify 36
- Stock prices are based on expectations 37
- Invest because there is a reason that stock will be a multibagger 37

2. Build Your Multibagger Edge 39

- What is an edge? 39
- Keep a record of your investment decisions 41
- Understand who you are up against 43
- Foster independent thinking 43
- Find an investment theme which the market believes will change the world 44
- Avoid narrative investment 45
- Lose to win, or make mistakes and learn from them 45
- Keep your multibagger portfolio separated from regular investing 46
- Focus on re-rating candidates 46
- Skip Warren Buffett style investing for multibaggers 47
- Keep your strategies and stock picks to yourself 48
- Read financial history — that is your trump card in the markets 48
- Disregard the noise 49
- Buy the stock before the price setters do 49
- Don't be emotional about losses 50
- Don't make decisions based on your most recent memory 50
- No single multibagger should exceed 20% of your portfolio 51
- First test your theory 51
- Don't let media do the stock picking for you 52
- Continuously test your multibagger investment process 52
- Unlearning everything you know about investing 53
- Focus on the methodology 54
- Find out why stocks didn't turn multibaggers 55
- Dry run for at least one year 55
- Develop second level thinking 56
- Develop a process for identifying multibaggers 56
- Deconstruct ideology, construct discipline 57
- You have an edge only till a few investors are investing in the stock 57
- Work on developing a multibagger attitude 58
- There's no substitute for experience 58
- Figuring out the odds 59
- Choosing a style 59

3. Multibagger Investing Myths 61

- Myth: Long holding period is beneficial 61

- Myth: Multibaggers will be found by following market gurus 61
- Myth: Diversified portfolio is the way to go 62
- Myth: Technology and 24-hour financial news give a competitive edge 62
- Myth: Investors know when to buy and sell stocks 64
- Myth: Buy and hold strategy leads to multibaggers 64
- Myth: Risk and reward have an absolute correlation 65
- Myth: A strong economy is good for stocks 66
- Myth: Markets are efficient 67
- Myth: Investing in low PE stocks is the way to find multibaggers 68
- Myth: Buy low and sell higher 68
- Myth: Knowledge of nuances of sectors and stocks may lead you to multibaggers 69
- Myth: Markets change and so does human behaviour 69
- Myth: It is easy to make money in the markets 70
- Myth: Invest over the long term for multibaggers 70
- Myth: Buy stocks for the long term 71
- Myth: Fundamental analysis is essential for multibagger investing 72
- Myth: Markets are rational 72
- Myth: Anyone can have a lucky streak and make money 73

4. Beware these Traps 74

- Buying stocks as products on discounts during a sale 74
- Trying to find multibaggers all the time 75
- Listening to business founders and managements 75
- Buying a stock because its "intrinsic value is low" 76
- Looking for confirmation of your beliefs instead of dissent 76
- Selling winners and holding losers 77
- Wasting time in meaningless financial calculations 78
- Basing decisions on recent rather than relevant information 78
- Preconceived notions of overvaluation based on the past 79
- Falling for the sales pitch 79
- Expecting a multibagger to pay for other things 80
- Investment errors caused by two dimensional information 80
- Don't be trapped by storytelling 81
- Be careful about correlated multibaggers 81

5. Principles of Multibagger Investing 86

- Understanding boom and bust cycles 86
- Understanding cycles and trends 86
- Investing in cycles and trends requires different techniques and produces multibaggers of different magnitude 87
- The point of reversal is when IPOs flood the market 88
- Investing with asymmetrical information 89
- A stock's price rests on consensus 90
- Learning to take losses 91
- Why we pick wrong stocks 91
- Don't sell out too soon 92
- Market behaviour is cyclical 92
- Exit if the crowd does not follow you in 93
- A few stocks allow the focus you need 93
- Correlation is not what we think it is 94
- Multibagger stocks have fat tails 94
- Superior returns are temporary 95
- You are in the business of absolute returns 95
- No single investment defines your success 96
- You must have a significant position size 96
- The rules of engagement 97
- Don't confuse winning streaks with good decision making 97
- How to value a stock 97
- IPOs will rarely be multibaggers 98
- All buyers and sellers of stocks are not value investors 99
- You don't have to wait for years for stock to turn into a multibagger 99
- Don't confuse economic growth with stock price rise 100
- Don't confuse revenue growth with operating cash flows 100
- Avoid anchor effect investing 100
- Invest in tandem with institutional investors 101
- The opportunity must be overwhelming 101
- Pick stocks in which institutional investors may get interested 102
- Pick stocks where supply takes time to adjust to demand 102
- Buy at points of extreme pessimism 103
- Look for new sectors where there are fewer listed stocks 103
- Selling principles 104
- ETF inflows portend multibaggers 104
- Stocks that will not turn into multibaggers 104

- Investment manias are your chance to make big money 105
- Sailing against the wind 106
- Look out for the unexpected 106
- It's the cycle which produces the opportunity 107
- Anticipate the anticipations of others 107
- You are your own best investment guru 108
- Managements make companies 109
- Leveraging irrationality 110
- Multibagger opportunities disappear when others catch on 110
- Risk and return are not completely correlated 111
- Multibagger opportunities comes up more frequently than we think 112

6. Psychology of Multibagger Investing 113

- Why we are unable to participate in bull markets 113
- Opinions, beliefs and ideologies 114
- Your market psychology has to be similar to that of a Samurai's 115
- Human behaviour is the single biggest driver of prices 115
- Accept that you are fallible 115
- Human behaviour doesn't change, whatever else might 116
- Guard against overconfidence in your investing decisions 117
- Take a break if you have a losing streak 117
- The importance of feedback loops on stock prices 118
- Logical reasoning does not work in multibagger investing 119
- Mistakes multibagger investors make 120
- Understanding the behaviour of crowds 121
- If you cannot lose, you will not win 122
- Don't let your mood decide your stocks 122
- Losses have serious psychological consequences 123
- Don't stick to ideology 123
- Rejoice in failure — but only if it improves your stock picking abilities 124
- The courage to act on your beliefs 124
- Being the lone ranger 125
- Acceptance of fallibility / paranoia 126

7. Multibagger Secrets Market Insiders Won't Tell You 127

- Getting rich is easy — it is the road less travelled 127

- Define your style 128
- High level of speculative activity is good for multibaggers 128
- Take advantage of the market's limited memory 129
- Put concentrated diversification to work 129
- Follow Warren Buffett's investment philosophy only if you have his money or clout 130
- A broker is a salesman of stock. And a salesman never says, "Don't buy what I have" 130
- A great economy or sector does not mean the stock is great 131
- In multibagger investing, individual investors have a distinct advantage over institutional investors 131
- Buy when investors are on their pain thresholds 132
- Take advantage of the human thinking process 133
- Picking multibaggers when price discovery is yet to happen 133
- If everyone is making money, it may not last for long 134
- Focus on the flow of money 134
- Multibagger opportunities 135
- Multibaggers in options 135
- Multibaggers need the appropriate environment 135
- Be prepared for clustered multibagger opportunities 136
- You cannot buy stocks that will be multibaggers in the long term 136
- A multibagger will start to stagnate at some point 138
- Invest when the market is not able to put a price on a stock 138
- Small changes create big multibaggers 139
- Trial and error investing 139
- The market must eventually agree with your assessment 140
- Historical data is little guide to a stock's future price 140
- Change your views to fit the market's dynamics 141
- Look for loss of investor diversity 141
- Why future projections of earnings don't translate into multibaggers 142
- You can rely only on yourself to find a multibagger 142
- Identify an illogical price and why it may correct 143
- How to protect your multibaggers 144
- The normal can change forever 144
- Multibaggers are like diamonds — what is the real value of a diamond? 145
- You don't invest in stocks, you invest in risk 145
- There is no right price in a discontinuous market 146

- Look for multibaggers when rational investors have exhausted their patience 146
- Multibagger opportunities do not depend on the quality of a stock 147
- Multibagger stocks are like rockets 148
- Even if you have to pay a higher price, wait for the move to begin 148
- Averaging never works 149
- After a bubble, interest will shift to another investment class or group of stocks 149
- Look for the mispriced bet 150
- How long has a bull or bear market been around? 150
- Multibagger buying secrets 151
- Watch for deception in the information you are relying on 151
- Advantages of being a multibagger trader 152
- Watch the flow of money to mutual funds 152
- Keep an eye on low float and low capitalization stocks 153
- IPO stocks will rarely turn into multibaggers 153
- Blue chip and index stocks are rarely multibaggers 154
- Multibagger investing is context based 154
- The market's cycles 155
- The listed stock fallacy 156
- There are times when you should not think rationally 156
- Wait for everyone to turn a believer before you sell or buy 157
- If you feel the excitement, it may not be time for multibaggers 158
- Multibagger investing is akin to a leopard hunting 158
- Don't stop listening to divergent views 159
- Don't be influenced by your current investments in picking the next multibagger 159
- Multibagger opportunities abound at the start of a bull cycle 160
- A cheap stock may fall even further 160
- Why do stocks continue to rise when they seem expensive? 161
- Low priced stocks turn into multibaggers in mid- and small-cap rallies 162
- The bull market cycle 162
- Blue chip, safe and popular stocks rarely make multibaggers 163
- A frenzied bull market turns into a Ponzi scheme towards its end 164
- There is no cheap and expensive stock because there is no mean or bell curve in a stock's price 165

- Correlation between a business and its stock price 166
- How multibagger stocks emerge and sustain themselves 167
- Why options work for finding multibaggers 167
- The dawn of a new era or new asset class is ideal breeding ground for multibaggers 168
- Small in size does not mean small in returns 169
- The easiest time to find multibaggers 169
- Stocks can fall way lower than you think 170

8. Multibagger Investing Rules 171

- Stay invested in a winning stock 171
- Opportunities arise when investors are focused elsewhere 172
- Limit your losses 172
- Mastery of technical charts is a must 173
- You must be liquid when you expect multibagger opportunities 175
- If you are convinced, your investment must be of a significant size 175
- Wait for the easy kills 176
- How to invest at the lowest risk 176
- Exit when everyone notices a problem with a stock's price 177
- There is safety when the entire market moves 178
- Don't confuse multibagger investing with value investing 178
- Pick stocks that turn into multibaggers in the shortest time 179
- Dealing with the wealth created by multibaggers 179
- Stocks near their lows don't become multibaggers 180
- Don't look for reasons when a stock begins to stall 181
- How do you make money being right only 10% to 20% of the time 181
- Staying in the proper frame of mind 181
- There are no multibaggers to be found in stagnant markets 182
- Multibagger investing rules 182

9. Types of Multibaggers 184

- Multibagger types 184
- Supply lag time multibaggers 184
- Multibaggers from a structural shift in demand caused by regulations, lowering of price points, etc. 185
- A company with a brand that has pricing power 185

- Risk free multibaggers 185
- Foreign buying into a local market 186
- Multibaggers based on the "mass psychology of a large number of ignorant individuals" 186
- Forced selling opportunity 187
- Dodo multibaggers 187
- Wave or bubble multibaggers 187
- Scarcity premium multibaggers 187
- Trading multibaggers 188
- Conventional multibaggers 188
- Valuation multibaggers 189
- Commodity multibaggers 189
- Penny stock multibaggers 190
- The mania multibaggers 190
- "New era" or "new asset class" multibaggers 191
- The crash multibagger 192
- The liquidity squeeze multibagger 192
- Can trading give multibaggers? 194
- Asset class multibaggers 195
- The low float multibagger 195
- Low volume / low float stocks in a changing economic trend 196
- The "boys club" multibagger 196
- Multibaggers in down and out stocks in a consolidating industry / M&A 196
- Stocks that will never become multibaggers 197

10. Strategies for Multibagger Investing 198

- Puts for M&As 198
- Check the level of pledging 200
- Multibaggers in long term commodity cycles 200
- Multibaggers are found in the extremes 201
- Sell as the plane takes off 201
- The greatest returns lie in the worst markets 202
- Multibaggers in a liquidity squeeze and a bubble 203
- Excessive leverage is the real cause of market falls 204
- Multibaggers for a living 205
- If you cannot comprehend it, skip it 206
- Why you should not buy in a falling market 207
- In a bear market, buy penny stocks 208

- Supply Squeeze 208
- Multibagger investment styles 209
- Trade money, not markets 210
- Special situation investing strategy 211
- Don't buy falling stocks 211
- Stocks waiting to become multibaggers 212
- Multibaggers through options 212
- Cheap is not what you think it is 213
- When multibaggers are available 214
- What not to do 215
- Managing risk 215
- Penny stock multibagger strategy 216
- Bull market momentum buying 217
- A few good stocks is all you need 217
- Opportunities in crappy stocks 218
- Who will buy from you? 218
- Be sceptical of management claims 220
- Multibagger vs multibagger 220
- Playing the increase in capitalization 221
- Cause and effect don't work for multibaggers 221
- Don't overrate your ability to comprehend the markets 222
- Making a living with multibaggers 222
- The market phase determines your multibagger investing strategy 224
- When to exit a multibagger 225
- Don't count forever on a winning strategy 225
- Multibaggers in manipulated stocks 226
- How to pick a multibagger 226
- Scarcity premium provides one of the best multibagger opportunities 228
- Speculative markets are required to turn stocks into multibaggers 230
- Look for sectors that investors are treating like a step child 230

11. The Multibagger Quiz: Test Your Multibagger Expertise 232

- Answers to the Multibagger Quiz 253

Introduction

~

Decoding the Secret World of Multibaggers

"The gods perceive things in the future, ordinary people things in the present, but the wise perceive things about to happen. In their intense meditation, the hidden sound of things approaching reaches them and they listen reverently while in the street outside the people hear nothing at all."

– Philostratus, Ancient Greek Poet

IF MULTIBAGGERS WERE THERE FOR THE PICKING, they wouldn't be multibaggers. By definition, then, the investment style required to pick multibaggers has to be different. The way we think and perceive information, news and other data about stocks needs to be both deeper and counter-intuitive to human nature. We need to find opportunity where others find risk, and see risk where others find comfort.

Investing in stocks has fascinated and confounded investors for centuries. Their supposedly wild nature has brought some of the greatest investors to their knees, in many instances to abject poverty, by the end of their lives. They have also created massive wealth for those who many of us would consider intellectual buffoons. So, is there some method to investing, or is it as random as randomness itself? The answer may not lie in the markets at all. It may lie deep in our individual psyche, temperament and behavioural patterns.

Contrary to popular belief, you don't need to be a accountant, a market guru, or an MBA in finance, or have an engineering degree for multibagger investing. If that were the case, accountants — since they can read financials, librarians — since they have access to all the financial history, or MBAs in finance would have been the best multibagger investors.

Contrary to popular opinion, and the liberal use of logic and facts to explain them, the markets have little to do with logic or facts. Logic and facts are, in most cases, overruled by human emotions and dreams. The same logic and facts make one person sell, and another buy the same stock at the same price.

In fact, there is no magic whatsoever in creating unbelievable wealth from stocks. For now, just take my word for it. I hope to convince you by the time you finish reading this book.

Multibagger investing requires a mastery over two broad areas. The first relates to elevating your knowledge and thinking to the level of legendary market gurus. Just as you cannot be a doctor before you complete an MBBS and an internship at a hospital, you cannot hope to pick multibaggers without a mastery of how markets work.

This part is much harder than it looks. The usual materials we rely on to invest are the very reasons we encounter investment failure and losses. Relying on financial data, reading or watching financial media, listening to all kinds of market gurus, or feeling optimistic of about stocks, seeking confirmation from others after you have picked a stock, are some of the common investment mistakes we make. Much of what you hear about markets and stocks are carefully cultivated myths and sales pitches to entice you into buying something or the other. Much of what you know about markets from public sources like financial TV and literature will cause you to lose money rather than make any.

To start with, we may have to unlearn a lot of what we know about value investing. For multibagger investing, value is not a scientific concept but a contextual concept that can change with the context and stage of the market. Multibagger investing is also contextual.

Markets fall and rise because of two sets of flows. The flow of money into stocks, and the flow of money out of stocks. For the most part the flow of money in and out of stocks is more or less balanced and so the movement of stock prices and indices is within a range. From time to time, the flow of money in and out of stocks becomes unbalanced, or one-sided, in that either the outflow outstrips the inflow, or the inflow outstrips the outflow. When the outflow of money dwarfs the inflow, multibaggers are born. That could be in a bear market, or in a temporary credit freeze. It could also be when disinterest in a sector reaches rock bottom. But don't confuse temporary investor disinterest in a sector as fundamental and structural problems that could lead to a long term downward fall in the sector. The two situations are very different.

When outflows far exceed inflows into stocks, or a sector, or when disinterest in a sector is at an all time low, that by definition is a time when most investors and traders either don't have the money, the gumption, the stomach, or the foresight to buy stocks. These are precisely the times when multibaggers are born. So, by definition, multibaggers are available only under certain market condition and because these are times when you won't find others to confirm your beliefs, at such times you have to act alone and on your own convictions. Extreme power laws apply in multibagger investing. It is on the gloom and losses of others that you pick up stocks which are poised to become multibaggers.

From time to time, a news event or change in policy sends most investors in one direction. At other times, excesses either in an industry or a stock take time to explode. So while a stock's price takes time to appreciate, its fall can be swift if investors decide to exit. But exits driven by real and structural changes in the business or outlook for a stock must be differentiated from fall in stock prices driven by a credit freeze or need for cash by investors.

So what drives stocks? It may not be the information, the growth prospects or the quarterly results that are key to a stock's performance. They provide the foundation but they are in themselves not the key to a stock's moves.

Multibagger investing requires you to develop an ability to understand the way markets really work — as opposed to how they should work.

Multibagger investing also requires you to develop a personal edge. Even after finishing an MBBS, few doctors acquire fame. The latter has more to do with an individual edge that a doctor cultivates. Mutlibagger investing requires you to cultivate just such an edge. An edge built on discipline, right temperament and a distinctive stock picking style that is unaffected by crowd behaviour. Such an edge takes at least 5 to 10 years to build. During this journey, you will lose often but you have to learn to lose small amounts in order to acquire fortune-making multibagging skills.

Trial and error, and losses, are the only way for genius and greatness to emerge. It is the law of nature. One out of a million sperm cells finds an egg to ovulate. Millions of our brain cells are destroyed before we develop cognitive skills. So, too, multibaggers must necessarily be found in markets where millions are losing money.

While the traditional way to pick multibaggers is to buy at times of a credit freeze — namely at times when lack of money makes stock sellers sell at any price — or at extreme bear markets, or points of extreme market pessimism, multibagger investing does not have to be limited to such markets. It can be done in bull markets as well, or in futures and options markets though there it comes with much higher risk and fewer chances of a stock turning into a multibagger.

You must build a knowledge base from where to learn, improve and develop your edge. You should keep a diary to record both your learnings and also how your stock picks actually turned out *vis-à-vis* your expectations. If you do this for a few years, you will be amazed by the improvement in your investment performance. You will reach a stage where you can see a multibagger staring at you.

Almost nothing that you are told or know, about stocks or investing works in multibagger investing. You have to start with reorienting your entire approach about how you perceive markets and pick stocks.

Multibagger investing is different in Asia

There are a number of books on value investing or multibagger investing written for US audiences. You may have tried to implement some of those strategies in Asia. Chances are you may have not ended up with multibaggers.

Investing in Asian stocks requires a different set of tools and skill sets for the following reasons:

- In Asia, promoters exercise a disproportionate amount of influence on their companies. Many companies are run like family concerns. No one talks of a company as an entity but as owned by some "tycoon" or the other.
- There are hardly any hostile M&As in much of Asia, and it becomes impossible to determine what the market is ready to pay for a stock, or control, of a company.
- Minority shareholders have little ability or influence, and are rarely a factor in a company's decision making process.
- Accounting standards are twisted and turned to fit whatever the company wants. This creates financial data of dubious quality.
- When Asian companies make enough money, they have a tendency of finding a way to spending it wastefully, use it for unrelated activities, or put it to use for founders/promoters rather than sharing it with its shareholders, including minority shareholders.
- The concept of the company being a trust for shareholders and that the founders are its custodians is absent in most Asian companies. This makes

stock picking a challenge, and buy and hold is not an ideal strategy. Investors have often to flow with the rise and exit when the stock stops rising.
- Entrepreneurs think the company as their personal business and minority shareholders as a source of capital.
- Companies are used as conduits to park owner assets, and remove them, when required without a proportionate payment to individual shareholders.
- In Asia, institutional investors are typically passive and rarely force companies to do the right thing.
- Your only hope is that you ride the wave. If you are going against it, you don't stand a chance.

Why reading US books and authors on investing does not work in Asia

Relying on US books, authors and market gurus to invest in Asia can take your money right into the garbage can. Here are some key differences between US and Asian stock markets:

- No buy and hold: Asian investors have a trading mindset driven by decades and, sometimes, centuries, of uncertainty. They want to make a quick buck.
- Fewer global brands: US markets have hundreds of global brands and a stock can rise multiple times as the US company expands globally. US companies get to enjoy the benefits of a rise in wealth just about anywhere in the world.
- The investing culture is relatively new in Asia, and there is little empirical material to rely on. Sales pitch, tips, and listening to others dominate investing styles.
- Retail's influence on the market's movement far outstrips institutional influence. Even the institutions that invest depend heavily on retail money.
- Asian countries have limited institutional depth in terms of number of institutional investors and their diversity.
- The role of government is often overriding. Government policy changes due to political whims create havoc for stock prices. Sudden changes in regulations can even kill businesses overnight.
- The interference with markets, such as closing down markets on extreme volatility, or banning futures and options, or suspension of stocks, causes

physical interruptions in market forces. Local regulators tend to suspend markets if there is a demand supply imbalance. Such circuit rules can lock you out of gains.

- The overriding role of company founders and promoters: Most Asian founders consider listed companies their family property and its wealth their personal fortune to be dealt with as they please.
- Passive institutional investors and the role of local pension funds in "permanent hold" of stocks: Institutional investors tend to tow the line of the owners/promoters and rarely turn active, when companies do things harmful to minority investors.
- Lack of contrarian views: no one wants to take up a fight with the promoter or the government. The repercussions for anyone going against the company's owners, the government or vested interests can be so severe that there exist very few contrarian and activist investors.
- Lack of local intellectual capital which can give a real picture: financial media owned by foreign owners and a generally condescending attitude towards Asian markets and governments skew the real picture.
- Market manipulation is rampant: The lack of deterrent penalties for manipulating stocks and the lack of prosecution have kept market manipulation rampant.
- No one wants to make a hostile takeover, while friendly takeover is another name for backdoor deals. Without hostile takeovers, incompetent founders and promoters have no fear of being removed even when they run companies inefficiently.
- Markets are still looked upon by 90% of investors as a lottery for making a quick buck.
- Lack of quality fund managers and lack of thought diversity in fund managers makes for a different market behaviour.
- Too much reliance on the financial press: Asian investors have a tendency of hoping and wishing that someone will save them.
- Belief that stock markets are easy money: Stock markets require years of high level knowledge and experience. Investors are not in the habit of recording their experiences and building on their experiences.

1

~

Multibagger Axioms

"One with a hundred longs for a thousand, one with a thousand yearns for millions, one who lords over millions wants to rule a kingdom, the kings aim to gain Paradise itself."

– Panchtantra

BEFORE WE DISCUSS HOW TO FIND MULTIBAGGERS, let's get a low-down on how stock markets really work. Many of these market realities are unknown to investors fed on a regular dose of investing sales pitch which causes more harm than benefit.

Multibagger Investing is a game of odds, not right or wrong. Only 1 or 2 out of the 10 stocks you pick may have the potential to become a multibagger. As you gain more experience on what you got wrong, your odds of getting a multibagger may increase, but still only marginally. The market is a complex adaptive system and not given to replicating past actions or reasons for a stock's rise or fall. Approach the 5 to 10 stocks you select as your multibagger candidates with the twin goals of preserving your capital at all time, and letting profits run. Don't stay with any stock, no matter how well you think of it, if it falls more than 10% below your purchase price. Exit the stock if it falls more than 10% below your purchase price. You may have guessed right that the stock will turn into a multibagger, but you may have entered too early. Or the stock you picked has problems and issues not known to you, and the fall of 10% below your purchase price may indicate that you made a wrong call.

Multibagger opportunities will be there all the time, but the odds may be very different depending on the market.

You can either do "fish in the barrel" multibagger investing, or "fish in a pond" multibagger investing, or "fish in the sea" multibagger investing.

At times of a credit freeze when cash is at a premium, no price is too low for panicked sellers to exit. Either redemption pressure, or a need for cash can send stocks crashing way below anything to do with their business. This will create "fish in the barrel" investing scenarios.

It becomes that much more harder if you try to pick multibaggers when investors have begun to realize the value of being in a stock or sector.

The timing of your buying and selling is critical

"Reality is much more vicious . . . . First, it delivers the fatal bullet rather infrequently, like a revolver that would have hundreds, even thousands of chambers instead of six. After a few dozen tries, one forgets about the existence of a bullet, under a numbing false sense of security."

– Nassim Nicholas Taleb, *Fooled by Randomness*

All of life is being at the right place at the right time. The timing of your entry before money flows in, and of your exit before money flows out of the stock is the edge that will stand you out. But timing is more difficult that we think. Investors are hardwired to believe that timing is a bad idea or that they should invest regularly. This kind of investing does average out the high and low points in the stock markets but delivers only average returns. And it works best if you are investing in mutual funds, or buying index futures. It does not work for multibagger investing.

Multibagger investing is all about timing. But what is timing? It is not buying in the morning and exiting in the evening, nor buying today and exiting after a month. It is recognizing the opportunity to buy a stock, and then not being tempted to sell even when it has appreciated 5, 10 or 20 times.

A stock will rise 5, 10 or 20 times only because the market has not recognized its growth potential or because it is in a business whose potential is not understood by the market, or because it has been taken down 90% or 95% in price because other stocks have taken a similar hit.

That would necessarily require that you understand the potential of the stock before the market does, or you can see what will emerge in the business the stock is in and assess whether the stock is poised to take advantage of emerging opportunities. It will also require you to enter only when the stock is so far removed from its intrinsic value that it can move nowhere but up.

Timing is also critical for selling a multibagger. The temptation to take profits too early kills the multibagger and reduces it to a stock with strong returns. No one know how much a stock can appreciate when it begins its ascent. That will depend on how much more money flows into the stock. And the flow of money into a stock that catches the fancy of investors is literally unlimited and that means the stock can move up 5-fold, 10-fold or even 10-fold higher. So holding on to the stock till the pace of its rise slows down appreciably is required to get the best out of the multibagger.

The timing of your entry and exit is critical for consistent multibagger investing. A stock moves up only when money flows into it, and heads down when money flows out of it. All great investors are masters at getting the timing of entry and exit right. Yet even they get it wrong as many as 8 out of 10 times. But even 2 multibaggers obtained from great timing more than make up for small losses in 8 wrong calls. For the 8 out of 10 times your timing of entry does not match what happens to the stock price, you don't need to fight the market. You should accept it and sell the stock without waiting. Thus, while you got it wrong 8 out of 10 times, but the important thing is not to let your negative score get out of hand. The 2 stocks in which you got your entry right, will then more than make up for the relatively smaller losses in the others.

No matter how sound your reasoning, the winds of money have to be right to make your stock a multibagger. When the mood in the markets shifts, liquidity dries up — and without liquidity even the best stocks languish. And if the markets have moved away from their anchor valuations, it is then anyone's guess when the earlier trend will return. The same applies in reverse. If investors feel positive, there is no saying how high they could run up a stock or a market.

Anticipating the flow of money and the mood about a stock, a sector, or the market will help you find multibaggers at low risk.

Re-rating of the market reduces investing risk

Extreme optimism in the markets on the prospects of a country or a sector, or the valuations being paid for M&A deals, indicates the revaluation of a sector or market. Investing risk drops significantly in a market or sector which is consistently running north. The challenge for multibagger investors in such markets is to find stocks that will turn multibaggers in the shortest period of time.

For example, if a pharmaceutical company has been acquired at ten times the value of what similar sized listed companies are trading at, it may signal a revaluation of the entire sector and give you a multibagger or two.

Anticipate the flow of money

"A speculative merchant exercises no one regular, established, or well-known branch of business. He is a corn merchant this year, or tea merchant the year after. He enters into every trade when he foresees that it is likely to be more than commonly profitable, and he quits when he foresees that its profits are likely to return to the level of others."

– Adam Smith, *The Wealth of Nations*

The flow of money is one of the least focused features of how a stock turns into a multibagger. No amount of focus on PE ratios, earnings growth, or other traditional measures of value will get you anywhere close to finding multibaggers. These factors may be prerequisites, but by themselves are never enough to produce a multibagger. What turns a stock into a multibagger is the flow of money into a stock. And when the flow outstrips the availability of the stock, the stock's price can rise very fast.

What can cause the supply of stock to drop or disappear? The stock may either have low float, or the public shareholding may be low, or the stock may have moved into the hands of institutional investors. Now combine this with mutual funds getting too much money to invest, which they usually do when a stock or sector becomes mainstream, and the supply dries up.

If a stock's got the momentum, we don't need to concern ourselves much about the reasons for the momentum but simply ride it. Multibagger investing requires us to anticipate a stock's move early, and then go with the flow. Your single minded focus must be on finding the likely multibaggers.

You must limit your losses

"Predict? Yes. That's implied when you make a trade. Just don't stick to your predictions if the market tells you something different."

– Jason Leavitt

Look at multibaggers in terms of a portfolio and not in terms of a single stock. If you have a multibagger but the other stocks in your portfolio are losing value, the returns on your entire portfolio may be limited. Cutting stocks with losses is critical to maintain high returns on the entire portfolio. Make it a rule to get out of a stock if it falls 5% or 10%, no matter what you think about the company. To find one multibagger, you may have to buy ten stocks. Most of them will either not do well, or head into losses. Multibagger investing requires you to accept that you are fallible and that most of your investments will go wrong.

Multibagger fundamentals are not what you think they are

"No action can successful be If expended on the unworthy. As parakeets the stork cannot. Be made to speak, however taught."

– Hitopadesa

What we believe are fundamental prerequisites for investing are rarely the fundamentals required for picking multibaggers. Most of our fundamentals are picked up through public media or publicly available information. There is an inherent assumption that those providing us the information we consider fundamental, such as the promoters, companies, financial media, etc., do not alter or manipulate that information. Fake news is also now common enough.

Then, too, there is also a tendency to mistake opinion with facts. When someone says a PE ratio is high or low, or earnings are good and bad, it is an opinion and an opinion is nowhere near a universal truth. Not that factors like PE ratio or are of any value in identifying multibaggers, anyway.

Then there is the question of who you are getting the information from? Is it in someone's interest to give you information that is important to you? Or to them? Companies, promoters, financial media, etc., all have very different objectives than you do. Companies and promoters will present earnings, prospects and growth information in a way that benefits them. Financial media presents information that is the most juicy, not the most relevant for investing. That is why it becomes critical not to take any information either at face value or consider it fundamental. Otherwise, your starting point itself will be wrong.

The way you know a business is growing is because that's what promoters, companies and financial media tell you. You know only as much as you hear and see, and this may not be enough to translate into an increase in the stock's price. There is no way for you to know things that the insiders know, or don't want you to know. It is like a couple that looks picture perfect for years, and then suddenly heads for divorce. There are going to be many times when you think a company's growth will show up in the price but it does not. When that happens, you must exit the stock. There may be things you don't know, or things that are not public information. The management or the brokers may give a picture that helps them sell more stock but which may not reflect the real picture. If they want the stock to go up, they will "talk up" the company's prospects. If they want to buy out the company's stock, they will "talk down" the stock down try and get the lowest price.

That is why a stock's price does not necessarily rise even when you buy the stock on company-, media- and analyst-fed fundamentals.

What, then, are the relevant fundamentals for multibaggers? If a stock falls significantly (say 70% to 80%), either because of large scale redemptions by mutual funds, or a sudden credit squeeze in the markets you probably have a multibagger in place. Or, if a stock has been drifting for years at a 90-95% price drop from its highs, and the market is beginning to pick up, or the industry prospects have started to look up, you might have a multibagger at hand.

You can pick potential multibaggers using the above approaches, and the many more approaches you will find in this book, but keep in mind that there is no such thing as a sure-shot multibagger. You can improve or lower your odds of finding a multibagger, but it's never a sure-shot game.

Stock prices may drop, rise, or rise exponentially on the same fundamentals

"Those who seek to relate stock movements to the current statistics of business, or who ignore the strongly imaginative taint of stock operations, or who overlook the technical basis of advances and declines must meet with disaster, because their judgment is based upon the humdrum dimensions of facts and figures in a game which is actually played in a third dimension of the emotions and a fourth dimension of dreams."

– Barton Biggs

One of the biggest fallacies of investing, and one that ensures that most investors never make money let alone find multibaggers, is the belief that investing is like solving some neat mathematics or physics problem. That when you apply the right formula, you will get an exact solution. Nothing could be farther from the truth. Investing is like studying philosophy where your argument may lead to an answer but also create many more questions. You cannot invest without keeping the market context in mind. Investing has to adjust to bull and bear markets, high liquidity and low liquidity environments, high economic and low economic growth environments, and many other factors. And even if you have picked a multibagger using one set of rules, don't assume that the same rules will work the next time. That is why you should never rely on brokerage research reports. They are plain wrong and try to create an impression that there is a predetermined formula based on which they have arrived at a target price.

There are times the public and institutional investors will take a fancy to a stock, a sector or the market. Whatever the reasons, large amounts of money will flow in that direction. The same stock may fall, rise, or rise exponentially, under the same set of fundamentals depending on the level of interest and money flow into the stock.

The weight and number of the stock's buyers has to overwhelm the sellers of the stock for a stock to turn into a multibagger. This, then, is what you need to become a master at anticipating — in which stocks will the inflow of money overwhelm the outflow. You must anticipate if a vast majority of investors will start liking a particular stock. A stock can be priced as low as possible but without others ready to put money into it, it will be no multibagger.

The way we are generally told to buy value stocks is to buy stocks that are trading at low PEs or have low levels of investor interest. But the reason they have low levels of interest is because no one is interested in them, or the supply of the stock is far greater than its demand. That kind of stock is not going to get you a multibagger, and you may be stuck with a dud for a very long time.

Time of least interest in the market is the best time to buy

"The opinions and beliefs of crowds are specially propagated by contagion, but never by reasoning."

– Gustav Lebon

The least risky time for a multibagger investing is when the market itself is at a point of least popularity. There are riskier starting points, such as a point of least popularity in the sector or the stock. When, however, you buy a quality stock because there is disinterest in the market as a whole, the stock is down only because no one is ready to put money into the market. That drives down all stocks, irrespective of whether they are race horses or donkeys. If you pick race horses at such a stage, it is only a question of time before you will have a multibaggers.

Defy consensus at the extremes

"He who lives by the crystal ball soon learns to eat ground glass."

– Edgar R. Fiedler

Consensus forms only after a stock has completed most of its run. Stocks follow the same theory of early adopters and late adopters. Multibagger investors are usually early adopters, while the majority joins when a fashion or trend has already become mainstream. But there are also times where the crowd or majority does not follow early adopters into a stock. If a stock does not do what you expect it to do, and falls around 10% from your purchase price, your assumptions may be wrong. Or, you may have entered the stock too early. Or, there maybe something more chronic and troubled about the stock than you are aware of. Whatever the reason, if your multibagger pick is not doing what you expected, keeping your losses in check is a very important part of the multibagger investing process.

Develop a contrarian view of markets, sectors and stocks from angles which the large majority of markets are not looking at, and which mainstream financial media has no current interest in. A good starting point for this kind of contrarian investing are periods of low interest in markets, a flight of foreign capital, or a sector beginning to emerge from a down cycle.

Expertise in fundamentals plus psychology plus technicals is a pre-requisite for picking multibaggers

"Price movements only have meaning in the context of the fundamental landscape. To use a sailing analogy, the wind matters, but the tide matters, too. If you don't know what the tide is, and you plan everything just based on the wind, you are going to end up crashing into the rocks. You need to pay attention to both to make sense of the picture."

– Colm O'Shea

There is a misconception that you must be a value investor to pick multibaggers. Multibagger investing requires you to develop an expertise not only in knowing which fundamentals matter but also in what the stock's technicals indicate and, above all, in your psychological make up. Even more important is the interplay of fundamentals, technicals and psychology in picking multibaggers. It is like an orchestra. Great music is produced by several musical instruments and their masters coming together in symphony.

While the right fundamentals read correctly in the context of the prevailing stage of the market will help you identify a potential multibagger, you need technicals to tell you when the stock will begin to move and when it will gather the speed to appreciate multiple times. To use a train analogy, fundamentals may tell you the platform from which to board a train but may not tell you when the train leaves the station or when it will gather speed. Stocks can have value for years and never move in price, and when they do begin their ascent, the speed and swiftness of the rise can only be explained by technicals. Your psychology plays an overriding part in being able to see a stock turn into a multibagger. Most investors tend to get out of a stock way too soon. They get out when the stock still has a lot of juice left. You have to allow your profits to run the full course — and that requires practice and patience.

Big money comes in short bursts

"The way to build long term returns is through preservation of capital and home runs. You can be far more aggressive when you're making good profits."
– Stanley Druckenmiller

It is almost always true that the vast wealth of big investors has been made in short spurts of market mania. As much as fundamentals may be important, even more important is the anticipation that there is someone else out there who will be ready to pay higher prices.

While there are several factors that must come together for a market mania to occur, manias are most often caused by the revaluation of a country or a sector, or the excitement about a new technology. At such times, stocks can rise beyond your wildest imagination but the majority of players will not be part of the rise. Most investors freeze in their tracks and rather than running with the stocks, move away from these stocks and buy into cheaper stocks. This fatal flaw in reading fundamentals leads to the vast majority missing the boat. If you see signs of a market mania, stick to the market or the sector where the mania is manifesting itself. The mania will take time to run its course and you will see the most exponential gains in the shortest periods of time in such a phase.

The best strategy in times of a market euphoria is to buy stocks whose prices are seeing the maximum appreciation in the shortest periods of time, no matter how their prices have already moved up significantly. There is no predetermined level to how high a stock may go from now to some point in the future. The usual practice for investors is to steer clear of high priced stocks that are appreciating the fastest and look instead for "cheaper" priced stocks that had not done much through the rally. This is a mistake. If a stock has not done well and has not seen a significant appreciation in its price in a market mania, there is no reason to believe it will appreciate very greatly going forward.

The 1990s saw a market mania in what was then a new frontier, the Internet. In the past, railroads and other inventions that were expected to bring a new world order generated similar manias. But such manias come once in a lifetime. That may not be surprising because when these manias end, so many investors have lost so heavily that it takes an entire generation to get attracted to a new fancy.

In the 1990s, for example, Internet, technology and media stocks rose the fastest when most mature market players thought things were out of hand. They did not factor in what strong demand, and the desire of every individual to cash in on a boom, can do to prices.

Once any sector, stock or investment theme becomes fashionable — and that theme could even include countries, such as India and China, it brings in the biggest numbers of investors at the last stage. These investors follow a rule I call "LILO," a take from LIFO and FIFO in accounting. LILO stands for "Last in, last out." Such herd investors — "dumb money" as they are pejoratively dubbed by market professionals — are the last to enter the markets and thus end up entering at price peaks, and also the last to cash out, often holding on to the stock till it is not even worth the paper it is written on.

Uncertainty takes over if you think too far ahead

"There is nothing so disastrous as a rational investment policy in an irrational world."

\- Maynard Keynes

You must think ahead, but just enough ahead to know when money will start flowing into a stock. Five or ten-year projections of a stock's potential are irrelevant for multibagger picking. If you look very far ahead, the reliability of the prediction drops.

Think of your own life. Did you know five years ago how things would be in your life, or do you really know how things will be five years from now? Now stretch this to ten years and you will immediately realise how difficult it is to predict the course of future events.

We are repeatedly told to buy for the long term. But we don't factor in the havoc the long term plays with stocks. In the long term, governments may change, the dynamics of the industry may change, the company's competitive position may change, the owners may change. Even more extreme, there may be a war or a catastrophe that wipes out the company altogether.

Focus on the immediate and medium term, and if you cannot see a multibagger opportunity in the stock, there may not be one in the long run either. In any case, the longer your outlook, the greater the chances of multiple interruptions derailing a stock.

Investors also tend to project the present into the future expecting things to move in linear trends. They rarely do. Stocks with multibagger potential have as symmetrical odds which means that the returns that can be generated by taking the risk is in multiples of the returns you can get from taking the risk in other stocks. Look for situations or patterns that indicate that a new trend is emerging, or a sector or stock where as symmetrical opportunities of returns are emerging.

Don't rely on past data

"There are four things from which you must be entirely free. Foregone conclusions, arbitrary predeterminations, obstinacy and egoism."

– Confucius

Extrapolating the past into the future is usually considered as working with fundamentals. But the market is in constant flux, it reacts differently to economic and financial news, which itself is in constant flux. On top of this, we turn optimistic and pessimistic about the markets depending upon our perception or judgement about recent events. Relying on past information to predict the future is an exercise in futility for the most part. The markets and stocks are inherently volatile and not given to neat mathematical projections.

If you feel comfortable, you are not trying hard enough

When you do what others are not ready to, you feel the discomfort of breaking away from the crowd. If you are investing in the same stocks that everyone else is, they may not be potential multibaggers. If you feel you are picking those stocks that others don't believe in or are not ready to invest in, you may be taking the risk that brings exponential returns. There is a difference between impulsiveness, recklessness and risk. Impulsiveness and recklessness indicate uninformed decisions. Risk refers to an informed decision where you expect the rewards to far outweigh the pain you could suffer.

Risk taking is critical to multibagger investing. Calculated risks where the downside is limited and the upside in price appreciation is unlimited is a prerequisite to finding multibaggers. Such opportunities will stare you in the face when the mood turns overly pessimistic, people disregard long term potential for avoiding short term pain, or a move to cash drives money out of stocks.

Value is what the market attaches to a stock

"Charles Dow, the founder of Wall Street Journal, *divided stock market movements into three classes: the result of changes in intrinsic value, the product of manipulation, and the outcome of daily trading."*

– Edward Chancellor, *Devil take the Hindmost*

There is no permanent measure of value. It changes with the perception of investors. When no one cares about a stock, its perceived value is minimal. Once an increasing number of people start taking interest in the stock, its perceived value increases. At points where everyone wants to be in the stock, its value is determined largely by the extent of cash entering the stock. It is no different than a global athletics shoe brand that retails for US$300 or $400. Its selling price has nothing to do with its cost of manufacture. The shoe may be manufactured in China and may have cost only US$20 to make. But its perceived value is obviously US$300 or $400, or no one would buy it.

So what you have to do is to find stocks where you believe the perceived value will be much higher than the value currently being assigned to it by the market.

We tend to pay far less importance to the opinion of those whose money drives the markets, and even lesser importance to what type of stocks are in fashion, than we pay to irrelevant considerations like PE ratios, dividend yields, etc. Money flow, fashion and opinion can be far greater definers or redefiners of value than any conventional measure of value.

Investors consider the price they first notice the stock trading at as its normal price. Now, if the stock appreciates from there, they consider it expensive, and if it falls, they consider the price cheap. This can be dangerous for multibagger investors because they may hesitate to buy the stock if it has moved above its "normal" price, only to see it appreciate another 5- to 10-fold. They may also hesitate to sell a stock that seems "cheaper" than the normal, only to subsequently see the stock then lose another 50% to 60% of its value. The moral: there is no such thing as a normal price, and the stock's price from when you started to observe the stock is not of any consequence to your investing decisions.

A stock does not know you and does not know when you first noticed it or its price. So the price you get used to, or consider the normal price for the stock, is just one price quote in a series of stock quotes over days, weeks, and years. It is neither the normal price of the stock, nor a cheap or expensive price. In fact, the price at any point is irrelevant. The stock's price acquires a meaning only when it is seen in the context of the circumstances under which it is trading. For multibagger investors, then, the stage of the market, the excess or shortage of liquidity, etc. are critical, and not the stock's price in isolation.

Don't diversify

"Behold, the fool saith, 'Put not all thine eggs in the one basket' – which is but a manner of saying, 'Scatter your money and your attention,' but the wise man saith, 'Put all your eggs in the one basket and watch that basket.'"

– Mark Twain, *Pudd'nhead Wilson (1894)*

Multibagger investing is not a daily pursuit. There will be months when you will find nothing to invest in. There may be days when you find many stocks with multibagger potential. Most of your time goes preparing and fine tuning your mutlibagger process and investing when the time comes. But when you are convinced of the odds that the stock will turn into a multibagger, go for the jugular and invest large chunks in the stock.

Because of the peculiar nature of multibagger investing, and the time gaps between finding mutlibaggers, most investors get impatient and lower their standards to pick up stocks that don't have the odds to become multibaggers. They diversify into too many stocks that have been picked when opportunities are not many and crowd out multibagger stocks when the opportunity arises. If you have already invested the money you have and now opportunities arise, you will have to pass them by. So don't diversify but hold the money for the few times you get a chance to buy potential multibaggers.

Then there is the issue of trying to keep track of too many stocks. If you can shoot "fish in the barrel" why would you try to shoot fish that is not in the barrel (or stocks that don't meet your multibagger identification standard).

Diversified portfolios also defy the basics of multibagger investing. If your portfolio is "diversified" or has more than 10 stocks, your returns will start to gravitate to the mean or towards the returns of the index. If this is what diversification does, how can you have multibagger returns. Ten should be the maximum number of multibagger stocks. When you have a threshold for picking a stock which is a return of 5 to 10 times your investment, even finding 10 stocks requires an effort.

Stock prices are based on expectations

"The market's action reflects the interaction of many agents, each with varying knowledge, resources, and motivation. So a disproportionate focus on individual opinions can be hazardous to wealth creation."
– Michael Mouboussin

The price of a stock changes with the expectations of buyers and sellers. For most of the time and for most stocks, prices move in a range because buyers and sellers are balanced. In severe bear markets, sellers overwhelm buyers of the stock, while at the peak of bull markets, buyers overwhelm sellers. This has very valuable implications for multibagger investing. You must enter stocks when sellers overwhelm buyers in a stock — and exit them when buyers overwhelm sellers.

Always remember that stock prices are based on expectations, and expectations are fickle. I have not known anyone who expects anything in his life to be moving in an upward trend in a straight line for the next 3 to 5 years. Yet we are made to believe that this is the right way to invest. This makes us focus on information, such as earnings, financial ratios, etc. without realizing that the stock's price is driven by all sorts of people with very different time horizons, many of whom such as traders, don't have any use for fundamentals. Don't waste your time on the academic exercise that makes most investors end up losing money.

Invest because there is a reason that stock will be a multibagger

A stock will become a multibagger only if it appreciates 5- to 10-fold from its current price. That is a very tall order and it eliminates most stocks unless special market conditions come about where there is very high disinterest in equities. It means that you will have long periods of inactivity, and often have to reject all stocks after spending time to analyse them. A high level of patience will be involved. But the beauty of multibagger investing is that it produces the same returns with a very little part of your time as compared to regular investing.

Your investing decision must be based only on identifying a stock that you expect will turn into a multibagger. We buy stocks because we got a bonus, or have sold out of another investment and are looking for something new. If you happen to come into money, keep it in a bank till you can find the right multibagger opportunity.

2

~

Build Your Multibagger Edge

"You only need one or two great ideas a year to get rich."
– Warren Buffett

YOU WILL NEED AN EDGE TO PICK MULTIBAGGERS. The edge is a multibagger investing process that is refined over the years using your experience and learnings.

So the first step in developing an edge is to keep a diary in which you specify how you made your decision and after you made your decision what happened to the stock. If the stock turned into a multibagger, did it do so because your assumptions were correct or did the stock turn into a multibagger even when things did not happen as you had assumed. If a stock did not do what you wanted it to do was it because your selection process was wrong or was it because of factors you did not anticipate. If you follow this process in a disciplined manner and never invest without keeping a diary of the process and the results, you will increase your returns exponentially.

If you invest using the conventional "fundamental" methods, follow conventional chart methods, have not figured out how your investments fit your mindset, you don't have an edge.

What is an edge?

"What do you know about this investment that
the rest of the world doesn't."
– Michael Steinhardt, hedge fund manager

What do you consider an edge? You know how to read financial statement? You watch financial TV? You read annual reports? You read broker research? Your edge may or may not be any of the above unless you can put it in context of the type of thinking you have. If your thinking is "non linear", this and other information may be an edge. "Non Linear" thinking has to do with looking at something from angles that others cannot or will not see. If you have that ability, may be good at finding stocks with multibagger potential. Sometimes, you have to get away from mainstream sources of information and look for stocks that are not covered or researched or have been overlooked. It's harder than you think. Most stocks worth covering are already covered. But it is important to remember that research reports, views, etc. are merely opinions about a stock. It is not necessary that they reflect a stock's potential.

The thing with widely covered stocks is that almost everything the company or founders are ready to tell you publicly is known. If there is something they don't want to tell you, it is usually bad stuff. But there are times even managements don't realize their potential. For example, a management may be too pessimistic about when an economic cycle would pick up and drive their growth, or it may not be aware of a change in regulation that can transform their prospects. If you can visualize or figure out such changes, you will be ahead of even the management and may see the potential of a multibagger.

As you can imagine, it takes considerable time to develop a thinking pattern that can see opportunity that others don't see structural shifts in industries before other investors can visualize it. In fact, listening to financial media or opinions of people whose bonafides and expertise are not known, or trusting annual reports prepared by management can give you standardized views at best, and mislead you at worst.

You have to look at stocks from a broader perspective and visualize the potential of the sector or stock as it unfolds. Trying to analyse financial statements and reading research reports is generally redundant for multibagger investing.

If you are wondering why you have not been able to find enough mutlibaggers till now, it's not your ability but your approach that may be flawed. There are no scoops and there is nothing you will hear on financial media or anywhere else that is not already baked into the price. Most of what individual investors think they know is market noise, and they end up investing on the noise. Differentiate yourself by building a style, a strategy or a method which is uniquely yours to separate your stock investing from others.

Keep a record of your investment decisions

"It takes a man a long time to learn all the lessons of all his mistakes. They say there are two sides to everything. But there is only one side to the stock market; and it is not the bull side or the bear side, but the right side."

– Jesse Livermore

Keeping a record and constantly improving your technique based on the mistakes that made you pick a wrong stock will help you improve your performance, reduce the number of incorrect stocks you pick, and will help you to identify multibagger stocks much quicker.

Keeping a record of your investments and reviewing it before a new investment helps you keep in mind all the points that are important to pick the right stocks and to avoid mistakes that you made in the past. Our brains are programmed to only remember the most recent experiences and to use those to extrapolate your future. When you do the same in stocks, you turn optimistic if the most recent events were happy ones and pessimistic if the most recent events were unpleasant. This is a fatal investing pitfall that the diary you keep will help you avoid.

Here is an example of what your investment diary can look like:

Stock purchased

Which stock are you purchasing and at what price?

Reasons for purchase

What makes you think the stock will become a multibagger? Specify why you think money is going to flow in and why there will be more demand than supply for the stock? Refine this process continuously based on which reasons or factors lead to identifying multibaggers and others that ended up nowhere.

Expected returns

Specify how much you expect the stock to return — it must not be less than 4 to 10 times your purchase price. Don't specify any holding periods. This is the most critical aspect. A multibagger has to deliver 5- to 10-fold returns.

This makes your selection process extremely selective. You can pick stocks that will go up 20%, 30% or 50% in a year. But when you expect 5- to 10-fold returns, your process has to be primed for rejecting 98 out of 100 stocks.

Odds

Write down the odds you believe the stock will deliver your expected returns. This is where your super thinking, evolved over a period of time, will kick in. The odds have to be exceedingly high that returns will be in multiples of current price for you to pick a stock.

Action

Specify that if the stock moves the other way, you will exit the stock if it drops 10% from your purchase price, no matter what. There are two advantages to this discipline. If you really believe the stock is a multibagger and it moves back up again, buy the stock. You are expecting it to rise 5- to 10-fold. What's missing a few percentage points in lieu of reducing your risk. And if the stock continues to head down, you can reanalyse it to see if you missed something, or buy it at a cheaper price. If the stock heads much lower than your purchase price, and you are tempted to buy it back, don't let your previous purchase and sale cloud your mind. Treat picking up the stock again just like buying a new stock and follow the stock picking process again.

What went wrong?

Write down what you think went wrong. You may have gone wrong because your assumptions were incorrect or because external factors beyond your control caused a change in the stock's outlook. Putting down what went wrong leads to improving your decision making significantly.

What can I do to improve?

Write down what you can do to improve your stock picking and performance. I cannot emphasize a truthful look at self improvement. It not only improves your stock picking ability but you will see a change in your personality in terms of increasing calmness, ability to deal with uncertainty and making a realistic assessment of things.

Anticipating the flow of money, or which stock will find the market's interest, doesn't come naturally to most investors. You will increase your odds of picking the right stocks if you keep such a diary of all investments.

Understand who you are up against

Fund managers are usually the top of their class in school and college. They have access to companies and managements. They have access to top of the line research from the best brokerage houses. They are also part of an ecosystem that gives them access to top tier investment ideas.

So how do you beat them? You don't need to beat them. You just need to look at stocks in ways differently from them, and get into stocks when or where they are constrained to enter stocks.

Your advantage also lies in not having anything to lose if you pick the wrong stock. Fund managers and institutional investors don't have any such benefit. They are on fat salaries and get used to expensive clubs and expensive dinners. They tend to become risk averse as a mistake could make them risk the comforts.

Foster independent thinking

> *"The mind is an attribute of the individual. There is no such thing as a collective brain. An agreement reached by a group of men is only a compromise or an average drawn upon many individual thoughts . . . . The primary act – the process of reason – must be performed by each man alone . . . . This creative faculty cannot be given or received, shared or borrowed. It belongs to single, individual men."*
>
> – Barton Biggs in *Hedge Hogging*

The majority view about the prospects of a stock is the antithesis of multibagger investing. If the majority agrees that the stock is good, the stock's price will reflect the crowding of investors into the stock, and if too many investors are in the stock, there will be little money left over to drive the stock up further. Now what if the consensus is that the stock is horrible and most investors leave the stock? There could be two reasons. If the company has problems of a chronic nature, like regulatory issues, or a permanent change in demand for its products, the stock may be priced correctly. But there are times when the crowd is wrong. There are times when institutional investors have to exit a stock in order to meet redemption, etc. In such circumstances, you have a multibagger opportunity.

Stay away from consensus. Multibaggers emerge in brief periods and in various market conditions. The problem is that most of us seem to be struck with disbelief, or frozen into inaction during such periods.

You must develop the ability to catch investment themes before they become mainstream. Instead of spending hours researching stocks, spend days in identifying where money will flow and what you believe will get investors attracted. Finding stocks to play out your strategy then becomes easier.

Find an investment theme which the market believes will change the world

If you can find a "change the world" investment theme and the market subsequently ends up believing in the same theme, you have the multibaggers of a lifetime. In the 1990s, the Internet was expected to change the world. It did change the world but the expectation was compressed by the market into a bull run that took Internet stocks up 10, 20 and even 100 times. At different times, railroads, telegraph, telephones, automobiles, aircraft, radio or paved roads were all investment themes which were perceived to change the world. And all these produced stock price rises of 10, 20 and even 100 times. But while almost all of these great investment themes changed the world, almost 80% to 90% of the stocks in these businesses vanished. The few that were left settled at prices that were in line with the market. This is one of the reasons for not buying stocks after a major investment theme has ended.

With time, you will come up with a system to invest. Continuously evaluate your system because the market's dynamics are shifting and you will need a system that works in different market scenarios. It is only when you repeatedly improve your investing system that you will end up with a system that starts to deliver multibaggers.

Avoid narrative investment

"A questing mind, the gambling instinct, and the ability to make tough decisions on inconclusive evidence are all essential characteristics (for investing."

– Barton Biggs in *Hedge Hogging*

Humans are suckers for stories. And we take this habit to investing. A story from the market's perspective is the construction of a stock's potential by someone who has a charismatic personality and a way with words in order to convince you to buy into a stock. This is also how companies get you to buy everything from shoes to cars.

Investing because you like the story means you are relying on someone's construction of the real events. Listening to promoters, experts, financial media, etc. to make decisions is investing on a story. Multibagger investing requires building a rigorous investment methodology which is constantly improved by making investment in stocks, getting out of those where you went wrong, writing down how you went about investing and what went wrong and what turned out right, and testing your method again and again. This experience will give you knowledge of what works for you and what does not, rather than relying on someone else's narrative of the market.

Lose to win, or make mistakes and learn from them

"The prospect of getting rich is highly motivating, and few people get rich without taking a gamble."

– Peter Bernstein

Making mistakes and picking the wrong stocks is a prerequisite to identifying multibaggers. When you risk your money and lose it, and figure out why you lost it, consider it a tuition fee.

You must differentiate between picking the wrong stocks using a strategy or a process, and those picked on impulse or recklessness. If you are picking the wrong stocks using your strategy and process, you can use the feedback to improve your strategy. Continuous improvement will increase your odds of picking multibaggers using your strategy.

If you are buying stocks on impulse, stock picking ends up being random and does not generate multibaggers; nor does it serve as a source of important learning required to develop a multibagger picking strategy.

As long as you can limit your loss to a predecided level — say, no more than 10% of your purchase price, losses can be the best way for you to understand the mistakes and pitfalls of multibagger investing. No matter how many stocks you think will be multibaggers, and no matter how many of them in fact turn into multibaggers, you will never improve your performance until you put up the money to back up your idea. The minute you put money into an investment, self doubt, conviction and all the other things that plague a person's investing psychology come into play.

You are better off taking several small losses early in your multibagger investing phase. Losses teach you ways to protect yourself while easy, early, accidental gains make you reckless and give you a false sense of having understood the market, or having some superior intelligence.

Keep your multibagger portfolio separated from regular investing

Multibagger portfolios should be held to a very strict standard and any stock that does not meet those must be sold. You will often find that the stock you picked does not turn into a multibagger but gives a gain of 30% or 40%. In itself, the gain is good and you will be tempted to continue to hold that stock. But you must sell such stocks from your multibagger picks. Either a stock rises to multibagger status, namely goes up 5 or 10 times in price, or it does not belong in the multibagger portfolio.

Focus on re-rating candidates

"Nothing could be more useful, than to be well instructed in his Hope and Fears; to be diffident when others exalt, and with a secret Joy buy when others think it their interest to sell."

– Sir Richard Steele

Multibagger investors should focus on stocks which will get the largest reassignment of value in the shortest period of time. The value of a stock gets reassigned by the potential of the business, or by the right brokerage firms or institutional investors taking it upon themselves to get the stock's story out. Value also gets assigned when the amount of money flowing into the stock, the number of investors in the stock, and the number of institutional investors in the stock start to change the value assigned to the stock by the market. When value gets pushed up significantly by such influencers in the markets, the stock price automatically follows higher.

Traditional value investors often fail to realize that the company's value does not necessarily transfer to value in the stock. The stock and the underlying company or business are not linked in some mathematical model. Multibagger investors have to find what value investors are ready to give a stock. Whatever value heavyweight investors accord a stock pouring their money overrules any standard measure of value, like PE ratios, etc.

Skip Warren Buffett style investing for multibaggers

One of the charms of Warren Buffett for investors is that he makes investing look simple and something everyone can do. That's his charisma and skill in telling a story, but it does not translate into multibaggers for you. The initial hurdle of following Warren Buffett's style is that neither do you have his kind of money, nor his psychological make up, nor his market influence. In fact, you may have none of the ingredients that makes it possible for Warren Buffett to be the outstanding investor that he is. Trying to use his style out of context can run you into losses, let alone getting returns.

Investors should be careful about following Warren Buffett's one-liners, folksy annual reports and other utterances. Investing is not easy. And you cannot reduce multibagger investing to one-liners. It is like saying you can become a brain surgeon by reading one-liners of some Nobel Prize winning brain surgeon.

It will not be easy for you to disregard this folksy wisdom. Warren Buffett's one liner "Investing is so simple" type of quotes also provide a way for pretenders and alchemists masquerading as asset managers and money managers a veneer of respectability in their unending appetite to grab more and more money form hapless investors who are hypnotized into believing that in some way there is some magic to the Warren Buffett way, whatever that is.

A whole industry worth trillions of dollars has been built up by leveraging the alchemy of the Warren Buffett way (if there is any such way) and with so many asset managers, money managers and others peddling financial products and services living on it, it has perpetrated a cult of investing which is doomed to fail.

Keep your strategies and stock picks to yourself

"Rommel, you magnificent bastard. I read your book."
– Patton in the movie *Patton*

Patton won the battle because his adversary general wrote a book discussing his strategies. If you know the adversary's strategies, not only can you prepare for them but you also enjoy the advantage of the adversary not knowing your strategy.

When too many people start to use the same multibagger strategy, it ceases to be a successful strategy. You don't need others to confirm your strategies. Put them to use in picking stocks you expect to be multibaggers, and you will know if the strategy works or not. Don't discuss or give out your strategies that work.

Multibagger investing is a lonely business. If you find yourself justifying to others why you picked a stock, it probably is not a multibagger. Most investors enter wrong stocks because they enter whatever is popular. You, on the other hand, have to enter stocks that are unpopular and need a high level of conviction.

Unless you are financial media personality, an influential broker or a fund manager, no one is going to believe you even if you told people that you have identified a multibagger. So why waste your time?

Read financial history – that is your trump card in the markets

"The market is endlessly fascinating, endlessly complex, always changing, always mystifying. There is always something unknown, undiscerned."
– Mister Johnson

Human behaviour is repetitive. Financial history gives us an insight into how stock markets rise and fall, how investment themes emerge and how investment manias take hold. This information allows you to be prepared to invest when the opportunity presents itself.

Reading financial history is like finding a treasure trove of the investment diaries of master investors. What could take you decades to understand and avoid can be obtained in reading the history of financial markets around the world. Since market cycles take decades to play out, financial history gives you a flavour of the how markets can rise and fall in ways that current market conditions will not show.

While reading financial history, focus on when and why markets turn around, and sustain their gains or fall. Study the role of money and the psychology of investors in driving up stocks.

Disregard the noise

"The credibility of any item in finance is inversely proportionate to the amount of publicity it receives."
– Michael Scott

The biggest challenge you will face is trying to separate the noise from valuable information. Most of the information you will get from the financial media, experts and others will be noise. Filtering out all the noise requires you to stay from reading too much of news reports, expert views or broker views on a stock. We don't know the motivation behind such information, and we don't know how it impacts the stock. Even if it does impact the stock, is it enough to get the stock to deliver 5- to 10-fold returns?

Buy the stock before the price setters do

"All life is speculation. The spirit of speculation is born with men."
– James R Keene, Celebrated 19th century American trader

Those with the deepest pockets set a stock's price, including domestic and foreign institutional investors. As a multibagger investor, your task is to buy the stock ahead of institutional investors. But how do you know if institutional investors will subsequently invest in that stock? This is the kind of knowledge and information you should be looking for. That's the edge you need. You can either develop a network among institutional investors, or look out for what influential fund managers with the money to back them say and do, or what the influential brokers who buy stocks for these fund managers are beginning to talk about.

Don't be emotional about losses

"Fragrant is the sandal tree, but on it snakes are also found,
In water there may lilies be, but also crocodiles abound.
And in pleasure there always are, villains who its merits mar
One cannot have felicity entirely of problems free."
– Hitopdesa

If you picked the wrong stock, all you need to do is exit it. In this book, I have set out a set of rules you can follow on how and when to exit but over time, and with experience, you can build your own set of rules. Develop the habit of never sitting on losses beyond the thresholds you have set for yourself.

Losses should be embraced and considered a tuition fee to learn multibagger investing. In fact, you should be exiting from 8 to 9 of the 10 stocks you shortlist at a predetermined loss level. After every loss, make sure you keep notes on how the loss occurred in your investing diary.

At no time should losses cause you emotional distress. Losses are an inevitable part of multibagger investing and as long as you keep them in limits, the stocks that turn out to be multibaggers will more than make up for the small losses you take.

Don't make decisions based on your most recent memory

Our bias to base our decisions on our most recent memory rather than our most rewarding or painful memories sets the tone for most trading mistakes. For example, if the market is rising, options will be priced in a linear fashion as if markets will continue to rise forever. But markets actually tend to have asymmetry and today's trend may not continue.

If recent events are viewed as bad for the market, it will cloud your future outlook. But recent events may be irrelevant for how a stock may look one or two years from today. Multibagger investing requires you to look at stocks beyond their current stock prices and the circumstances currently surrounding them.

No single multibagger should exceed 20% of your portfolio

In a potential multibagger, start by putting in 5% of your portfolio money. If the stock price, moves up 50%, put up another 5%, and if it moves up 100%, another 10% of your total portfolio size. But don't exceed that number. With experience, you can come up with your own formula but positions above 20% of your total portfolio can lead to emotionally disturbance you if you start to lose money in the investment. The limit is more to ensure that you do not lose your calm and make impulsive decisions in other multibagger investments.

We have to build multiple walls to ensure that losses are limited and, even when there are losses, they should have no impact on your investing psychology or emotional balance. One way we do this is by limiting our loss in any stock to 10% of its purchase price. Another way to do this to limit the amount we put in a single stock. No matter how good our decision making, we are still dealing with odds in investing. And there is always an outlying chance that the stock collapses the next morning, and never gives you the opportunity to exit at your pre set level.

First test your theory

"The scarred sit, frozen by memories, through the ebullient markets, and the unscarred are sliced apart by the Black Horsemen of greed at the end. Only a longer time span reveals the truly prudent man."

– The Money Game

Many books and market gurus make it look as if multibagger investing is simple and based on folksy wisdom. Nothing is farther from the truth. You may have gotten a multibagger using a particular set of rules, strategies or styles. But on the next stock, you may see losses using the same set. What did you miss?

The only way to capture as many factors or points you need to come up with for a personal formula for finding multibaggers is to test your theory and write down the results. If one stock turned into a multibagger and the other into a dud, write down what you could have missed. As you continue to go through this process of evaluation and testing, you start to arrive at a proprietary formula for multibagger investing.

Don't let media do the stock picking for you

The media presents news that's important to them, not to investors. So, don't let media guide your investing decisions. Every thing that is news worthy is not necessarily of much use for making investing decisions. Much of what you hear on financial media is noise and can be very distracting to making sound investing decisions.

Investing is a lonely pursuit. No one is interested in telling you things that will let you make money. They are interested in you telling them what will make them money.

You get raw information and opinions on financial media. Disregard opinions entirely. Since these opinions are available to the widest audience, and because they are opinions, they are rarely of use in picking stocks. Raw information in itself is not of any relevance. But if information helps you to think at another level, it may have some use. But for the most part, you must first decide what you are looking for and then search for it. For example, if you wish to identify stocks in industries which are reaching full capacity, do your own research rather than depend on the media.

Watching financial TV is more like random investing.

Continuously test your multibagger investment process

"The spectacular George Soros, when making a financial bet, keeps looking for instances that would prove his initial theory wrong. This, perhaps, is true self confidence: the ability to look at the world without the need to find signs that stoke one's ego."

– Nicholas Nassim Taleb in *The Black Swan*

Pay importance to the process not the final result. The result will improve if your process is good. Start with defining a set of criteria to pick multibaggers. Identify 2 or 3 multibaggers using the criteria. See if the stocks turn out to be multibaggers or fail to take off. Sell out if they fail to take off and keep notes on what went wrong. The stocks you identified as multibaggers may not have appreciated either because of factors beyond your control or because you used the wrong criteria. Make improvements to your criteria and identify another 2 or 3 potential multibagger stocks. Repeat this process and you will see your process improving your odds of finding multibaggers. A great process will improve the odds of identifying multibaggers but it will never give you 100% results. But this method of multibagger investing is any day superior to an ad hoc, impulsive system. A process or method also eliminates the havoc your emotional state can play with your investments. If you stick to the process, the human frailty of swinging from one end of the spectrum to another is kept in check.

Your goal should be to improve your investing process by leveraging the investing mistakes you have made using the process. You must continuously test the assumptions you have made in the process and see why your stock picks may not deliver.

Unlearning everything you know about investing

"In any military operation, it is important to first know the lay of the land. When you know the distance to be travelled, then you can plan whether to proceed."

– Sun Tzu

You can be educated, uneducated or ill educated in financial markets. Being ill-educated is worse than being uneducated. At least when you don't know, you can start afresh. But when you are ill-educated, you have to unlearn what you know. Think of it this way. Countries that never had mobile phone started out with state of the art technology but countries that had mobile phones for years had to migrate from several legacy systems to reach the current level of technology.

Unlearning what has been sold to you as financial wisdom is not very easy. It gets hardwired into your brain by numerous repetitions. Let's deal with a few things that you will need to unlearn to succeed at multibagger investing.

Diversification is the first hurdle. Anyone who diversifies his or her portfolio beyond 10 shares is sure to end up making returns similar to the index, or somewhere near it. Diversification is like engaging your mind in too many things. And we all know what happens when we try to do too many things at once; nothing gets done with excellence.

Averaging is another hurdle. Mutual funds and other products encourage you to "average" or "invest systematically." This is just not conducive to multibagger investing, though. Averaging destroys the benefit of getting your timing right. Think about your own life. The biggest achievements we have made are usually in short spurts of time. The rest of our lives are usually mundane and routine.

"Don't time the market!" This is one of the most preposterous suggestions and a major hindrance to finding multibaggers. You *have* to time the market. You *have* to be in the right stock at the right time.

Focus on the methodology

"Investors generally dwell on attribute-based categorizations (like low multiples) versus circumstances based categorizations. A shift from attribute to circumstance based thinking can be of great help to investors and managers."

– Michael Mouboussin

Developing and refining a process to pick multibaggers in various market situations and contexts can only come from years of multibagger investing. It is a trial and error process because stocks can turn into multibaggers in dozens of contexts. Only by investing in different market conditions and contexts will you gain this experience. The experience will help you increase your odds of picking multibaggers but can never make the process foolproof. Nevertheless, multibagger investing based on a process is far more superior than ad hoc decision making and builds on a body of knowledge that only past experience can produce.

Anyone can get lucky and get one or two multibaggers. But getting multibaggers based on an investment methodology and process developed with knowledge and experience gives you a tool to find multibaggers consistently and understand which stock picking techniques work best in which market conditions.

Find out why stocks didn't turn multibaggers

"If opponents suddenly run away before their energy is faded, there are surely ambushes lying in wait to attack your forces, so you should carefully restrain your officers from pursuit."

– Sun Tzu

If a stock continues to fall, don't assume it is getting cheaper and buy more, or sit with the stock. No matter how good your multibagger selection process, you can never know everything about a stock. And it is possible there is a problem with the stock that is known to the insiders or some investors, which is why it's falling. The easiest way to deal with a falling stock is to get out of it.

We only hear from people who were successful in finding multibaggers, but almost never hear stories of those who picked stocks that never turned into multibaggers. If we know the mistakes others have made, we can steer clear of these mistakes. Talk to other multibagger investors and find out the methods they used, and why their stock picks did or did not turn into multibaggers.

Dry run for at least one year

"Almost anyone can make money on imaginary trades because there is no risk of any kind – the mind is free from the strain and apprehension that accompanies an actual trade; fear does not enter into the situation; patience is unlimited."

– Richard Wyckoff in *The Day Trader's Bible*

Before buying any stock, dry run your multibagger picks. Pick them, but don't buy them, and follow them to see if they are behaving the way you expected. A dry run is crucial before you put up real money.

However, do not take the returns you get on your dry run as a proof of your competency to find multibaggers. Putting up money on an investment idea comes with a different set of pressures.

To do a dry run, define a set of criteria for identifying the multibagger opportunity. The criteria cannot be low PE or low Price to Book Value and other conventional nonsense that is sold to you as value indicators. Instead, think of how far a commodity cycle can go if you buy into a commodity cycle, or how significant can be a regulatory change for the prospects of the business. Whatever the criterion would, it must be based on superior investment thinking and an ability to look beyond today. Test this by assuming you bought the stock. Check how the stock moves and whether your assumptions were correct.

Develop second level thinking

Stock markets confuse two levels of thinking. The first is the base level thinking which is what most investors have. Such thinking generates losses or average returns. Then there are a few who possess the ability of second level thinking — and this is what generates high returns and limits losses. At the peak of second level thinking you start to generate multibagger returns.

So what is base level thinking? It's when you depend on watching financial TV, use textbook methods to identify stocks, think low PE and other such conventional methods will help you pick stocks, listen to other people's recommendations, and believe that reading stock market books by itself will make you a millionaire soon.

Second level thinking is investment thinking that has evolved by refining one's investment process over years of investing, reading investment wisdom that is not available off the shelf, understanding that markets don't work on facts and figures alone, that esoteric dimensions of hopes and dreams are important, as is learning how to find investment opportunities to execute your high investment knowledge.

When you reach the highest levels of second level thinking, you will begin to see multibagger opportunities when they arise, and skip stocks that will never be multibaggers.

Develop a process for identifying multibaggers

"This attitude is also culturally reinforced, as exemplified by the advice; Seize opportunities, but hold your ground in adversity. Better advice to a trader would be: "Watch idly while profit taking opportunities arise, but in adversity run like a jackrabbit."

– William Eckhardt

Focus on the process — and develop the discipline to stick to the process. You may sometimes get an odd multibagger in going by your intuition but just as soon you will lose the money in other, wrong stocks you pick. A process that is tested continuously by investing — and corrected to remove its shortcomings — ends up delivering long term success in picking multibaggers.

This would require you to focus on evaluating your decision making process rather than the outcome. Even the best decision making processes have some probability of failure. So in order not to get badly hurt, you must put a limit on your losses.

Deconstruct ideology, construct discipline

Since stock prices are based on consensus, you must wait for the consensus to reach extremes. If almost everyone agrees that a stock will not move up, you have found the low point of the stock's price.

Just because you find value in the stock does not mean others agree with you — and without other agreeing that the stock you picked is indeed undervalued, it is not going to move. The trick then is to have the same view as the rest of the investors but much ahead of them, and at a price much lower than what they decide to enter at.

This is harder than we think. Investors often believe that they have superior insight into a stock, a sector, or the market in identifying value stocks and that eventually the market will catch up with their view. Most investors end up holding value stocks for years without seeing any significant move, let alone a multibagger. This may be because a majority of investors don't have any superior insight into the market and rely on publicly available information which may be of dubious quality, or relying on clichéd value parameters like low PE. They have often not given enough thought as to why other investors will find the stock undervalued over a period of time.

You have an edge only till a few investors are investing in the stock

"What everyone knows is what has already happened or become obvious. What the aware individual knows is what has not yet taken shape, what has not yet occurred."

– Sun Tzu

Over a period of time your edge in picking a stock will disappear. As other investors pick up on the theme and buy into the stock, a point will be reached where the reasons for investing in the stock are common knowledge and anyone who wants to be in the stock has invested in it.

Your point of entry is the point where others have not yet figured out the reasons why the stock will rise, and your point of exit is the point where everyone agrees that the stock has potential to rise.

Work on developing a multibagger attitude

"Investing in stocks is an art, not a science, and people who've been trained to rigidly quantify everything have a big disadvantage."

– Peter Lynch in *On up on Wall Street*

I have often heard investors tell me that they will do well with stock picking because they have an engineering or mathematical background. Multibagger investing has nothing to do with anything you learnt in engineering or in math. It is a game of dealing with the psychology of people and being able to anticipate the market.

Whatever your educational background, do not assume it gives you any real edge in multibagger investing. This is an entirely different subject and you must work on understanding it accordingly.

There's no substitute for experience

"Many people get involved in the markets without any edge. Most small speculators will never be around long enough to find out whether their system could have worked, because they bet too much on their trades, or their account is too small to start."

– Monroe Trout

There is no substitute for experience. Every mistake is a learning experience and adds to your mastery of the art of investing. That's one of the reasons why overexcited analysts and fund managers with 3 to 5 years experience start believing in the cycle they are in, i.e bull or bear market. That's also the reason why the majority of market players cannot warn you of an impending crash. In euphoric markets, most analysts/fund managers are raw being added to fuel an unending investor appetite for stocks.

Figuring out the odds

Think of stocks as race horses. If you go to the races, you can figure out the odds of a horse winning. You have to pick a horse where the chances that it will win the race is in total disconnect to the odds the punters are giving the horse to win.

You will not make money in races where you pick a horse which is a sure shot winner. That's because everyone will bet on such a horse, leaving little chance that you can get outsized profits. But if you can pick a dark horse, or a horse who is not fancied to win, and this horse then wins the race, your winnings will be large. The same principle applies in multibagger investing.

Looking at stocks in terms of odds is not easy. Investors are programmed to believe that there are blue chip stocks and risky stocks, and they tend to pay higher prices for blue chip stocks and discount riskier stocks. But what they need to do is to find a stock generally categorized as risky which has very high odds, namely great discrepancy between its price and price potential.

Picking stocks with excellent odds of turning into a multibagger will take a few years of practice. At all times, get out of stocks where the odds seemed good but the stock price did not move to justify your expectations. Keeping losses in control is key to enhancing both your odds as and your returns.

Choosing a style

"Don't think about what the market's going to do; you have absolutely no control over that. Think about what you're going to do if it gets there."

– William Eckhardt

Improving your odds of finding multibaggers requires an independent thought process. It requires you to develop your own approach rather than follow an established approach expounded by a market guru. Just as you won't become a tennis ace by watching a five-time champion, you won't get multibaggers by following Warren Buffett or some other guru. One of the key reasons why following others does not work in multibagger investing is that you may not have the same level of market influence, market knowledge, market access, etc. compared to the person you are looking to follow.

Think of your expertise and personal psychological make up. Pick a style that works for you. Don't try and implement too many different strategies and styles. Focus on areas of your relative expertise, whether it be your knowledge of real fundamentals, technicals, or markets. You may have developed an expertise in picking multibagger stocks in commodities and in anticipating when commodity stocks react to commodity cycles. Stick to this expertise rather than trying every other multibagger style.

Don't confuse investing style with investing rules. A style defines a way you go about picking stocks, and it deals with the process rather than a result. Investing rules deal with the results produced by following a particular style. While having a process is critical for multibagger investing, it can produce different results. But because you can exit stocks where results don't match your expectations, it does not dilute the quality of the process.

An investing process must be based on second level thinking. Second level thinking refers to looking at things beyond the superficial way financial media and run of the mill investors look. It requires you to develop a process that can define why a stock has the odds of becoming a multibagger.

3

~

Multibagger Investing Myths

Myth: Long holding period is beneficial

You will often hear experts, financial planners and others on financial media talk about a stock returning a certain return over a holding period of one year, three years, etc. This is pure hogwash. No one knows how long a stock will take to deliver a return. It is almost certain that if a stock needs three years to get to a certain price, it will not get there. Stocks move up when money moves in, and money moves in when there is enthusiasm. Enthusiasm is infectious and ensures a stock's price rise will be swift and steep — or not at all.

The general tendency of stocks is to rise in short spurts. And it makes perfect sense that stock prices get most of their gains in short spurts. A stock begins its real move when the float or number of shares available with the public, becomes limited. In bull markets you also find a combination of sellers not wanting to sell their stock in anticipation that it will appreciate combined with buyers flocking the market to buy stocks at ever higher prices.

In fact, a stock that does not move for a long time indicates either a lack of interest or too many buyers to match sellers.

Myth: Multibaggers will be found by following market gurus

You may try to imbibe or seek inspiration from some of the psychology or principles used by market gurus but you will need your own investment methodology. Every market guru has a very different level of knowledge, money and influence on the market or a stock. For example, it is impossible to follow Warren Buffett because his profile, stature, influence and money has nothing in common with you. From his high pedestal, it is easy for him to give simple folksy investment wisdom but putting it into action with your knowledge, money and level of influence is a whole different ball game.

A multibagger by definition has to be discovered by a few early investors. If a market guru's views are publicly available, what are the chances that you are an early investor?

Myth: Diversified portfolio is the way to go

"The king should not simultaneously go to war on many fronts. An arrogant snake is bound to be killed if hunts inside insect holes."

– Hitopdesa

Diversification is like opening too many fronts in a war. It stretches your resources and capital too thin to make money anywhere. If you invest a small amount in a stock, the amount you get back is also small even if the returns are exponential. For this reason alone, you must have a significant amount in any multibagger stock to generate enough money to make it worth your time. Too many stocks in your portfolio also means that underperforming stocks will drag down the return on an entire portfolio. And it is the rule of the market that most stocks underperform.

Concentration of portfolio is essential for multibagger investing. It allows you to concentrate your capital and thinking on a few stocks. Diversification generates average returns at best, and rarely helps you in reducing risk.

Contrary to popular belief, the more we diversify, the more our returns will look like the index returns. Our portfolios are all umbilically linked to other holders of the stock. And that holder is not nearly as rational as we expect him to be. When he starts to behave irrationally, i.e. when he is overcome by either greed or fear, he starts to treat the portfolio as one whole and either sells the family silver with the trash, or buys trash along with silver.

Myth: Technology and 24-hour financial news give a competitive edge

"There is no observed improvement in the emotional stability of the average investors, notwithstanding dramatic advances in financial literacy or in the sophistication of computer software."

– James Grant

Mass media discussing a stock ensures there is no multibagger opportunity in that stock. If everyone is in a stock, the upside becomes limited. But when mass media drives a large number of investors out of a stock, and the stock collapses way below its potential, a multibagger opportunity may arise.

Access to increased information and technology have not improved our emotional stability or temperament. Moreover, once something becomes available to all, it ceases to be a competitive advantage. It turns into a commodity. Take the example of computers. Twenty-five years back, no one used them. So if we had a computer, it was a competitive advantage. Now if we don't have one, we are at a disadvantage; but having one, is no competitive advantage.

In a complex financial world, it does not help to be ignorant. Financial media plays a significant role in bringing us the same information that institutions have and does not leave us groping in the dark. To the extent it saves us from losses, it is very valuable. To what extent it can help us make money, I am not so sure. While the information provided by the financial media can protect us from losses, it cannot make us money. With universal access to information, it makes it is also less likely that the insiders can make money out of information others don't have — a phenomena referred to as information arbitrage. But financial channels are in the business of reporting on markets, not predicting or leveraging the markets. Often, we take what is said on financial television as the gospel truth.

Financial media provide no leads on how important the information is for us, or what we should do with it. For the media, the importance of news is based on its journalistic considerations. But what is important, or makes a great story, is not necessarily what is important in making investment decisions.

There is also the problem of cheerleading. The livelihood of financial TV channels depends on rising markets and active trading. That, inevitably, leads to financial news being given a bullish bias and, often, a need to create something out of nothing. While it is critical for financial TV to generate and sustain such interest for its own health, it is not clear whether it is required, or whether it improves investment returns in any manner.

By its nature as a mass medium, television targets the largest possible audience and channels which have a mass appeal are the ones that make it to the top. However, what is popular is not necessarily sound investment rationale. Picture this. If any anchor or reporter presents a contrarian view as the market rises, he would simply be dismissed as bearish. His popularity would wane. The popular anchor would be the guy who tows the public line, which would include hyperbole.

Financial TV magnifies the ups and downs of the market — usually the ups. Financial TV's profits depends on viewership and it must keep up the viewer's enthusiasm for investing even if in the process it makes a serious activity appear as though "everyone can do this. It is so easy." TV anchors and reporters speak breathlessly of stocks that rise 10% on any day — omitting to mention that they may have dropped off 80% in the past 2 years! Equally, most market experts and commentators have an interest in keeping the market from declining as going short is not everyone's cup of tea. In the process, their cliched explanations mostly border on the naïve and are also repetitive.

Myth: Investors know when to buy and sell stocks

Advances in behavioural finance show that we remember events that are the most recent, and not necessarily the ones that are the most important or powerful. So if prices have not risen for years and then do so suddenly, small investors quickly sell off. Having gotten used to depressed prices, they assume that's how markets will remain. Most investors buy and sell stocks using their purchase price as a benchmark and the longer they are stuck in the stock, the more they are tempted to sell if the stock moves higher than their purchase price. But relying on the price you bought the stock at to decide the price to sell it causes investors to lose a major chunk of the rise in a stock's price.

Stocks don't know when you bought them or at what price. They move on their own steam and the market conditions that prevail at that time. If you can stay away from buying and selling stock on some personal notion of what is a cheap price, you will be able to get into stocks that have multibagger potential.

Myth: Buy and hold strategy leads to multibaggers

"People who have the notion that buying and holding for the long term is the way to go can easily go bankrupt."
– Victor Sperandeo

Buy and hold depends on factors way beyond your control to drive your multibagger. The timing of your entry and exit from a stock is a prerequisite to successful multibagger investing. You can buy and hold only as long as the technical charts indicate that the stock has price and volume momentum on its side or that the price is backed by increasing volume over a period of time. If volumes drop and the stock price stagnates, it indicates a loss of interest and buy and hold will not then work.

Buy and hold was devised as a strategy when only a few industrial firms dominated the world. In today's context, companies rise and perish within years. It took Google less than ten years to dominate the world, and less than that for its competitors to perish.

Should you hold overvalued stocks when the mood of the market is euphoric? When does one sell out in a market mania? These sell questions are critical, not buy and hold. For example, at the end of a market mania most analysts say, "It's a good time to buy." Actually, it's often a good time to sell since the race, namely momentum, is over. A dynamic mix of value and momentum which takes into account the mood of the market for that particular stock or sector at a stage when it seems the stock has moved away from value could help us capture gains that may not make sense, but are on offer because a large swathe of investors will push prices up. It is not important if we have made, lost or will lose money by selling off. It is whether we can get much more, or lose much more, that should drive our selling decisions.

Myth: Risk and reward have an absolute correlation

Multibagger investing is about picking stocks with exponential return potential at the lowest possible risk. There is no direct relationship between risk and reward. You may get very different returns for the same risk depending on where the market it. When markets have fallen a great deal and you are told stocks are risky, they may provide you multibagger returns at almost no risk. And at the height of bull market when you are told to stay in stocks, they may have been extremely risky and may result in losses.

Not only is there no formula that says that you have to take more risk for more return, neither does one work. Multibagger investing is all about buying low risk very high return stocks.

Investors who bought stocks in the US after the 1930 crash when the markets were off 50% from their highs would have lost another 80% as markets fell that much more by 1932. In 1955, the Dow Jones again touched its 1929 high — yes, it took it 26 years to get back to the same point — again then rose 3-fold thereafter. The correlation between risk and reward in stocks is not clear.

The maximum rewards are also reserved for those who take the least risk. Investment bankers, brokers, "market gurus," company promoters usually have a first cut at stocks. And it is not always because they have some insider information. It's simply because they are so close to the action, they can see the structural shift happening before others can.

Myth: A strong economy is good for stocks

"A severe financial crisis can occur for a number of reasons including excessive speculation . . . and not necessarily because of a general and long-lasting downturn in the real economy."
– Marc Faber in *Tomorrow's Gold*

A growing economy may drive a market to move up but the degree of rise can vary sharply. Moreover, a growing economy creates severe competition causing several listed companies to either generate lower profits or shut shop. Multibagger investors have to be exceedingly careful about equating a strong economy with multibagger stocks. In fact, multibagger opportunities at much lower risk arise in economies where economic growth is slowing or has turned negative. Stock markets tend to overreact to slowdowns and discount stock prices in ways that could only be justified if the economic downturn was permanent. But most economic downturns are not permanent and if investors are averse to stocks, it may be an investing opportunity.

Economic growth, especially of the exponential kind, is not always good for stocks. As a business shows exponential profits, more companies rush in to the sectors concerned, more companies raise money, margins get squeezed and a squeeze out leaves only the best around. So while railroads are still around, railroad stocks have been relegated to museums. Internet has brought about the most profound changes in our lives, but only a fraction of the Internet stocks are around.

We often equate a strong economy with rampaging bull markets. But if so many companies rise to world standards and can produce at such cheap rates, how can it be good for investors?

In strong, globalized economies, the rate of failures and fallen companies increases exponentially. Margins become wafer thin and companies compete either on volumes or because they have an intellectual capital edge. Only the best survive. There is no place for inefficient companies.

And that's why at such times stock picking, as opposed to sector picking, becomes the order of the day. Betting on entire sectors is then nothing but outright dangerous. For example, it is preposterous to assume that all banks will be able to survive the burst in productivity and efficiency improvements in the digital era.

Few stocks survive economic booms and busts. Fewer still survive beyond a decade, let alone a century. Unless we happen to be invested in the 5 out of 50 companies that survive on an overall basis, we end up losing. A growing economy increases competition, productivity and puts to test management quality. In such a scenario, those ahead in the race get ahead even faster. Those falling behind, fall further behind. Google is a prime example of the "power law." The Internet changed the world, but look how the winner namely, Google took all. A majority will fall by the wayside being the victims of easy money, ill conceived plans, poor management quality and an inability to price products higher in a surplus economy.

Myth: Markets are efficient

"Observing correctly that the market was frequently efficient, they [the efficient marketers] went on to conclude incorrectly that it was always efficient. The difference between the two propositions is night and day."

– Warren Buffett

Share prices reflect both information that we know and information that others know. For example, I may not be able to explain why a stock has moved based on the information I have but that does not mean that others who bought or sold the stock don't have information based on which they traded the stock. The information does not necessarily have to be fundamental in nature. It is all kinds of information, whether it be fundamental, market mood, etc.

Sometimes, however, the markets are unable to factor in all information, especially in times of extreme moves where the force of liquidity, or the lack of it, moves the markets either more or less than what all the information is likely to do. These are precisely the points in which we can make significant returns.

Myth: Investing in low PE stocks is the way to find multibaggers

"Almost everything investors are taught about the relation between earnings and stock market returns, whether in business schools or on the stock market pages of newspapers is wrong."
– Victor Neiderhoffer

Low PE stocks rarely turn into multibaggers. A company with a low price earnings ratio should make you wonder why others are not interested in the stock despite its low PE. The information is there for everyone to see. Could it be that the potential of the company's growth is limited, or, is it in a sector with no investor interest, or is there a question on the management's integrity? Low PE may indicate a problem that you may not be aware of. On the other hand, a stock that has growth potential will always trade at high PE multiples. That is because investors are expecting the stock's price to rise. The only time low PE investing may work is when there is investor disinterest in stock markets as a whole, or investors have been forced to sell shares because of liquidity issues, or the entire market is suffering from lack of demand or money to invest.

Myth: Buy low and sell higher

"The greatest misconception is the idea that if you buy and hold stocks for long periods of time, you'll always make money."
– Victor Sperandeo

"Buy low and sell high" is one of the most popular market clichés and fallacies. How does an investor know what is "low" and what is "high." How does one know if a stock can head even lower from what we consider "low." Buying stocks that are drifting lower will not create a multibagger. Buying stocks that are in an uptrend is one of the first rules of multibagger investing. Buying low is like getting into an aircraft that is heading to the parking bay and not an aircraft that is on the runway gaining speed to take off.

Buy low and sell high does not produce multibaggers. Buying high and selling higher does. You need a stock where money is flowing in but there is investor interest. Stocks that have fallen may fall further as a falling stock reflects lack of confidence or a problem with the stock. When investors lose confidence in a stock, it usually takes a long time for that confidence or investors to return to that stock.

Myth: Knowledge of nuances of sectors and stocks may lead you to multibaggers

"Knowledge that does not go beyond what the generality knows is not really good."
– Sun Tzu

Investors often assume that they stand a better chance of getting a multibagger in an industry they understand. While it is helpful to know about a sector or industry, working in it or knowing it well provides no guarantee of finding multibaggers in that industry or sector. In fact, knowing about a sector or industry may prejudice you or give you preconceived notions about a stock's prospect.

Stocks don't move when industry experts invest in it. They move because a very large pool of buyers submerge sellers to such an extent that prices rise significantly.

Myth: Markets change and so does human behaviour

"There is no observed improvement in the emotional stability of the average investors, notwithstanding dramatic advances in financial literacy or in the sophistication of computer software."
– James Grant

If human behaviour is the key driver of markets then we know why it is not different this time or any other time. Markets always get back to their mean. If they have a meteoric rise, they will have a violent fall. If they rise nominally, their fall will be nominal. And this holds true across markets from the US to Europe to Asia, from developed to the emerging, from boom economies to stable economies, from sectors to stocks. What foreign investors are currently doing in the favourite market of the moment, is the same as what they earlier did in China or in South East Asia, or for that matter in America, Japan or Peru or elsewhere. It is also the same thing they did in railroads or airlines or technology, i.e. push stocks up to great heights expecting the company they invested in to leverage the benefits of a new technology, country or asset class.

Myth: It is easy to make money in the markets

"They (people) believe you can make tons of money with little work. They think you can make 100 percent a year doing a little bit of research on the weekends. That's ridiculous."
– Monroe Trout

Either making money in stocks is easy or there is a lot of money to be made in stocks. But both cannot be true. Because if it was true, too many investors would rush into stocks and drive prices up, leaving no multibagger pickings. So, it is not easy finding multibaggers but because most people don't even make an attempt you have a good chance to find them if you put in the hard work.

Multibagger investing requires tremendous self control. Control over both greed and fear. Multibagger investors are a rare breed and a gifted one at that. They are masters of behavioural finance and have conquered ego and ideology. They have a feel for not just the mood of the market but don't confuse hard decisions on returns with ego and ideology. Their thinking is counter-intuitive and, in fact, rational. This very fact makes multibagger investors one in a million.

Myth: Invest over the long term for multibaggers

"Those who get in early during an upturn – and have the luck or presence of mind to get out before someone shouts 'fire'– reap huge awards. But those who come late to the party, often through no fault of their own, are hammered. Markets do not punish the greedy; nor do they necessarily reward the virtuous and frugal saver. Markets are amoral. 'Good decisions' and 'bad decisions' play a role in the outcome, but much depends on the wanton accidents of timing-when you get in and when you get out."
– Maggie Mahar, *Bull!*

The long term is a continuum of short terms. If a stock does not show the potential to be a multibagger in the short term, it will find it difficult to become a multibagger in the long term. Spending years for a stock to turn into a multibagger is like spending a week to catch a fish. Waiting for the long term also defies the logic of how stocks rise. Stocks rise in short spurts and there is nothing to show that if you stay invested in the long term, your returns improve.

Most market theories are based on an assumption of a rational investor. If markets did work rationally, then we could mathematically calculate a stock's over- or undervaluation and buy or sell it accordingly. And since everyone would know the extent of overvaluation, all of us would buy and sell at the "rational" price, in effect, killing arbitrage. Such a situation would kill all trading and give us prices that would move only because there is a material change in the financial position of a company. We can pick "value" or "fundamentals" or whatever we call it but if we mistime our purchases, it could be years before there are any returns. "Consensus" or the "interest of crowds" is a key factor. And if stock picking is done on fundamentals or value, etc. combined with excellent timing about the crowd's interest, we can be sure of making exponential returns.

Logic rarely drives stock prices. At best, logic is used to explain "consensus" prices, especially at peaks of bull markets. And consensus is rarely based on logic. It is driven by perceptions of economic growth, confidence, etc. Of course, markets do reflect what the economy says, but they are almost always in overreaction both up and down. As Burton Malkiel says, "God Almighty does not know the proper price-earning multiple for a common stock."

"Don't time the markets" is a myth. While it is not helpful for investors (as opposed to traders) to time the market for a few days or even a month, it is essential to time the markets based on a structural shift.

Myth: Buy stocks for the long term

When we cannot even predict how our personal and professional lives will look in the next 3 to 5 years, what makes us think that we can predict what will happen to a stock price, after that period something over which we have no control. If you don't expect the stock to be a multibagger based on your current information, giving it a long rope of 3 to 5 years is not going to turn it into one. Competition, over-capacity, delay in disinvestment, new taxes, change in taxing capital gains or dividends, price controls will sooner or later average out very high returns in some years.

The best returns are always made in short spurts. You can either buy a stock and hold it for a long time and it will generate large returns in a short burst, or you can time your entry into the stock just before it starts its exponential rise and not have your capital locked in a stock for years doing nothing.

Myth: Fundamental analysis is essential for multibagger investing

"The historical-average price-earnings ratio provides investors little or no guidance about market returns over the typical investment horizon."
– Michael Mouboussin

Fundamental analysis will not tell you how much the stock will rise. It will not tell you why people are interested in the stock. Nor will it tell you if buyers will overwhelm sellers in the stock and give it a meteoric rise in price. Fundamental analysis may save you from being in a dud but it gives very little information about finding multibaggers. Compounding the problem of using fundamental analysis to find multibaggers is that it is impossible to define what fundamental analysis is. If your view of fundamental analysis is looking at low PE ratios or low Price to Book value or some other mathematical stuff, you are on the wrong path. There is no formula or mathematics to figuring out a stock's price.

Investors using fundamental analysis to identify multibaggers may end up holding immobile stocks for years. You may find out how a company works or earns by fundamental analysis but it will tell you nothing about when money will flow into the stock or how the stock's price will rise.

Myth: Markets are rational

"Few men, who follow Reason's Rules, grow fat with South-Sea diet. Young rattles and unthinking Fools are those that flourish by it."
– Edward Ward, *A South Sea Ballad*

Wherever humans are involved, the activity cannot be rational. Where crowds are involved as they are in markets, there is no chance of any rationality. Stock markets are driven by people's perceptions of the future and their hopes and dreams from the stock. Perceptions can change overnight. And with a change in perception the stock's price can vary significantly no matter what the future holds. This is an opportunity for multibagger investors. If stock prices drift significantly below what the future holds for the stock driven by immediate perceptions of the majority investing in the stocks, it will sow the seeds for the stock to rise significantly as the mood changes.

The job and expertise of a multibagger investor lies in understanding the emotion and mood of investors towards a stock. The biggest gains in a stock come when a large mass of investors who have no clue of the value of the stock and have done no research enter the market driven by their impulse, emulation of others, and current perceptions.

Myth: Anyone can have a lucky streak and make money

"We look back at investors who have made a lot of money and we tend to think, 'They made it because they were good.' Perhaps, we have turned the causality on its head: maybe we consider them good just because they made money."

– Nassim Nicholas Taleb, Options trader

Luck has nothing to do with stocks or investing. You may get lucky but then it is like walking through a minefield. Just because you did not get blown away by the first mine does not mean the next one will not get you.

Multibagger investing requires you to build a process and then refine it continuously. You have to be good at not just controlling your risk but of identifying stocks that will rise 5- to 10-fold in 2 to 3 years.

4

~

Beware these Traps

"An appreciation of our need for explanation can be an inoculation against making mistakes. Investors who insist on understanding the causes for the market's moves risk focusing on faulty causality or inappropriately anchoring on false explanations. Many of the big moves in the market are not easy to explain."

– Michael Mouboussin

HUMAN COMPREHENSION IS LIMITED. At any given time we can only deal with 6 pieces of information. Even then, we will need the IQ of a genius. Yet 24-hour financial television and round the clock hour access to financial information exposes us to so much information which is impossible for any human mind to comprehend. This information's worthlessness and confusion value is multiplied exponentially by anchors and analysts trying to find a cause and effect for every piece of information, and adding their own opinions to it.

Most of this information is only a distraction for multibagger investing and at times it is harmful. It may make you buy or sell a stock that would otherwise have never met your criteria.

The best approach is to stick to your process and wait for low risk, high return opportunities to enter stocks.

Buying stocks as products on discounts during a sale

"Never buy a stock because it has had a big decline from its previous high. The likelihood is that the decline is based on a very good reason. The stock may still be selling at an extremely high price – even if the current level seems low."

–Jesse Livermore, *How to trade in stocks*

Stocks are not like products. There is no real discount, only a perception that there is a discount. What seems like a discount may be a loss of interest in a stock which could take it much lower.

Think of stocks like vegetables. They are only worth buying if they are fresh. No price is too low if they are rotten. Buying stocks at "bargains" only translates into buying stocks at a lower price than they were trading at earlier. But what if the stock is trading at a lower price because it has turned rotten. Then no amount of discount on the stock can turn it into a future multibagger.

Buying on discount or a bargain presupposes that we are getting something of the same worth at a much cheaper price. For multibagger investing it would suggest that we are getting something of the same value for a fraction of the price. It's like saying that we are getting a luxury car at the price of a small sedan. But while we can differentiate between a luxury car and a small sedan, it requires several years of experience to identify a stock of great value to be selling for the fraction of its value.

Trying to find multibaggers all the time

"When you know you do not yet have the means to conquer, you guard your energy and wait. When you know that an opponent is vulnerable, then you attack the heart and take it."

– Sun Tzu

It is difficult to sit tight and do nothing. But activity is fatal for multibagger investing. You only invest when the "fish is in the barrel" and when you take a shot it has nowhere to go. At most times, such opportunities do not exist. But when they do come, you must have the money and the psychology to put up the money. You have to go for the jugular when you are convinced, no matter what the market, the financial media or the analysts are saying.

Listening to business founders and managements

Your multibagger investing agenda is not in sync with the agenda of company founders and management. They tend to be more optimistic than required because they need cheap capital all the time. They tend to hide major hits till the time they have to disclose them. By keeping the narrative on their stock positive, they keep adding investors including institutional investors.

This creates price bubble in stocks which burst with severe intensity. So buying on management view is usually a dangerous exercise.

When markets are down and out, however, managements tend to be overly pessimistic. Because they have to deal with the daily grind of lower revenues and lower profits in bad times, they tend to bring that view and feel to their stock and its price. Moral: You must analyse a stock independently without paying much attention to what the managements or the analysts say.

Buying a stock because its "intrinsic value is low"

One of the most common investing errors is assuming that you have a multi-bagger at hand just because its intrinsic value is low. First, what you consider as intrinsic value may be based on information that itself is incorrect, or is based on your perception of information that may be incorrect. What you must focus on is what the expectations of other investors are and whether those are reflected in the stock's current market price.

Intrinsic value and other concepts and measures of a stock's value and safety are opinions — and opinions are often wrong. When opinions are based on the majority's perceptions, they are almost always wrong.

You do not need to look at stocks based on conventional definitions of value, like PE ratio, etc. They were invented with the purpose of enticing people to buy a stock and to make buying a stock look like an intellectual activity.

Instead, you must focus on things that make a stock move up. Excellent market conditions, high barriers to entry, few influential investors, top quality management, innovation, etc. These factors are not easy to put in a value formula, but so you need to make up your own criteria.

Looking for confirmation of your beliefs instead of dissent

We look for information and people that will confirm our views on a stock. We tend to disregard or skip information and people who punch holes in our investment rationale. Actually, we must look for information and informed people who can give us clues on where we could have gone wrong, or missed something, in deciding to pick a stock.

In bull markets, cognitive dissonance takes over. We want to hear what makes us feel good about stocks, not how things really are. "Shoot the messenger" if he does not communicate what we want to hear is the theme of a bull market. As the frenzy builds up, any constructive criticism or review of the market is disregarded or simply mocked at. As the crowd of cheer leaders (read brokers, analysts and financial media) grows shriller, any realistic look at the market seems impossible. Those who have such views are not invited on TV shows, shunned by brokers as bears, and disregarded by investors for being overly pessimistic.

One sided information creates a vacuum of views in the markets that leads markets and stocks to extend themselves very far one way or the other. These extremes of one sided information and view are the best time to find multibagger opportunities. If such views are pessimistic, stocks may have reached rock bottom and may be ready to deliver multibagger returns. If views turn to the extreme optimism, it may be time to exit stocks and keep cash ready to enter after a massive fall.

Selling winners and holding losers

Selling a stock with gains feels like a victory and selling a stock with losses means accepting a bad call. Psychologically, we prefer feeling like winners and postpone anything that makes us look like a loser. When this psychological make up transfers to investing, we end up selling stocks which show a profit even when the profit is small and may not reflect the profit potential of the stock. We also end up holding stocks that show a loss. Postponing the day of reckoning keeps a window open for the stock to recover and helps us avoid pain. This investing behaviour is exactly the opposite of what is needed for stocks that show profits and stocks that show losses.

But that's like throwing an orange which is half squeezed and retaining a rotten orange. The exact opposite needs to be done for multibagger investing. The rotten orange should be thrown out and the juicy orange should be squeezed till you have extracted all the juice.

A knowledge of technicals is critical to fathom how much more juice is left in the stock.

Wasting time in meaningless financial calculations

There is no hidden magic in accounting or financial statements. There is almost no chance of finding multibaggers by looking at financial statements, except during long term bear markets. Financial statements are not based on some mathematical formula. Despite seeming mathematical in their exactitude, they are based on very subjective judgements and the ratios and other data you come up with from such statements are misleading at best and useless at worst for multibagger investing.

In buying stocks, stay away from any financial projections or calculations about a company's potential. Brokers often use financial projections as a means to justify their target price for a stock. Such information has zero value for picking multibaggers.

Basing decisions on recent rather than relevant information

Our brains are programmed to remember the most recent events and information. The about creeps into our investing. We invest based on the most recent information about a stock or our most recent perception of the stock. But recent information is not necessarily relevant information. Cultivate a habit of looking beyond recent information to see if you have missed other relevant information that may be valuable but has been missed. This also gives you an edge because the vast majority of investors make the fatal mistake of making decisions on their most recent perceptions, mood and information.

Multibagger investing is based on two types of information. One, information that creates your conviction to invest in the stock, and two the information that is required for picking the most appropriate time to enter the stock. The information that creates the conviction to invest in the stock is usually related to the stock's potential, management, etc. The information about timing is related to external factors like the stage of the market rally or fall, the level of interest in the stock or the industry, etc.

Preconceived notions of overvaluation based on the past

"If the enemy suddenly abandons their food supplies, they should be tested first before eating, lest they be poisoned."
- Sun Tzu

When the market is rising, many investors stay away believing the stock is overvalued. Their concept of overvaluation is based on a point they have chosen as their base. For example, if a stock was trading at a PE of 5 and moves to a PE of 20, an investor may consider it overvalued. But who is to say that the stock will not move to a PE of 100. In these preconceived notions, investors end up missing rallies because they anchor any new price to a base price they have in mind. They then compound the mistake by buying a stock because it has fallen 50% or 70% from its high. They now consider the new price as cheap. This is a mistake because there is no way to know if the stock will not continue to fall. The stock is below the price an investor considered as the base, but it is not necessarily cheap.

Falling for the sales pitch

"The systematic dissemination of false beliefs is called propaganda. The seven main techniques of propaganda – name calling, glittering generalities, transfer, testimonial, plain folks, card-stacking and bandwagon. Regrettably, nobody tells investors how to recognize these techniques in the financial field."
- Victor Neiderhoffer

In investing, more than in any other field, most of the information you get is given by interested parties, i.e it is a sales pitch. Brokers, mutual fund managers, financial media, company owners, etc. all have their own interest in getting you to invest. What gets treated as fundamentals by most investors is nothing but a sales pitch or information that has been structured or presented in a manner to meet the goals of the presenter.

Differentiating a sales pitch from investing wisdom is very difficult. Many financial products are sold under the garb of investing advice. Research written by brokerage houses is meant to sell a stock, and is no different than a brochure meant to sell a car.

Expecting a multibagger to pay for other things

Investing must be done without any reference to what that money can and will be used for. Investing is not the same as savings in a bank account or in an insurance plan where the final return is known. Moreover, multibagger investing lacks a specific time frame making it impossible for anyone to use expected returns as a means for financing anything in life.

If your starting point is to get a multibagger to buy a car or satisfy some other dream, you will end up losing money. When you invest expecting the market to pay your bills, it breaks your discipline and does not allow you to build a system of finding multibaggers. You may get lucky and find one or two multibaggers but the market will as soon take all of it and more back.

Investment errors caused by two dimensional information

While investing is perceived in terms of facts and figures, it operates in the human dimensions of hopes and dreams. This acquires significance for multibagger investing because no stock can go up 5- to 10-fold unless there is large surge in public popularity for the stock or the industry. Analysing stocks in financial terms will not produce any results. But anticipating the changes that could cause an industry or sector to generate large investor interest will produce multibaggers.

At no point will we have all the news that could make our decision right. What we can do is to decide if the information is substantial enough from a financial perspective to make us buy a stock at its current price?

It was only in the 1990s that the Asian Tigers (Thailand, Malaysia, etc.) saw their stock prices evaporate. This was a revulsion to the boom in the 1980s when stock prices got bloated beyond recognition. Money found its way into stocks and real estate in these countries. Property prices gained as more people came to cities and rapid growth led to new employees and higher wages. Foreign companies pumped in foreign direct investment into offices, factories, etc. which then led to another spiral in real estate prices. A construction boom followed, leading to a supply overhang that took almost a decade to clear.

Don't be trapped by storytelling

"The honey-bee, forsakes blossoming lotuses in ponds free of perils, and goes for sitting behind the ears of elephants, not counting the risks of what a flapping ear can cause. It is in the nature of those in hot pursuit of something, not to pause and reflect upon the final outcome."

– Panchtantra

Stocks are sold by brokers and made to appear attractive by financial media and experts by making an interesting story out of a stock. And we are suckers for stories. But a story is just that. It is a way of playing with your mind in a way the story teller wishes. As a multibagger investor, you cannot rely on stories because they come with psychological twists. You have to build your own story.

Stock prices are a result of investors picking stocks based on building a story to justify buying the stock. Financial numbers are used to justify the story rather than numbers leading to the story. The problem with storytelling is that it fails to build a process or method that works in various scenarios. Multibagger investors must steer clear of basing their stock picking on a story building to justify their investment but develop a method, that is continuously improved from mistakes, for identifying multibagger opportunities.

Be careful about correlated multibaggers

"I have two basic rules about winning in trading as well as in life: (1) If you don't bet, you can't win, (2) If you lose all your chips, you can't bet."

– Lally Hite

The multibaggers you pick must have low correlation with one another. That does not mean they must not be in the same sector or in a similar business. It means, the reasons why they are rising must not correlated. If one is rising because of institutional buying, the other should be rising because the promoters are buying back their pledged shares, and so on.

Keeping the correlation low between stocks acquires increased significance in multibagger investing because of the high concentration of your portfolio in a few stocks. But you must be careful of not picking stocks on the opposite sides of the spectrum where if one stock does well, the other stock will necessarily underperform. For example if you invest in an automobile stock betting on increase in electric cars, you may want to avoid another automobile stock making gas guzzling SUVs. Either your conviction says electric cars will do well or they won't. But it cannot be both.

Investing and trading mistakes of my life

"It's amazing how difficult it is for a man to understand something if he's paid a small fortune not to understand it."

– John C. Bogle

I have seen several spectacular multibaggers and have also seen several spectacular blowouts among my investment choices. But this is part of the journey of becoming a multibagger investor and the lessons I learnt from these investments are well worth the tuition I paid by way of the losses I suffered or the profits I missed.

Investment 1

I bought a pharmaceutical stock which appreciated 24-fold from my purchase price. The promoter died and the company lost its course. But I did not sell out. The stock then dropped 95% from its highs. At that point, I identified another pharmaceutical company whose stock I was sure was going to be a multibagger as their strategy was to sell out their molecules for hundreds of millions of dollars before they were commercialised into a drug. I could have switched out of the first stock and bought the second one as both were at about the same price. But I procrastinated. The result was that the first pharmaceutical company dropped to 1% of its high, while the second pharmaceutical stock rose 50-fold in a period of 5 years.

(contd . . .)

Lesson

Let go of a losing stock. I should have sold off the stock as soon as it dropped by more than 10%-15% from my purchase price. The other mistake I did was to link my entry into a multibagger to exiting another stock. Each entry and exit of a multibagger must be independent of the other and the decision to enter and exit a stock must be based on each stock's potential.

Investment 2

I purchased another pharmaceutical stock after a chance meeting with its promoter/founder. It was a small cap stock but the promoter's enthusiasm and singular sense of purpose made me believe the stock was going to rise. Indeed, the stock duly rose 10-fold in a period of one year. Over this time, I realized that the owners were using speculators to drive up the stock's price. Such stocks never sustain their momentum. Despite that, I did not sell out and continued to hold the stock. I finally sold the stock after it had fallen over 90% from my purchase price.

Lesson

Never let losses run out of hand. A mastery of reading charts and technicals is critical for multibagger investing. It allows you to figure out if the stock is on a strong footing or if it is being manipulated.

Investment 3

I purchased the stock of a multiplex cinema chain. In those years, multiplex tickets were considered expensive and the owners had a goal of setting up just two multiplexes a year. Then the owners sold out to a large media group. The large media group was only looking for a platform to scale up exponentially. During that time, changing habits and increasing disposable incomes made multiplex tickets affordable to mainstream movie goers. I held on to the stock knowing that it would be acquired sooner or later and the new owners would use the operational base to scale up the business. I had held the stock for three years and seen no change in price before the large media group bought out the original owners. The stock then jumped 3-fold from my purchase price. As I had waited so long to exit, I sold out immediately. The stock

(contd . . .)

continued to rise and appreciated more than 20 times from my purchase price in just a year after I had sold off.

Lesson

If the dynamics of the business change, or if a company is acquired by someone with a much larger scale, a stock can appreciate exponentially. I also learnt to sit with winners till they run out their full return potential.

Investment 4

I bought an SUV manufacturer's stock when the company launched its first internationally acceptable SUV. I sold the stock after six months at three times my purchase price. But the very next day, I bought the stock back expecting the stock to rise much more now that the company had a platform to design and launch modern SUVs. I also expected the SUV market to explode from being non-existent to reaching the high levels seen globally. The stock rose 20-fold from my purchase price in 2 years and I sold it. After I sold out, the stock continued to rise but at a much quieter pace and appreciated another 50% in year.

Lesson

If you sell out but see the stock continuing to rise, don't let your ego stop you from buying it again. I also realized that when a company develops a new competency, the stock's price can scale up in multiples.

Investment 5

I purchased a real estate stock at a time when there were only 2 or 3 listed real estate companies, the entire business was unorganised, and no investor wanted to buy real estate stocks. I held on to the stock for 5 years but the stock did not move an inch from my purchase price. Then, all of a sudden, global investors started to pour money into real estate and they could not find any listed companies to invest in. The few that were there had low floating stock and appreciated exponentially. The real estate stock I owned appreciated 10 times in less than 6 months! Finally, I sold it at 10 times my purchase price. But with no new listings in the horizon, and billions of dollars chasing the few available stocks, the stock went on to rise 550 times from my purchase price!

(contd . . .)

Lesson

Low floating stock or only a few listed stocks in an industry where global investors begin to buy can take stocks up multiple times. Another lesson I learnt was that there is no knowing how high a stock can rise. I thought 10 times my purchase price was great, but the stock then moved up 550 times.

Investment 6

During the dot com boom, I purchased the stock of an animation company at the peak of the frenzy. When the frenzy ended, the stock began to fall. I continued to average and bought more stock, unable to accept that the game was over. I averaged repeatedly till the stock lost 99% of its value. Finally, I was not even able to sell it as the stock stopped trading altogether.

Lesson

Never average a losing stock. Second, when an investment mania comes to an end, stocks which are the subject of that mania never recover.

5

~

Principles of Multibagger Investing

Understanding boom and bust cycles

When a bull market starts to emerge from the depths of a bear hug, it usually means that shares have moved from weak hands to strong ones, because experienced investors buy at points of extreme pessimism. Investors sitting with losses for years at a stretch are happy to sell out as soon as they see a stock finally rising. As the rest of the market begins to realize that markets may finally be out of the woods and try to buy stocks, there is little supply available from the weak hands as they have already sold out. The markets can then double or triple in no time.

The same also holds true for the IPO market. As a market emerges from a depressed phase and moves into the first stage of a bull rally, IPOs are rare. In the second stage, some IPOs come to the market and they are of good quality and will appreciate significantly and turn into multibaggers. In both these stages, the demand for stock is higher than supply. In the third stage, the stock appetite is high and so is the sale of stock and IPOs, though in this stage they are either of poorer quality or are very aggressively priced. It is in the fourth and final stage of the bull cycle that the sale of stock and the flow of IPOs begins to outstrip demand, leading to a bust cycle. Consequently, it is rare to find multibaggers in the third and fourth phases of a bull run.

Understanding cycles and trends

The odds of finding multibaggers, and the choice of multibaggers available, are extremely high at the bottom of a market or industry cycle. That is why getting in at the right points of the market cycle are critical for multibagger investing. At the lowest points of the cycle there is an aversion to stocks, investing is at a low point and trading volumes are extremely low. As the market cycle picks up, multibagger opportunities shrink and the prospects of the stock turning into a multibagger are significantly reduced.

Your investing style has to adjust to the stage of the market cycle. A common mistake we make is to average our purchase price by buying more stock. That is a losing strategy if the market is in a down cycle. At such times, what is low will go even lower. An understanding of cycles could have indicated that the game was over and it was time to cut losses and book profits at the earliest.

Markets work in cycles. A cycle lasts for years. Within cycles, there are trends. So we could be in a bull market cycle and yet see the market lose 5% to 10% in a month; and this could occur a number of times in a bull market cycle. Such a fall is a bearish intermediate trend in a bull cycle.

Why is this important? If we can make a call on the start and end of the cycle, we are almost sure to come out a winner as we will sit through the intervening bearish intermediate trends.

Investing in cycles and trends requires different techniques and produces multibaggers of different magnitude

Before you pick a stock, determine if the sector or the stock belongs to, or the entire market, is a long, mid or short term bull or bear cycle. The best multibaggers at the lowest risk are found in long term bull cycles. If the stock is in such a cycle, you can give yourself greater leeway when a stock drift downwards. Intervening downward trends are common in long, mid and short term cycles.

The risk increases and the probability decreases of finding multibaggers as you try to invest in a mid or short term cycle as these can reverse anytime.

If the market is in a long, mid or short term bear cycle, multibagger investors need to keep out. There may be strong upward trends in these down cycles but they are usually not strong enough to produce a multibagger.

A distinction between cycles and trends is critical for buy and sell decisions. How do you read a cycle? Usually it lasts for years and is unrelenting in its up or down moves. Cycles will also go through phases with the last phase perhaps the sharpest in its moves upwards. And inevitably the cycle will end in a blowout and then it will take a couple of years before it can recover. The Japanese markets are a case in point. After touching surreal levels of 40,000 the Nikkei lost almost 75% of its gain and languished for over a decade at those lower levels.

Another opportunity for multibaggers presents itself when a market begins to emerge from the depths of a bear market cycle. Shares move from weak hands to strong hands. Investors sitting with losses for years at a stretch are happy to sell out as soon as they see a stock rising. Only experienced investors buy at points of extreme pessimism.

Stay out of the market when a major market mania (like Technology) or a country mania (like Japan or China) goes bust. Investors develop an aversion to stocks, especially a large proportion of first time investors who suffer the most. It then usually takes a new generation to come up to start buying stocks again.

The point of reversal is when IPOs flood the market

"Nowhere does history indulge in repetitions so often or so uniformly as in Wall Street. The game does not change and neither does human nature."

– Edwin Lefèvre, *Reminiscences of a Stock Operator (1923)*

A market flooded with IPOs gives the first indication of a market prepping up for a fall. A point is reached where any IPO manages to sail through irrespective of the quality of the company or the management sowing the seeds for the market to collapse. The more the frenzy in the IPO market, the more likely the market will collapse.

Only once or twice in your lifetime, will you get a multiyear bull market. Grab such an opportunity and you will have several multibaggers. This bull market will take almost every stock up, if it is a broad based bull market, or every stock in a sector if it is a sector based bull market. In such a market, you have to stay till the market is flooded by IPOs. When there is too much supply of stock, the market will reverse with a vengeance and lose over 80% to 90% of its value. There is no "cheap" stock at the end of this phase. Such severe reversals in a long term bull market don't just affect investors but also destroy businesses. Easy money drives many companies to scale up to levels they will not be able to sustain. Loss of liquidity is so severe at the end of this phase that companies end up scrambling to keep their operations running.

Investing with asymmetrical information

"Limited opportunities – Even when you know what you're doing and play under ideal circumstances, the odds still favour you less than 10 percent of the time. And rarely does anyone play under ideal circumstances. The message for investors is that even when you are competent, favourable situations – where you have a clear-cut variant perception vis-a-vis the market – don't appear very often."

– Michael Mouboussin

Cause and effect investing is our conventional style. We expect that every move in stock market price can be explained by some cause. But stock prices react asymmetrically to information. It is not the information itself but who considers which information important enough to act upon that decides how the stock reacts. If a very large institutional investor finds information about a small cap stock important enough to invest heavily, the stock could rise exponentially. If millions of individual investors get excited about a stock or a sector, their combined financial muscle could drive stock prices up.

So what is asymmetrical information? It is information where returns are exponentially higher on a given level of risk, or where the cause produces an exponential effect. Asymmetric information exists all the time in the markets. Every time buyers and sellers are in imbalance or a stock is overwhelmed by an excess of buyers or sellers, the stock's returns may turn asymmetric.

Mastering asymmetrical information is the unique ability to look at information and picking a multibagger. It is like knowing how to fire a gun when everyone else has swords. The gun gives you have an asymmetric edge. Even the best swordsman may be no match for the gun.

For example, you may well read that significant amounts of power will be needed in many advanced companies in order to run servers. This may sound comical to someone who is focused on fundamentals and, looking at the current excess supply of power, may consider power stocks a sell. You, on the other hand, may believe that given growing Internet use, power consumption from servers may be so significant as to create a multi year power shortage, driving power stocks through the roof. This is an example of asymmetric thinking.

A stock's price rests on consensus

A young trader once asked his boss, "Why are the markets up?"

"There are more buyers than sellers," replied the boss.

John Law who was a land bank accumulator and one of the originators of the Mississippi bubble said that, ultimately, all values for money or gold or assets rested on consensus.

Most market theories are based on an assumption of a rational investor. If markets did indeed always behave rationally, then we could mathematically calculate a stock's over- or under-valuation and buy or sell accordingly. And since everyone would know the extent of over-valuation, all of us would buy and sell at the "rational" price, in effect, ending all arbitrage. Such a situation would kill all trading and give us prices that would move only because there was a material change in a company's financial position. As we know, however, that's not how markets work.

A trade only happens because at each price there is someone who wants to sell and someone else who wants to buy a stock. Each is following his own perception of what he believes is the value or the upside of the stock or availability of liquidity in his hands. If more investors believe the stock should move up and buy with that belief, the stock will move up as its demand would outstrip the supply. That is why stock prices seem to appreciate so dramatically in euphoric bull markets. As larger and larger groups of people come to believe that stocks are the way to go, they push up the prices. The converse is equally true, too.

We can pick value or fundamentals, or whatever else we call it, but if we mis-time our purchases, it could be years before there are any returns from our stock picks. To get it right, "consensus" or the "interest of crowds" is a key factor. Thus, if stock picking is done on fundamentals or value, etc., combined with excellent timing about the crowd's interest, we can be sure of making exponential returns.

Logic is used to explain "consensus" prices, especially at peaks of bull markets. But logic rarely drives stock prices. Also, consensus is rarely based on logic. Instead, consensus is driven by perceptions of economic growth, confidence, sentiment, etc. Of course, markets do reflect what the economy says, but they are almost always in overreaction, both when going up and falling down.

Learning to take losses

"A military force has no constant formation, water has no constant shape, the ability to gain victory by changing and adapting according to the opponent is called genius."

– Sun Tzu

Our psychological make-up does not allow us to take a loss even when the loss is after a windfall gain. For example, you would feel much better if you sell a stock with a 100% gain rather than sell it after it went up 200% and then dropped 20%, even though the gain would still be much higher in the latter case. We are just not wired to take losses and feel good about it. So what we end up doing is to sell out too early and miss out the opportunity of the stock turning into a multibagger.

Why we pick wrong stocks

Humans have a natural tendency to find a cause for an effect. We try and see patterns where there are none. Investors compound this tendency by not being able to factor in variables that affect a stock's price and often don't have the ability to appreciate that there is at reflexology work — namely changes in the stock price affect investor sentiment, a company's business, and in many other ways cause ripples that come back to further drive the stock price.

Because there are so many factors that are beyond human comprehension, if you pick a stock that heads down, get out of the stock instead of waiting for it to recover. There may be things that you don't know, or are just beyond your comprehension, which are driving the stock's price and they may not be in consonance with the assumptions you based your investment on.

We can improve the odds of picking more stocks that can turn into multibaggers by making a few changes in our thinking process. The first change relates to cause and effect. In stock markets, what causes which effect is rarely clear. And that creates a great opportunity. If you can figure out the magnitude of the effect based on a cause that the market has not anticipated, you will have multibagger returns. Another change you have to make is to keep in mind that rarely do things go up and down permanently and it is in the reversals of the market's cycles that opportunities wait.

We tend to forget that even if the stock does not do what you want, you can get out of the stock. As long as you are firm on that decision, even mistakes in investing will not hurt you. You have also to remain invested in profitable stocks as long as they are profitable.

These few minor changes can improve your investing performance significantly.

Don't sell out too soon

"Its amazing how sometimes something important will happen, and the market will keep going despite that . . . just because I see something doesn't mean that everyone sees it. A lot of people are going to keep buying or selling just because that has been the thing to do."

– Jim Rogers in *Market Wizards*

There is no defined point for a stock to stop moving higher. There is no PE ratio too high or low, no valuation too high or low and no stock price too high or low. There are only prices that are set by the preponderance of sellers or buyers.

Don't make your selling decisions based on preconceived notions of price but on anticipating how much more money can flow into the stock and how limited the availability of the stock is at any point of time.

The risk of being too keenly aware of value is that you tend to realize a stock is overvalued too much in advance of the market. You may be tempted to get out of the stock, or decide not to buy more. But this may be precisely the time to remain in the stock, or actually buy more, and also find more multibaggers. You must develop a keen ear for the time the majority in the market realize that the stock's price is overdone. And this usually happens way beyond any rational or logical point.

Market behaviour is cyclical

Markets react to the economic cycles. However, the pace and time investors take to change their perception, or form new perception about economic cycles may occur with a time lag. Take, for example, an economic cycle in a commodity like copper. When copper supply outstrips demand after a long upward move in copper prices, prices of copper stocks may not even react and may, in fact, continue to head up. The knowledge that copper supply is outstripping demand is known first to copper miners and smelters. Given their large capital outlays and expansion plans — which incidentally happen without fail at the peak of a cycle, they continue to tell analysts and markets that demand remains strong. Beyond a certain point, the drop in prices start to show up in earnings. While institutional investors may decide to begin an exit at this point, individual investors and ETFs balance this off by buying more copper stock. At some point, investors realize the game is over and try to exit all at the same time. So while the copper cycle may have ended some time ago, prices of copper stock adjust after a lag.

Multibagger investors must exit the market, the sector or the stock when an economic cycle has come to an end.

Exit if the crowd does not follow you in

Multibagger investing is the art of picking stocks with the highest odds of going up multiple times. These odds work only if two things are in place. The first is that the stock itself should be selling at prices that reflect an inefficient price, or a price that is low either because investors are out of equities, or because cash is in short supply, or there is a liquidity freeze in the system. This sets the tone for a multibagger opportunity. But one more essential ingredient is needed to create a multibagger. And that is a flood of money into the stock. You have to be able to figure out if the stock will find its way back into investor portfolios at some point of time. Without the flow of money flowing into the stock, prices will not rise multiple times.

Identifying the right theme ahead of the crowd is critical, but only just ahead of the crowd. If the crowd has no desire to follow you into the stock, then you could have bought the stock for the right reasons but it will still not move. Investor psychology is to buy with the crowds and sell with the crowds.

A few stocks allow the focus you need

Concentration of your portfolio and your money in a few multibagger opportunities allows you to focus. Keep your multibagger portfolio separate from any other kind of investing you do. Multibagger stock picking requires you to think in ways and to look into potential future scenarios that cannot be done for too many stocks. Since multibagger opportunities change with market conditions, you will need to spend considerable time trying to figure out the scenario that may emerge and ensure that you have enough money to enter multibagger opportunities when the time is right.

In multibagger investing, all you need is a few stocks. The more you diversify, the more your returns will look like the overall index returns.

If you have set your multibagger threshold at 5- to 10-fold return on your purchase price, the number of stocks you will find that fit such a high benchmark will be few. And by the time you zero in on those few, the list will not be more than 10. The only exception may be when the markets are in a wild bull charge when investors invest without discrimination.

Correlation is not what we think it is

Try and buy stocks with very little correlation to each other. But this correlation is not the conventional correlation of stocks you are used to. Our portfolios are umbilically linked to each other by the holder of the stock. And that holder is not nearly as rational as we expect him to be. When he starts to behave irrationally, i.e. either taken over by greed or fear, he starts to treat the portfolios as one whole and either sells off the family silver with the trash, or buys trash along with silver.

One way to reduce correlation is to invest in a stock only if you will not need this money to pay margins to your broker or pay for your living. If at times of distress, you will need this money, you will be selling for reasons other than the stock's potential to be a multibagger. Stay with stocks where the investors are different; for example, one of your stocks may be dominated by institutional investors and another by individual investors.

Multibagger stocks have fat tails

Just as earthquakes, tsunamis and other catastrophes happen at a much higher frequent rate than any statistical projection, spectacular rise and falls in the markets happen more frequently than what you would expect. The occurrence of things more often than it seems likely is a fat tail. Stock markets demonstrate fat tails all the time. Stock market falls can be triggered in minutes and for reasons that don't seem remotely able to cause such falls.

But the fat tails also mean that stocks will be mispriced more often. It is the extreme mispricing of the stock that you are looking for. You have to differentiate between permanent change in price or a temporary displacement of price. Permanent change in price is triggered by change in regulations, a structural change in the demand for a product, etc. Temporary changes in prices happen because of global outflows, a sudden need for capital, etc.

Investors tend to get average data about investment performance in sectors and stock markets. Most stocks in a sector or the market stay around the mean financial ratios of their peers. The task for a multibagger investor is to find stocks that are not part of the average but are breaking out of the pack.

Superior returns are temporary

Select a stock based on an undervalued theme and exit when the theme becomes popular to get the maximum out of a multibagger. Over time, competitors, alternative products, government regulations and a host of other things make a business move from delivering above average returns to average returns. The stock turns into a commodity and investors then have multiple alternatives to the stock. As an increasing number of investors realize the multibagger potential of the stock and push the price higher, the stock suffers a diminishing ability to become a multibagger. The larger the discovery of the potential of the stock, the less the chance of any significant rise in the stock's price.

You are in the business of absolute returns

"A speculative merchant exercises no one regular, established, or well-known branch of business. He is a corn merchant this year, or tea merchant the year after. He enters into every trade when he foresees that it is likely to be more than commonly profitable, and he quits when he foresees that its profits are likely to return to the level of others."

– Adam Smith, *The Wealth of Nations*

Preconceived or popular notions of which industries or stocks are good or bad, or believing that you understand a stock or sector better than others is the undoing of investors. It also leads you to frame the wrong investment goal. If you frame your investing goal as returns of 500% to 1,000% in 3 to 5 years, you are more likely to find a multibagger rather than starting by saying, "Bank stocks will do well and I will invest in them."

Setting a goal for the returns you are looking for makes you look for opportunities wherever they are available and shift from investing to trading to futures to options. This flexibility in approach and in stocks is essential for reaching the high goals on returns you would have set for yourself.

Your single minded goal is to get a multibagger with the lowest possible risk. The only benchmark of your performance is the returns your investments deliver. The method you use, fundamentals, technicals, futures and options, or the sector you invest in or the part of the market cycle you enter must all be geared towards achieving multibagger returns.

Having an ideology of being only a value investor, or not believing in technicals, or investing on intrinsic values are fatal to your success. Keep an open mind, master fundamentals, technicals and futures and options and look for opportunity anywhere it presents itself as long as the odds of investing in the stock present you a return of 5 to 10 times your investment.

No single investment defines your success

Think of multibagger returns in terms of all the multibagger stocks you pick over a 5 to 10 year horizon. Don't look at multibagger returns from a single stock. It is one thing to get a 5- to 10-fold return on one stock but replicating this level of return over 5 to 10 years over a number of stocks requires a robust process and significant expertise. Over a lifetime, you may buy hundreds of stocks that look like multibagger opportunities. Some of them will turn into multibaggers. Most will not.

You must not shy away from trial and error. It is a critical process to develop your expertise and to provide you a method to pick multibaggers. Put every thought you have into action if it meets the criteria of having the odds of a 5- to 10-fold appreciation — and keep notes both on why your investment process worked or did not work.

You must have a significant position size

You must invest an amount sufficient to give you a significant return when a stock turns into a multibagger. Investors often find great stocks but put so little money in them that even when they turn into multibaggers, the proceeds don't give them the cushion or comfort of having extra money.

Multibagger opportunities do not present themselves at all times, and when they do occur, you have to go for the jugular. Putting in a significant amount of your capital also confirms your conviction about a stock's potential.

The rules of engagement

"Prices tend to come down much harder and faster than they go up."
– Jeff Yass

What do you do if a stock falls because the entire market is going through a liquidity freeze? Take your profits and exit. A liquidity freeze results in losses across the market and no stock, no matter how precisely it has been picked, can last a market meltdown.

But such market meltdowns are also prime times to pick multibaggers. A lack of money, or a sudden need for money drives stock prices to levels which are way below their intrinsic value. If you have money when others don't you are bound to get bargains, and if you can wait it out till markets find equilibrium again, you will exit at multiples of your purchase price.

Don't confuse winning streaks with good decision making

For consistent performance, improve your decision making. Investors tend to believe in their superior stock picking ability after finding just one or two multibaggers. Ask yourself if the multibaggers were a result of random decisions, impulse, a sudden "gut" feeling about the stock, or a methodical investment process. Winning streaks make you continue on the same course of picking stocks without any method and eventually result in losing whatever you have made. Think of it as walking in a minefield blindfolded. If you managed to skip 3 or 4 mines, you start believing the field is safe, only to be blown away.

How to value a stock

There is no sure-shot mathematical formula for putting a correct value to a stock. The value of a stock depends on how old you are, how much money you have, your level of knowledge about the markets, your past and most recent experience with stocks. It is when there is extreme non-alignment between your stock's value and the market, and when you are right and the market is wrong, that a multibagger is born. Over time, you have to hope that the market's view on the stock's value will move towards your view of its value. Only, you may have entered the stock much ahead of that.

Look for stocks where you believe your view of its undervaluation is a view the market will accept after some time.

At the bottom of bear markets, you don't need to value stocks. The general disinterest in stocks, or a shortage of cash, or large scale unemployment, or a recession ensure low supply of money.

So a general rule to value stocks is: "Stocks are undervalued when too much stock is available while too little money is at hand and stocks are overvalued when too much money is available but too little stock." You must look for extremes of this condition to get in and get out of your multibagger investment.

IPOs will rarely be multibaggers

An IPO puts you in an adversarial position with the company's founders, and it's the company founder pays the bills of the investment banker. So the investment banker is going to try and get the best (the highest) price for the company's founder. If the founder gets the highest price, then you, the subscriber to the IPO, are squeezed out of a significant potential of a price rise

Why do companies make IPOs? Either because they cannot get money from banks or the debt markets, or because they want to discover a price for the stock. Discovering a price is nothing but finding out what price the market is ready to pay for it.

There are exceptions to this rule — but they are few. There are companies that are going to change the way people do business or revolutionize a process. Such companies may turn out to produce a multibagger even at the IPO stage.

In general though, IPOs are meant to give the promoter the best price. If the company is good, he will extract the last bit of price from the market. If he is doing an IPO to raise money because he has few other options, you can be sure the stock will not hold.

All buyers and sellers of stocks are not value investors

"The outstanding fact is the extreme precariousness of the basis of knowledge on which our estimates of the perspective yield have to be made. Our knowledge of the factors which will govern the yield of an investment some years hence is usually very slight and often negligible."

– John Maynard Keynes, *General Theory*

Value investors tend to believe that if they figure out the undervaluation of a stock, it is bound to produce abnormal returns over a period of time. That would be a correct assumption if there was a mathematical formula to determine value, and also if all other investors in the stock too were value investors.

Neither is there a precise formula to determine value nor do all buyers and sellers in a stock share a similar philosophy, look for similar profits, or invest with the same time horizon. Multibagger investors must account for the play between rational and irrational investors, traders and speculators, and a host of very different motivations of those who buy and sell the same stock. The speed at which the stock moves and the direction it takes depends on the majority of those putting up the money. Disregarding the role of other players in the stock can lead to miscalculations about where the stock could head and what it could produce in returns.

You don't have to wait for years for stock to turn into a multibagger

"One of the best rules anybody can learn about investing is to do nothing, absolutely nothing unless there is something to do. They make a big play and say, 'Boy, am I smart, I just tripled my money.' Then they rush out and have to do something else with that money. They can't jus sit there and wait for something new to develop."

– James Rogers

There is no correlation between the chances of bagging a multibagger and the length of time you hold a stock. Sitting for a long time in a stock, in fact, indicates that perhaps you entered it too soon. You may have got the multibagger potential part of the stock right, but timed your entry too early. Another danger of being in a stock for too long is that you don't realize the loss of opportunity cost of being in that stock. And you don't know if you made a wrong call if the stock goes nowhere for 2 to 3 years. You keep believing it will rise "some day."

You can have a multibagger in a few weeks, a few months, or in a year. It will take a couple of years for you to compress the time you need to turn your investments into multibaggers. You will need to master investing and, trading, and develop a disciplined investment psychology before you see a reduction in the time it takes for you to convert stocks into multibaggers.

Don't confuse economic growth with stock price rise

Buying stocks on prospects of economic growth is not a good idea. There is a lag time between positive economic growth, its impact on an industry, and its impact on individual stocks. Extrapolation of economic growth on stocks will not result in multibaggers. Whenever an economy picks up after a lull, it throws up a few successful companies and also offers opportunities to exit for others.

Don't confuse revenue growth with operating cash flows

Companies may be taking orders to show revenue growth but without cash flows, namely without getting paid for what they are selling, in which case there is little chance for them to invest and grow their businesses. Only if you can find stocks where operating cash flows are growing as fast as revenue does it provide a possible multibagger opportunity.

Avoid anchor effect investing

Anchor effect investing refers to buying stocks after they have fallen significantly in price. It refers to finding a stock cheap at its current price in relation to a high price you were earlier used to seeing the stock. Anchor effect investing rarely ends up with multibaggers. In fact, investing in stocks which have fallen from their highs ends up in losses. A stock that is losing ground indicates a loss of confidence in the company or management, or a loss of interest or a withdrawal of money by those who know more than does the public. A falling stock is not cheap.

Invest in tandem with institutional investors

One of the best opportunities come when Institutional investors become interested in a stock. Institutional investors may have an interest in the stock but may not be able to buy it because its market capitalization is not high enough for them to invest or because the current interest in small cap stocks is not significant enough for them to set up new small cap funds. If you can identify stocks where institutional investors will enter the moment the stock reaches the market capitalization threshold of institutional investors or if small cap interest picks up and several new small cap funds are set up, the prices can go up several times.

The opportunity must be overwhelming

"He is a fool who goes to war without an opportunity. To fight the mighty, it is sure is flapping wings just like a bee."
– Hitopdesa

For a stock to appreciate multiple times, it should be a sapling ready to grow into a fruit tree ready to bear fruit or a vineyard reaching the inflection point in terms of the age of the vines where the wine produced can fetch a very high price.

There are millions of investors on the prowl for opportunities, and thousands of institutional investors with the sharpest mind in the business, you can't find an opportunity all the time. So you have to wait for when the opportunity arises. It may arise because most investors are migrating to cash, or have serious liquidity issues. Multibagger opportunities can also arise if you can graduate your thinking to "second level" thinking. It is the ability to look beyond the obvious and visualize changes in the way things are done and then identify the companies that are best placed to leverage these opportunities.

Pick stocks in which institutional investors may get interested

Buy stocks which neither the FIIs nor the brokers have noticed as yet. If you are right about the company's potential, institutional investors eventually will notice the company and you will be sitting on a multibagger. The rise in a stock's price is the best way to test if you have picked the right stock. If the basis on which you picked the stock is incorrect, the stock may languish at the same price for months, and sometimes years.

There are many signals you can pick up that indicate institutional interest in a stock. Institutional investors buy stocks based either on their own research or research from top tier institutional brokers. If institutional brokers start to cover an industry or a stock that has thus far not met their interests threshold, it indicates the eventual entry of the stock in institutional investor portfolios. Another indication is when a number of fund managers begin to talk about a sector where the stock market capitalisations have not so far been high enough for them to invest.

Pick stocks where supply takes time to adjust to demand

In several industries like hotels, cement, etc., there is a lag time for supply to catch up with demand. The period in between creates low risk opportunities for multibaggers. On the other hand, you must stay away from stocks in sectors where enough supply exists to meet even the increased demand.

When supply is abundant, companies are not in a position to increase prices. Where supply will take a few years to catch up with demand, companies can increase prices at will and create multibagger opportunities.

Look for sectors where the supply curve is not a smooth line but moves in steps. In such sectors, the pricing power of the companies shifts from the consumers to producers. This usually happens in sectors or industries where production is consolidated in a few producers or companies. Cement is a classic example. In such industries, capacity reaches a point after which new plants have to be added. Now, new plants take years to set up. In the interim, cement companies can increase prices several times and stocks can rise in multiples. Keep a watch on how far away companies are from reaching capacity utilization levels and enter before the inflection point is reached.

Buy at points of extreme pessimism

"Bull markets are born in pessimism, grow on skepticism, mature on optimism, and die of euphoria."
– Sir John Templeton

Markets can fall at any time and for any reason. All falls are not multibagger opportunities. Multibagger opportunities arise only when the psychology of investors changes. And psychology changes when investors start feeling pessimistic. Pessimism of the majority is the time when stocks start to trade below what they are worth and extreme pessimism is when stocks fall because no one wants to own them.

As pessimism grows, the risk of picking a multibagger falls and the chances of a stock turning into a multibagger rises. The seeds of a bull market are sown at the depths of pessimism.

Don't get swayed and stay away from the market when there is consensus that there is no way for things to improve. Things always improve. Stock markets move in cycles and the lower the market heads in a cycle, the greater the chances it will rise back.

Look for new sectors where there are fewer listed stocks

When a new asset class or sector is emerging, there will be few listed stocks in that sector. If the sector catches the market's fancy, prices of the few available stocks will move up exponentially. This rise in stock prices is because of an imbalance in the supply of stocks as compared to the demand for stocks in the new emerging sector. Over a period of time, IPOs in the sector will flood the market, bringing about a balance between the supply and demand for the stock. The time to get into such stocks is when there is too much demand chasing the few available stocks: Once there is an oversupply of stocks in the sector, it's time to get out of it.

Selling principles

"Don't sell stocks, when the sap is running up the trees."
– Jesse Livermore

When you sell has as much impact on your multibagger portfolio as when you buy. If a stock is not doing what you thought it will do, getting out of the stock before it starts to clock losses of more than 10% of the purchase price and staying with the stock for as long as the run continues are both important to enable the entire portfolio to deliver multibagger returns.

ETF inflows portend multibaggers

Exchange traded funds tend to receive the largest pools of money and reflect a pool of blind capital that enters a particular market or asset class because that's where there is a clear uptrend. Exchange traded funds can turn an uptrend into a massive tsunami by the amount of money they receive. The amount of money they receive may not match the availability of stock (for example small cap stocks or pharmaceutical stocks) and this could lead to a massive rise in prices of a group of stocks.

A multibagger investor then can focus on the rising tide of EFT money into a particular sector or industry and buy into it.

Stocks that will not turn into multibaggers

"Even if you manage to pick the bottom, the market can end up sitting there for years and tying up your capital. You don't want to have a position before a move has started. You want to wait until the move is already under way before you get into the market."
– Randy McKay

Most stocks fall in price, or are cheap for a reason. Low management quality, low margins, mature business are all reasons why a stock may not turn into a multibagger. Stocks with low PE ratios or high book value look tempting but they are investing traps. Stocks that end up having low PE ratios or high book value may indicate a mature industry or investor disinterest and may never recover. Then there are stocks that have dropped down 90% to

95% from their highs and have little or no chance of ever going back up again.

To avoid stocks that have a low probability of turning into multibaggers, you have to work on your psychology. You must have very high entry standards for multibagger stocks as compared to investing in stock for 20% or 30% return. This includes skipping stock investing on earnings growth, low PE, high book value and other such conventional measures. It also means avoiding stocks that have fallen 90% to 95%. It means thinking of how the world will look in the next 2 to 3 years, and how a company is poised to leverage the new world. A great example of a latter type of company is Google. In anticipating how Google could change the way people search for information you needed to look for companies that are not given to "projected growth rates" or growth rates based on number of products sold, but those that can scale up in revenues and sales so significantly that they have to be structurally valued. This also rules out companies in very heavy capital investment businesses and businesses with long gestation periods unless you are at the cusp of a new growth cycle in that industry and the stocks are selling for pennies.

If you are in a wrong stock, not only do you not get a multibagger, precious time is also wasted on a wrong course of action. It is critical to develop a method of avoiding stocks and markets that will not end up being multibaggers. A starting point for any process to identify a multibagger must be to ask yourself that if you bought the stock today, would it end up giving you a 5- or 10-fold return in the next few days, months or years.

Investment manias are your chance to make big money

What is an investment mania. It is a market where investors are in stocks not because they understand the market, or think that there is value, or for any of the traditional reasons to be in the market but simply because they can flip stocks to others at a higher price. This phase provides one of the best times for multibagger investing at the lowest risk. But you must not sell out too early in such a phase. Stocks may rise many times beyond what you consider a reasonable price, so don't be in too much of a hurry to sell.

Investment manias are once in a life time opportunity for generating exponential wealth from multiple multibagger opportunities. But you must fight off the normal human impulse to consider any significant price rise from the price level they are used to as making a stock overvalued.

In an investment mania, there is a structural mismatch between the demand and supply for stocks. If everyone wants to get into stocks, there is only a certain supply of stock available at any point of time. Unending demand can spike up stock prices in multiples at such times.

Sailing against the wind

We have been programmed to stick to group behaviour. The cost and penalty of digressing from accepted behaviour is usually severe. If you don't behave in a manner that is generally acceptable, you can become an outcast, lose your job, or even get thrown out of your own house.

Multibagger investing requires you to break away from group behaviour. Since it is not natural for human beings to behave differently, you have to consciously practice thinking differently about stocks. Different thinking enables you to find investment themes before others latch onto them, and gives you a head start in picking stocks at prices that are set to rise multiple times.

When stock markets collapse, the mood becomes despondent. It is not easy to buy when the entire world is selling. When those around you are focusing on preserving cash or turning stocks into cash, it will take courage to do the opposite. You don't have to go against the tide every time the markets head down but only when the falls are driven by a change of psychology of investors from optimism to pessimism.

Look out for the unexpected

"The expected never happens; it is the unexpected always."
– John Maynard Keynes

Certain risks, such as disappointing earnings, a fall in the market, etc. are known and expected. The risk in buying stocks where the risks are known is low. The risk in buying stocks where the risks are not known is high.

Investors do the exact opposite. They avoid stocks where the price has collapsed because of some known risk. They buy into stocks where there is no negative news. But no negative news does not mean that things are fine with the company or that information has not been suppressed.

Multibagger investing requires avoiding stocks where everything looks great and everyone is interested in getting into the stock. If everyone is in the stock, its price cannot be cheap — and the chances of a price collapse are high if any negative news hits the stock.

It's the cycle which produces the opportunity

Many trends — both up and down — make up a cycle. But the biggest and lasting wealth opportunities are thrown up in getting the cycle right even if we are wrong on the intervening trends. Watch for turning points in a cycle for multibagger investing.

Cycles start and stop when investors swing from optimism to pessimism, or *vice versa*. For investors to change their perspective about being in equities requires massive losses of principal by a majority of investors. Change in perspective rarely happens when investors lose some part of the gains; it happens when they have significant losses in their invested capital. For a majority to lose a significant portion of their capital would require the market to be at a euphoric peak but poised to collapse, a stage when the largest set of investors (most of whom have no idea how the markets work) enter at prices which they don't understand or appreciate. They unwittingly become the financiers and subsidisers of a savvy minority which begins exiting just around the time the majority of investors enter the markets.

Anticipate the anticipations of others

"To be able to do something before it exists, sense something before it becomes active, see something before it sprouts, are three abilities that develop interdependently. Then nothing is sensed but is comprehended, nothing is undertaken without response, nowhere does one go without benefit."

– Sun Tzu

Investing may be a lonely pursuit but successful investing requires you to anticipate what other investors are going to do. For a stock to become a multibagger, many others will have to pour money into it. Whatever the motivation of its other buyers, a stock will move only when a growing number of investors pour money into it.

Recognize an opportunity before the world does — or catch a momentum wave before it rises — that is the way to pick multibaggers, and not by averaging, discipline, long term investing, or any such market "truism."

You can buy a fruit tree sapling and wait for ten years to bear fruit, or buy a fruit tree old enough to begin bearing fruit. Not only do you have to wait for a long time when you buy a sapling, the number of things that can go wrong on the way are many. The sapling may not survive to become a tree, or may get infected, etc.

Multibagger investing then is not just a question of identifying the right multibagger stocks, but identifying them when they are ripe to bear fruits and not years before they reach the fruit bearing stage. In market terms, it means that you must be ahead of the crowd in entering the stock, but not too much ahead of it. The crowd is needed to push the price up, so if the crowd remains disinterested, the stock may not rise for years.

You are your own best investment guru

"As long as you stick to your own style, you get the good and bad in your own approach. When you try to incorporate someone else's style, you often wind up with the worst of both styles. I've done that a lot."

– Michael Marcus.

Sometimes we think we should emulate the Warren Buffett's of the world and play the market like them. But most of us are not Warren Buffett. We must each play our own game, a game in which we define the parameters of what we can possibly achieve, given our own distinct strengths and limitations.

Why would a market guru tell you about a multibagger early on in the game? He may tell you about it when the stock has already appreciated significantly, and at its current prices cannot deliver multibagger returns any more.

This opens up several questions you must ask yourself. Are you getting your market guru's information through financial TV? In which case, so are another million people. That would mean that the stock is already reaching its peak. Even if you have access to the market guru, how high are you in his chain of priority for him to tell you about real multibagger opportunities. There are some who blindly follow whatever their market guru is doing. This approach is fraught with danger and almost never produces multibaggers.

One other reason you cannot rely on market gurus or others to guide your investing is that nothing works all the time. Value works in some market cycles, momentum in others.

Taking responsibility for your investment decisions and developing an edge to pick multibaggers is the only way to invest. No one is interested in plucking multibaggers and handing them over to you.

Managements make companies

"There are routes not to be followed, armies not to be attacked, citadels not to be besieged, territory not to be fought over."

– Sun Tzu

When the opportunity presents itself, choose companies with management with potential, execution ability and scale. Management quality, integrity and sharing rewards with minority shareholders is the only way stocks can deliver even when you buy them at rock bottom. Rouge companies and rouge promoters may spike up the stock using dubious means but it will always end badly. Either a regulatory investigation or some other scam will destroy the stock.

All construction companies don't do well. Nor do all textile companies. It is their managements that make some companies do well. Just because the economy is doing well, there is no particular reason why all listed stocks in that sector will do well. In fact, the contrary is usually true. With easy access to capital, many more companies enter or grow in the area enhancing capacities and putting pressure on profits for everyone.

Severe economic conditions and poor markets don't discriminate between good and bad managements. They slam all stocks. In fact, better run companies may be slammed harder because their shareholders are usually institutional shareholders who often tend to exit a stock as a group causing very serious cracks in its price.

Leveraging irrationality

"Markets were not perfectly liquid and investors are not perfectly rational."
– Sebastian Mallaby

While talking long term is a favourite pastime, immediate herd mentality frequently overtakes the markets. Money flows in and out of markets within days based on changed perception of the investing crowd about a major event around the world or a market. If money flows reverse out of a market, especially an emerging market, it could slam stocks very severely as local investors are often unable to absorb foreign selling, at least not immediately. Such a scenario creates several multibagger opportunities.

Irrational behaviour is the hallmark of the stock market and leveraging this irrationality is why so many investors end up picking multibaggers. Investors tend to invest and exit stocks on impulse or for reasons unconnected to the stock, e.g. their need for liquidity.

Your investing direction must be opposite of that of the crowd. When everyone is heading out of the stock, you must head in.

Multibagger opportunities disappear when others catch on

"In the winter, I shovelled snow. At first, I charged a nickel, but I found that there was so much demand that I raised the price to a dime, and then to 15 cents. The first year, when I was eight, I made several dollars, but the next year the other kids caught on, and the markets changed."
– Edward Thorp

What differentiates a multibagger investing from regular value investing is that you have to time your entry to perfection. If you are too early, the stock may not move and if you are too late, the price may have appreciated to an extent that the stock cannot be a multibagger. And when you have identified the multibagger put enough money to be worth your while.

Multibagger opportunities cease to exist when everyone latches on to the same stock. If the market has recognized the stock's potential the price will rise to a level where there will be little profit left to be squeezed.

Risk and return are not completely correlated

"The desire for constant action irrespective of underlying conditions is responsible for many losses on Wall Street even among the professionals, who feel that they must take home some money every day, as though they were working for regular wages."

– Jesse Livermore, *Reminiscences of a Stock Operator*

Conventional wisdom is that higher risk has to be taken to generate higher returns. But this sounds absurd. If something can give you higher returns then, it cannot be risky. What holds true though is that when you take a higher risk you may have a chance of making a higher return. The "chance of higher returns" is not the same as "higher returns." Return is not certain just because you take a risk. Conversely, sometimes you can get exponential returns even with minimal risk.

Risk is often confused with ad hoc decision making, following the gut, impulsiveness, etc. But risk is not the same as recklessness or impulsiveness. Risk deals with only the odds of an investment turning into a multibagger. You improve your odds of multibagger returns when you make a low risk investment. You make a low risk investment when the chance of a significant further fall in stock is extremely small as compared to the upside potential of the stock.

Higher returns then are necessarily a consequence of consciously reducing risk.

Multibagger opportunities comes up more frequently than we think

"Much of the real world is controlled as much by the 'tails' of distributions as by means or averages; by the exceptional, not the men, by the catastrophe, not the steady drip; by the very rich, not the 'middle class.' We need to free ourselves from 'average' thinking."

– Philip Anderson, Nobel Prize recipient in physics

Look at the distribution of wealth in most countries. The top 5% control over 60% to 90% of the wealth. And they control the wealth because they don't constrain themselves to consensus thinking but are ready to look at opportunities that seem far fetched and where the downside is limited but the upside is unlimited.

Changing your thinking is perhaps the most important challenge you will face. To think of stocks as generating returns in multiples rather than percentages, to put a significant chunk of money in one stock, and in being ready to take opportunities of excessive volatility and uncertainty come with practice.

6

~

Psychology of Multibagger Investing

"We have seen much more money made and kept by 'ordinary people' who were temperamentally well suited for the investment process than by those who lacked this quality, even though they had an extensive knowledge of finance, accounting and stock market lore."

– Benjamin Graham, *The Intelligent Investor*

MULTIBAGGER INVESTING REQUIRES A ROBUST understanding of crowds and of investor psychology. Most multibagger opportunities will spring up from the irrationality or impulsive behaviour of the crowd of buyers and sellers in the market. It is known that the psychology of the crowd is usually inferior to the psychology of the investors who constitute the crowd. Inferior reasoning of a large part of the market gives rise to multibagger opportunities.

Much of your success in finding multibagger stocks will depend on the changes you make to your investing psychology. Much of what is needed in counter-intuitive and will require you to think against the values and principles you apply in your daily life. It will often be diametrically opposite to what you have been made to believe are the rules of investing or trading.

Why we are unable to participate in bull markets

"Great fortunes (are a) consequence of a long life of industry, frugality and attention."

– Adam Smith

Investors tend to treat stocks like grocery shopping. But neither are stocks like buying grocery, nor can you buy them in that manner. The comparison is fallacious. Have you ever seen grocery prices appreciate after you bought them?

Stock markets are more akin to horse racing. You have to put your money on the fastest horse, not the cheapest. Investors get used to a certain price of a stock and when it doubles from there, they look for cheaper alternatives. But how much the stock has risen from an investment's starting point is immaterial to the prospects of the stock. The only relevant point for an investor is to pick stocks which have the most potential to rise from the point of their purchase.

Because of the tendency to look for "cheaper" or "low priced stocks," or stocks that have not risen as much, most investors lose out on multibagger opportunities.

Since stock picking is so much about psychology and the flow of money, expertise in technical analysis or reading charts is an invaluable tool for knowing when to enter stocks and how long to hold them. Charts can show you which stocks are running the fastest and are backed by an increase in volume or the number of shares traded. This is the best indicator of the fastest running stocks and those which will deliver the best returns.

You will have to fight our inborn psychology of looking for "deals." And we consider prices lower than our anchor price as a deal. In investing, this can lead to fatal results.

Opinions, beliefs and ideologies

Each of us want to identify ourselves with some form of investing, be it value investing, trading, day trading, etc. This restricts our ability to see an opportunity for what it is because we look at opportunities from the limited lens of our investing style.

If you invest with opinions, beliefs and other ideologies, the markets will bring unrelenting punishment. Your only goal is to get a multibagger. There are no superior styles in getting a multibagger. Being a value investor does not make you any better than a trader, a chartist or a speculator. The sooner you can get rid of conventional ideas about how and who can come up with a multibagger, the faster you will start to invest in stocks that will turn into multibaggers.

Your market psychology has to be similar to that of a Samurai's

A good samurai knows that he is mortal. All he tries to do is to painstakingly master, over his entire lifetime, every potential move of the opponent. He does not tell the opponent what to do, nor what he believes in, nor what he expects. In this lies his victory; not in forming an opinion and then hoping the opponent will follow the course of his opinion.

That, as you will appreciate, would be fatal. It's the same for markets. You must understand that we have no control over what will move the stock and when — all we can do is to interpret its next move to the best of our ability. The market is indifferent to your wishes and hopes, and moves to its own rhythm.

Practice improves your odds of identifying multibagger opportunities but there will always be blind corners, hidden risks and surprise turns to a stock, no matter how much experience you have. The advantage an investor has over the samurai is that no blow has to be fatal. When the opportunity does not go the way you expect, you can exit the stock.

Human behaviour is the single biggest driver of prices

What is it that gives you the edge in picking multibaggers? It's not the amount of research you do or the reports you read, for they are based on publicly available information. It is your ability to look at things in ways others cannot, in seeing opportunities when others can't, in putting up money because of your conviction, and in holding on to stocks when they seem to have risen substantially that differentiates you.

The stocks in our portfolio automatically become related to one another because of their common owner — us. This factor especially comes into play in times of panic or bear markets. When we need to sell stocks, it really does not matter what kind of a diversified portfolio we hold. That is why we must invest only such money in stocks that we won't need in an emergency.

Accept that you are fallible

Successful investors know that they are not invincible, and that they can be wiped out at any time. It is in this grounding that they never lose focus or sight of risks and know when to exit the market and sit out, as much as they know when to enter.

The sense of fallibility, even paranoia about failure, is a key ingredient in the success of great investors and traders.

The beautiful thing about investing is that you don't have to fall. You don't have to lose much and you can control your risk. But to do this, you have to fight your ego. As long as you are ready to exit stocks at preset levels of losses from your purchase price, you will always be able to limit your losses. What happens in real life though is that we continue to believe we are right even when the threshold we have set for taking a loss is crossed, we continue to hold the stock hoping for a recovery.

Accepting fallibility is especially important in multibagger investing. We can have a multibagger portfolio only if we don't let losses go out of control. Otherwise gains from multibaggers can be lost by large losses in other stocks, and the portfolio will then deliver only average returns.

Human behaviour doesn't change, whatever else might

"One with a hundred longs for a thousand, one with a thousand yearns for millions, one who lords over millions wants to rule a kingdom, the kings aim to gain Paradise itself."

– Panchtantra

Look at stock picking from the perspective of human thought processes. Human thought processes are often influenced by their immediate term experiences, feelings at any point of time, etc. There are no rational investors because stock investing is not a rational activity. But the understanding of human behaviour gives you the most vital clues on multibagger opportunities.

Human behaviour has remained more or less constant over the centuries. Means have changed, but motives and goals have remained the same. In essence, the twin human traits of greed and fear set the tone for market's direction and swings more than any valuation story.

Don't be distracted by new technologies, the speed with which you get information, or any other such tool. At the end of the road, humans will make decisions and their decision making process or speed has not evolved over centuries. This allows us to learn valuable lessons from financial history and from those who have experienced market cycles and mastered stock picking skills before you.

Guard against overconfidence in your investing decisions

"It is not about how much you can afford to risk, but you also have to consider how many potential future winners you might miss because of the effect of the larger loss on your mental attitude."
– Randy Mckay

Overconfidence in your investing decisions is one of the reasons your investments may not deliver. Much of our investing decision making is based on incomplete or unreliable information, or too much optimism or confidence in our analysis. We also tend to find patterns and relationships between economic growth, market movements and stock prices that don't exist, or are at best tenuous leading, to serious investment errors.

Investors mistake opinions for factual information and most of what is dished out as financial news are financial opinions. Not only are opinions almost always wrong when they try to predict the future, they are misleading. Investing based on what one market guru or expert says may distort your thinking about a stock.

Independent thinking is essential for picking multibaggers. That thinking cannot be based on number crunching alone because financial statements themselves are opinions about the financial health of the company based on some accounting standards that often are bizarre. Also, managements have considerable leeway to present financial information in ways which suit them but not you.

So don't take anything as a given. Question everything. Question financial statements, management statements, market gurus, financial media. Questioning produces uncomfortable questions and if you can find answers to these questions, you get closer to finding multibaggers.

Take a break if you have a losing streak

"Losing begets losing. When you start losing, it touches off negative elements in your psychology; it leads to pessimism."
– Michael Marcus

Investing is as much psychology as it is prediction. And human psychology takes a hit when you lose a couple of times on the trot. Losing disorients us and makes us do things to recoup losses, act on impulse, etc., all dangerous to any longer time investing. Holding steady to your thoughts is important and when you have a losing streak, either your thought process has been infected or you are on a wrong line of reasoning. Either way, stop for a while and disconnect from investing. Get back to stock picking after a month or two of a total disconnect with stocks. During this period, don't watch financial news, nor read financial books, nor check market indices, nor stock prices. A complete and total detoxification from a losing streak will allow you a fresh perspective to multibagger picking.

The stock we invest in does not owe us anything. But we tend to expect the stock to deliver. And if it does not deliver, we either add more of the same stock to our portfolio or find other stocks to make up for the losses in a stock. This approach leads to a losing streak. Losing streaks are extremely damaging to your psychology and can disorient you for some time. If you have a losing streak, exit the stock and take a break. You must flush out feelings of making up for your losses, anger or impulse that can manifest themselves when we have a losing streak.

The importance of feedback loops on stock prices

"Most investors also seem to view the stock market as a force of nature unto itself. They do not fully realize that they themselves, as a group, determine the level of the market. And they underestimate how similar to their own thinking is that of investors."

– Robert Schiller in *Irrational Exuberance*

Feedback loops are critical for the formation of a multibagger. A rise in a stock's price bring in more investors and traders. Reporting and opinions on the stock improves. Stock prices don't rise in isolation but create positive feedback on the stock's potential that fuels further buying. If the positive feedback loop is fed by stock influencers like mutual funds, institutional investors or famous investors and traders, a stock can take a life of its own.

A rise in stock price with increasing volumes generates an interest in the stock. As the stock's price rises, the market capitalization of the stock rises.

This brings in investors who need a certain level of liquidity, volumes or market capitalization to buy the stock. A further rise in stock prices stops sellers from selling the stock in anticipation of rising prices. A feedback loop sets in where rising prices drive greater demand for the stock and reduces the supply of the stock.

Knowing when a feedback loop is in operation is important for staying with the stock. A reversal of the feedback loop, when sellers rush to sell and buyers retreat, also signals the exit point for multibagger investors.

Logical reasoning does not work in multibagger investing

"A chain of logical argumentation is totally incomprehensible to crowds, and for this reason it is permissible to say that they do not reason or that they reason falsely and are not to be influenced by reasoning."

– Gustave Le Bon, *The Crowdend of 19th Century*

You cannot apply logic in a psychological game. A psychological game requires us to anticipate the psychology of others and not the prospects of a company. The prospects of a company are mere opinions of management, market analysts, investors and traders. The investing challenge is compounded when you have millions of investors and traders trying to anticipate the stock price.

That is why multibagger investing is a trap for engineers, doctors or those trained in finding definitive answers. It suits those who have a background in fields where there are no definitive answers, like philosophy, etc.

There is as much gap between logical reasoning and a spectacular rise in markets as there is between night and day. And the only time a stock turns into a multibagger is when a vast majority of investors invest or trade because they expect profits rather than making decisions based on any systematic process or logic. Look for market conditions where a vast majority of investors and traders are participating because they think it is easy money and they feel stock picking is some kind of an exciting game.

The point of your exit is when people stop listening to anything that contradicts their thought process.

Mistakes multibagger investors make

"We're accustomed to thinking in terms of centralized control, clear chains of command, the straightforward logic of cause and effect. But in huge, interconnected systems, where every player ultimately affects every other, our standard ways of thinking fall apart. Simple pictures and verbal arguments are too feeble, too myopic."

- Steven Strogatz

- Being unable to think about a stock's prospects from various angles — investors form opinions about a stock and find it difficult to consider alternate views on why a stock may or may not rise.
- Thinking of stock price rise to be an effect of some cause — investors look for a rationale to justify the rise in a stock's price. But cause and effect are tenuous at best in a stock's rise. Stock prices are driven by multiple factors and depend on the psychology of thousands and millions of investors. Simple cause and effect analysis can lead to losses for investors in such complex systems.
- Investors find a stock and are convinced that it is undervalued. That is only a part of the stock picking process. The second and more important part is to determine what others are thinking about the stock or how they may perceive it in the future.
- Investors think they have a low risk stock pick when they have convinced themselves about its undervaluation based on conventional stock picking methods, such as low PE, etc. They tend to consider a stock high risk when they believe the stock is overvalued. The basis of the under- or overvaluation is flawed.
- Not giving a thought to who you are competing with. If the stock has a high institutional shareholding, it may indicate there is little upside left in the stock's price. If the stock has no institutional interest, think of where the money will come from to drive up the stock.
- Picking stocks based on financial statement, management statements, financial media opinions, etc.
- Not giving enough attention to the mood of the market and the direction of money flow.

Understanding the behaviour of crowds

Understanding the behaviour of crowds is a key skill for picking multibaggers:

- The reasoning of crowds is always inferior but it is enough to drive prices to extreme levels.
- The imagination of crowds can be a driving factor to take stocks to multibagger levels.
- Crowds are influenced by ideas that have a conviction to them and are simple. That is why they tend to be in the largest numbers when a market is at its peak. At that point, a market seems to confirm that good times will continue forever and that it is very simple for anyone to make money.
- Crowds enter the market when the investment theme has been overly simplified and made to look as though making money in stocks is a breeze. So if an investment theme is still being discussed at a conceptual level or scientific manner, it is the time to get into a stock.
- It will take time before an investment theme is planted in the minds of the public. This gives a multibagger investor time to pick on the theme that is in the process of being sold to the public and being simplified. A good sign for a multibagger investor to get out is when the crowds are right and sophisticated investors are flummoxed by the market's rise.
- Crowds tend to justify the rise in a stock or the market by finding correlations or causes that have little to do with the stock's rise. The public also indulges in using generalizations to justify the stock's rise.
- People are not driven by logic but by anticipation of easy money. Even when they assign reason which is rare to investing in a stock, the reasons are irrelevant.
- Crowds tend to disregard the prospect or the ability of a stock to hold a high price as impossible. In fact, the more impossible it seems, the more they seem to rush into the stock or the market.
- Crowds can change their opinions very quickly causing stock prices to rise or collapse in short spans of time.

If you cannot lose, you will not win

"While it's essential to respect the market to assure preservation of capital, you can't win if you're fearful of losing. Fear will keep you from making correct decisions."
– The New Market Wizards

Multibagger investing is like tennis. You can be World No. 1 but the No. 20 could beat you some days. But that does not reduce who you are nor the standard of the game. It is just the nature of the game that on some day and in some circumstances you may not win. Even the best investors will get multibagger opportunity wrong. The loss should not bother you nor should it go out of control. It should be used to improve your investing.

Taking risk is an essential part of multibagger investing. Risk requires us to invest in stocks where the odds of gains are high. Inherent in investing is the ability to take a loss. The way we manage risk is to limit our losses to a certain percentage of our purchase price. It also requires us to make the next investment without being influenced by a loss in the previous one. That is why it is important to limit your losses. Large losses impact our psychology and cause us to digress from our investment process.

Don't let your mood decide your stocks

Legendary investors can't even generate the returns of a novice in runaway bull markets. This should not surprise you because experienced investors rarely fall for the trap of following the herd. They wait for the herd to disperse before entering a stock, and for the herd to grow to its largest size to sell a stock.

Going against the herd or the market mood is one of the most difficult things to do. As social beings, humans want to belong and so you have to cultivate a specific mindset to be able to do things differently and not look for a confirmation from the market.

When markets are at their peak, the feeling of being left out is intense. You almost feel as if insulted or fleeced somehow. Then as markets move into a bear phase, we feel a distaste for stocks. Neither emotion is rational, but that is how our emotions work.

It takes conviction to see and put money into what others have not seen.

Losses have serious psychological consequences

"When you're in a losing streak, your ability to properly assimilate and analyse information starts to become distorted because of the impairment of the confidence factor, which is a by-product of a losing streak. You have to work very hard to restore that confidence."

– Bill Lipschutz

Multibagger investors must exit all stocks where their losses exceed their pre-set loss limit. You can set your loss limit at 10% or 15% of your purchase price. If you don't put such a limit and allow a stock to drift because you believe it will recover, or buy additional shares because the stock has become cheaper than earlier, you are priming yourself for being forced to sell at a much lower price. If a stock is drifting lower after you have invested, it is possible you have missed something that others know.

The bigger and more severe damage of taking large losses is the psychological impact it has on your other investments, or in finding future multibaggers. Human beings are programmed to become risk averse to anything in which they have taken a hit. It is a normal human reaction. In life, we cannot set limits to how badly we have been hurt, but when you can do so in stocks, why not set a loss limit so that it does not needlessly impact or alter your investment style.

Don't stick to ideology

If you are given to principles and don't like to give up, you must build up a new set of traits for multibagger investing. Multibagger investing requires you to exit and enter depending on the opportunity, and stay invested only if you see the stock rising. You must think of multibaggers as stocks that rise because the demand for the stock far outweighs the availability of the stock. Whatever the reasons for this, demand for the stock must outweigh its supply to make it a multibagger. Lack of ideology is a great asset in the market. Lack of ideology allows you to shift loyalties at a moment's notice. And, in the markets, loyalties always lie with the rising sun.

Rejoice in failure – but only if it improves your stock picking abilities

"There is not a single dabbler in scrip who does not steadfastly believe, first, that a crash sooner or later, is inevitable; and secondly, that he himself will escape it. When the luck turns, and the crack play is suave qui peut, *or devil take the hindmost, no one fancies that the last mail train from panic station will leave him behind. In this, as in other respects, men deem all mortal but themselves."*

– A letter in the *Times* in 1845

Every time we make a fool of ourselves, we must resolve to read up every possible material from financial history, hone up on various schools of financial thinking — fundamental, technical, behavioural, etc. Most of our mistakes originate from ignorance and a lack of knowledge. We could have avoided just about every mistake had we read up on financial history, understood the nature of crowd manias, the craziness of stock prices driven by a new technology or country.

The number of times we'll lose or make a mistake is drastically reduced if we analyse our failures. And the number of times we can get superior returns gets multiplied just by knowing how things work.

What we must work on throughout our investing life is to develop a temperament that investing needs. That includes being able to see things when others cannot, having the conviction of putting your money ahead of the crowds, being able to sit tight when markets are running up, and not getting carried away into buying when others are making loads of money.

The courage to act on your beliefs

"While some build Castles in the Air, Directors buil'em in the Seas; Subscribers plainly see'um there. For fools will see as Wise men please."

– Jonathan Swift, *The Bubble* (1720)

We all agree that there are so many stocks which we thought were going to become multibaggers, and they did become multibaggers over a period of time. Only, we never bought them. Thinking you were able to identify a multibagger without putting money in the stock leads to two fallacies. First, human psychology conveniently makes us avoid how many stocks we got wrong in order to identify that one multibagger. Second, your psychology about a stock undergoes a tectonic change as soon as you put money in the stock.

If you believe in your analysis, then put up the money and put it in quantities where a loss will hurt you and multibagger returns will make a material difference to your wealth. This also helps you refine your multibagger investing process and enables you to look at investing as something that can hurt you as much as it can generate a return.

Emotional temperament is key to taking action on the structural shifts the markets may be showing. It takes courage to follow our own beliefs and analysis because at the point of making such investment calls ahead of the market, the crowd is usually betting the other way.

Being the lone ranger

"Victories of good warriors are not flukes . . . they position themselves where they will surely win."

– Sun Tzu

Multibagger investing is a game for the lone ranger. If you like to follow your own road, make your own decisions and have faith in your own convictions, you will do well.

Think of yourself as the Columbus or Captain Cook of investing. You cannot follow others and find new worlds. You just have to go out there and find your way. Luck plays an important part but so does your vision and your perseverance to get to the multibagger.

Independent thinking also enables you to avoid the temptation of being busy in the markets without making significant returns, a bane of most investors. There is no reason to be looking for stock all the time or picking too many stocks. You can wait for the right opportunity or when there are significant opportunities to be in a stock.

Acceptance of fallibility / paranoia

"It's not merely a matter of how much you can afford to risk on a given trade, but you also have to consider how many potential future winners you might miss because of the effect of the larger loss on your mental attitude and trading size."
– Randy McKay

Every successful investor, including great traders, are convinced they are fallible, and not invincible, and that they can be wiped out anytime. It is in this grounding that they never lose focus or sight of risks. They know when to leave as much as they know when to enter. The sense of fallibility, even paranoia, is a key ingredient in the success of great investors and traders.

Fallibility enables you to take advantage of the overconfidence that a majority of investors and traders have in their ability to know the market's direction. This overestimation almost always leads to losses. But if someone is losing money, which is the majority, someone else is making money, the minority. And this minority is paranoid about being wrong, has an overwhelming sense of being wrong or not knowing everything, closes out of losing stocks immediately and allows profits to run their full course.

7

~

Multibagger Secrets Market Insiders Won't Tell You

Getting rich is easy – it is the road less travelled

Picking multibaggers and getting rich means doing nothing most of the time. The itch to do something is the most common reason why most investors are not able to pick multibaggers. Multibagger investing is driven by using strategies that fit a market. That is one of the reasons you will see your multibagger investing improve significantly if you have been in the market for 5 to 10 years. This period of time allows you to see all phases of the markets and come up with strategies that work in each of these phases.

Another reason why it is easy to get rich with multibagger investing is that a majority of investors are almost always wrong. Crowd psychology is inferior to a single person's thinking. And when a crowd thinks the same way about a stock or the market, it sows the seeds for the stock to do the exact opposite.

Historically, the best gains can accrue if we enter a market when foreign investors are drowning in losses and after they pull out their money in loads. This usually happens when they overpay for stocks and real estate. When the slide begins, they dump stocks, and they do it as a "herd." This results in stocks going way below what they are worth as a business.

Selling by foreign investors can also be driven by reasons unrelated to your stock market or stocks. If foreign investors either have losses in other markets or face redemption elsewhere, they sell out of all markets to get into cash.

It takes conviction to see and put our money into what others have not seen. It's counter-intuitive and it requires us to break away from the comfort of the herd.

Define your style

Your multibagger investing style will depend on your personality. If you like the excitement of the market, pick a trading style that relies on picking stocks based on technical charts, or picking stock futures or stock options for their ability to generate quick multibaggers. This style carries a high risk of losses and you must take 2 to 3 years to trade only small amounts to understand the risks and develop the discipline to exit stocks that are showing losses.

If you prefer to invest only when there is an opportunity and are not busy following markets or stocks all the time, invest only when you find the entire market heading up, or when you are convinced that an investment theme will take all stocks up in a sector or industry.

Avoid a style that does not suit your personality. Every style, nevertheless, comes with its own level of risk and you must start by investing smaller amounts and improve your investing style as you gain experience.

High level of speculative activity is good for multibaggers

Speculative markets are generally defined as those where expectations of capital gains are high, trading volume is high, and a large mass of the population, usually far removed from stocks, gets involved in buying and selling stocks.

As markets rise, uninformed investors — or those who are not investors at all, but seek to emulate those who got rich through the market — start to invest. As markets rise further, this trickle turns into a tide.

Uninformed investors buy stocks because they expect the stock's price to rise enough to give them high profits. When their expectations are not met, they tend to exit the market in panic. Large scale selling at any price creates a temporary imbalance between the demand and supply of stocks, dropping prices to very low levels. Such low prices have nothing to do with the prospects of the business but with the desire of uninformed investors to get out of the market at any price.

Low stock prices created by panic selling is one of the best times to pick multibagger stocks. When things stabilize, such stocks can gain in multiples in every short periods of time.

Take advantage of the market's limited memory

Multibagger investing works because a majority of investors leave the market after every crash, never again to return to stocks. A new set of investors comes in to repeat the same mistakes of those before them. Very few investors take a market crash or losses in stocks as tuition fee for learning investing. The few that do are at an advantage because they have seen all kinds of markets and this is a very potent edge against new investors.

Investors forget how much stocks can fall when stocks are at all-time highs, and also forget, or else are not aware of, how much stocks can rise. But multibagger investors can use their experience to pick stocks that an ordinary investor will never identify.

The market's memory is amazingly short. By the time the next bull market presents itself, most investors have forgotten the pain of the previous bear market. Also, new investors enter who have never seen a complete market cycle. Multibagger investors must keep in mind not just current scenarios but how the market behaved in similar situations in the past and take advantage of the repetitive nature of human behaviour.

Put concentrated diversification to work

Diversification by multibagger investors has to take a very different hue from diversification by ordinary investors. Multibagger investor must hold no more than 5 to 10 stocks in their portfolios at any given time though they must keep a list of 10 to 20 stocks that may become multibaggers based on different scenarios coming into play. If things are not going your way, or a market begins to collapse, you should not think twice before getting out of all stocks as long as you keep your losses limited to a certain pre-decided percentage.

Keeping the number of stocks limited to 5 to 10 also forces you to set very high standards for selecting a multibagger stock and to weed out non-performing stocks. It also shows high conviction you have in your stock picking.

The number of stocks in your portfolio may be zero if market circumstances are not favourable, but it must never be more than ten.

If you are sure of the stock you are invested in, put more money into it. If the stock you picked is showing losses, get out of the stock at a pre-fixed loss level. This constant pruning of your portfolio helps you focus on the few stocks that are turning into multibaggers. Without pruning, your attention will be divided among too many stocks. Keeping loss-making stocks in your portfolio has far reaching effects on your psychology. They tend to colour your outlook on picking multibaggers in the future and occupy most of your attention.

Follow Warren Buffett's investment philosophy only if you have his money or clout

When Warren Buffett speaks, investors listen. His investing then is as much about being able to pull investors into a stock after he invests into it as it is about picking the right stocks. There is no empirical evidence to show that Warren Buffett's investment philosophy works for other investors or if it works in all kinds of market environments.

We have no such influence in the markets. Large investors also have access to superior information and knowledge because they get to meet the best minds in the investment business. Following large investors to find multibaggers does not work for an individual investor. You can take some important traits from them but aping their styles will not deliver the same results.

Following Warren Buffett without having the kind of influence or following he has in markets will lead you to investing results very different than those achieved by Buffett.

A broker is a salesman of stock. And a salesman never says, "Don't buy what I have"

What is a research report? It is a sales brochure. What is a broker doing? He is selling stocks. A salesman uses a sale brochure to sell a product. A sales brochure is good to get the technical specifications about the product but tells you nothing about its reliability, durability or deliverability. A broker's research report is meant to get you to buy a stock. It is by definition a listing of the "fine" qualities of a stock. Why and how can you rely on a sales brochure to decide on a multibagger opportunity?

Broker research is good for reading but has nothing to do with what the stock will do. The best brokers don't give information to individual investors and work largely with institutional investors. Because institutional brokers are privy to the flow of money in and out of stocks, they have much better information to justify their reports. Stock brokers who cater to individual investors have no such influence on the market and their reports don't carry much value for multibagger investors.

A great economy or sector does not mean the stock is great

The question is not whether the company has great prospects or is growing. The question is whether you are paying too much to acquire the stock, given its current and future earnings. In booming markets, too many uninformed investors put their money into stocks. This excess flow of money makes stocks too expensive. Easy money also leads companies to make acquisitions, take up expansion and do other things that have little business rationale. The point about demand is that it adjusts very quickly. The problem with supply is that it takes a longer cycle to build up but once it builds up, you can't simply apply brakes to it. Thus, easy money sets in motion the ultimate collapse of stocks at a future date.

Stock prices are not hinged to, or tied to, any economic growth or corporate earnings growth, etc. They have the same relation that a balloon has to the earth. You have to fill the air on earth but how far it goes after that depends on the wind, the weather, and the air you filled. Stocks may need earnings and economic growth but it is not enough to get them to fly far.

In multibagger investing, individual investors have a distinct advantage over institutional investors

"A gem, by chance, may lie before you,
And be gleaming in the rubble,
But fate won't pick it up for you –
It expects you to take that trouble."

– Hitopadesa

An individual investor is best placed for picking multibaggers. This is where you can beat institutional investors or mutual funds hands down. Rules and restrictions on the market capitalization of a company, liquidity of the stock, etc., give institutional investors and mutual funds limited space and ability to buy potential multibaggers, even when fund managers are convinced about the stock's potential.

Institutional investors operate under significant constraints and cannot buy a stock just because it is a multibagger opportunity. They have to meet requirements of company size, market capitalization, etc., which don't constrain you. By keeping out of multibagger opportunities even when they know about them, institutional investors leave the field open to individual investors.

Institutional investors have large pay packets, club memberships, homes and a family that has gotten used to all these perks. They can ill-afford to get into a stock which may not turn out to be a multibagger. By nature, a majority follows the few institutional investors who have the ability to influence stock buying. Their return expectations are mediocre that finding multibaggers is neither worth the risk nor the expectations investors have of them.

Multibagger investing requires you to be wrong when others are right, and exit stocks that don't become multibagger stocks with pre-fixed loss limits. It also requires you to be right in a few stocks and ride the profits all the way. It requires you to stand away from the crowd, a risk institutional fund managers cannot take. It is similar to an individual investor being an entrepreneur and an institutional investor being like a corporate employee. The corporate employee will avoid actions that may stand him out as having violated the "corporate culture." An entrepreneur takes a risk. A majority don't make it, but a few who end up being the "multibaggers" in life, like the creators of Google or Facebook.

As an individual investor, you have no such limitations and compulsions. You can invest in a stock that you believe is going to capture the interest of other investors and see money flows into the stock. You don't have to justify to anyone why you believe money is going to flow into that stock. You can stick to your conviction, buy it, and hold it for as long as you like. This is what gives you an unbelievable advantage to find and profit from multibaggers.

Buy when investors are on their pain thresholds

"Time and sustained pain are what alter behaviour patterns and change society."

– Barton Biggs

There are times when investors will sell stocks involuntarily. These phases come when investors have large losses in their portfolios and sell otherwise sound stocks to pay for their margins or losses. Sometimes, a large part of homeowners in an economy face loan defaults. Thus, investors often have to sell shares because of losses in other asset classes or other stocks.

Whenever you see a large mass of investors getting out of stocks because of reasons not related to those stocks, namely for reasons of large scale loan defaults, high unemployment in the economy, losses in other stocks, etc. the time is ripe for picking multibaggers.

When a bear market has lasted several years, investors either develop a disinterest in stocks or start to believe that the prevailing price is the normal price for the stock. The only selling that happens at such times is either by investors who need the money or those who are fed up of holding a stock. The only buying that happens is because the stock is exceedingly cheap. Such markets are a buyer's market for stocks and an ideal time for stock picking for multibagger investors.

Take advantage of the human thinking process

"After each crisis, the financial markets invariably shrug off past follies and losses to confront the future with bright optimism and fresh credulity. Capital becomes 'blind' unable to remember the past, investors are condemned to repeat it."

– Edward Chancellor

Human thinking is tuned to remember the most recent events and not to analyse events over a period of time. When investors focus on the most recent events, they tend to follow the herd. For example, if markets have been down, you too feel down, or if markets have been great, you feel that you've some special skill in picking stocks.

But multibagger investing requires looking at opportunities over a number of years. Your stock picking has to think of how things have happened over a number of years and what sets the stage for the stock to rise exponentially at this point.

Picking multibaggers when price discovery is yet to happen

Price discovery refers to a price which the majority of investors are ready to pay to buy a stock. If a majority of investors are ready to pay a certain price for the stock, it will not have much more upside left. A multibagger investor has to find a stock whose price has not yet been discovered by a majority of the investors.

Price discovery can happen at the time of an IPO, or if a company has a structural shift in management quality or source of revenues, or a windfall improvement in margins.

If everyone is making money, it may not last for long

"The moral seems to be that any approach to money making in the stock market which can be easily described and followed by a lot of people is by its terms too simple and too easy to last."

– Benjamin Graham, *The Intelligent Investor*

There are short periods of time when a lot of people are making money. Most of these people are uninformed investors and are riding a Ponzi scheme where the next investor is compensating the previous set of investors. This can last only so long as there is another set of investors ready to buy out the previous set. But like all Ponzi schemes, the collapse comes when the largest number of investors are in the market and there is no one left to buy out their stocks.

Such markets can give you multibaggers, created by newer and newer investors ready to buy stocks from the previous set of investors at ever higher prices. If you believe a stock is in a Ponzi rise, sit through it. The price of the stock can rise exponentially if a stock turns into a Ponzi style rise. The point of collapse will only come when the largest number of uninformed investors are in the stock and there is no one to take the stock off their hands.

Focus on the flow of money

"There are no multibaggers if there is no money entering the stock no matter what its fundamentals."

– Ashu Dutt

You need a tsunami to get a multibagger. Normal flows of money will not drive up a stock. Investors concentrate on the wrong frame when they pick stocks on concepts like intrinsic value, low PE, etc.

There are times when money flows into stocks like the bursting of a dam and there are times when money flows out of stocks as though being sucked out by a vacuum. These extreme events are rarely driven by the economy or corporate growth but have to do with the majority's rush in and out of stocks.

It is the flow of money which throws up multibaggers.

Multibagger opportunities

- When overleveraged markets or the tops of bull markets explode, the need to pay margins draws down stock prices way below their intrinsic value. Buy whenever mismatch in liquidity drives stocks down.
- Look at the institutional holding and float. If the ownership of a stock is largely with promoters and institutions start to increase their stake, stocks will double or triple very quickly.

Multibaggers in options

There is an inherent fallacy in the pricing of options. It assumes an upward price or downward trending price and then attaches a time value, which means the same strike options get more and more expensive the longer their duration. This makes no sense because a market may be poised to go through an "accumulation" where it goes up 20% in 3 months or 50% in a year, and then falls 50% from its high point in 18 months. But the way options are priced, the price of the option will be the highest for 18 months. This is a structural pricing problem caused by our psychology and belief in trends and that there is a time value of money. Traders who understand this anomaly have an edge.

Multibaggers need the appropriate environment

The fatal flaw in multibagger investing is trying to find multibaggers based on conventional measures, such as low price compared to intrinsic value or book value, or low price earnings ratio. These measures are meaningless when used without a context. And the context is the market's stage at the time of buying the multibagger. For example, a low price to book value (P/BV) for a steel stock may be meaningless when steel prices are at multi-year lows. But it may have meaning when steel prices are at all time highs.

You will not find multibaggers using the same conventional measures in all kinds of markets. Stocks are like seasonal flowers. They bloom in certain seasons and certain weather conditions. The three steps you should follow to evaluate a potential multibagger are:

- Are these the right market conditions for the stock to move up?
- Is there enough interest and money flowing into the stock to take it up in multiples of its current price?
- Does the stock have any intrinsic value? While this is important in a bear market, too much emphasis on this aspect will make you lose multibagger opportunities.

A stock can become a multibagger in very short periods of time.

A surprise announcement, such as an acquisition or a change in earnings, change in management, or the turn of a market cycle in commodities can change the structural outlook of a stock for sophisticated investors. If that happens, a stock could become a multibagger in a few days. You will face two hurdles in picking such stocks. One is our hesitancy to buy a stock that is already up 20% to 30%. The other is our inability to understand the implications of the structural change early — or quickly — enough.

Be prepared for clustered multibagger opportunities

At the peak of a bull market, or when the market becomes dominated by uninformed investors, a stock can get into a vertical rise. It is a phase where sellers are convinced that they can sell at higher prices tomorrow, while buyers are convinced that they must be in the stock at any price. This creates an imbalance between the demand and supply of the stock. Prices rise as it is a sellers' market and a seller of the stock finds a buyer at any price he is ready to sell.

You cannot buy stocks that will be multibaggers in the long term

"Any predictions about the distant future are likely to be wildly off the mark. The only thing we can pretty much count on going forward is innovation."

– Michael Mouboussin

Even the best investors in the world cannot predict how things will be after 12 months, let alone 3 to 5 years. Buying stocks and hoping they will turn into multibaggers in the long term is wishful thinking. Such wishful thinking is sometimes incorrectly interpreted as long term investing when some stocks turn into multibaggers in the long term. But this may be random and may have nothing to do with good stock picking.

If you cannot convince yourself that the stock will be a multibagger in the next few months or a year, stay out of it. If there is nothing in the short term for the stock, the long term is a series of short terms. Why park your money in an immobile stock. You can always buy the stock later, if and when it starts to move.

You don't have to look far to see why long term investing does not work. Think of whether your life and circumstances are what you thought they would be 3 to 5 years ago. Almost without exception we will be way off the mark. No one can predict the future and that is why no stock turns into a multibagger merely by holding it for the long term.

It is almost always true that the vast wealth of big investors has been made in short spurts of market mania. As much as fundamentals may be important, even more important is the anticipation that there is someone else out there who will be ready to pay higher prices. As long as this virtuous cycle continues, chances of losing money are remote. It is in the recognition of opportunity before the world does, or on riding a momentum wave before it rises that the biggest fortunes are made, not by any averaging, discipline, long term investing or any such market "truism."

Major investment themes like technology, China, India, commodities, etc. become obvious to most investors somewhere in the middle or peak of the cycle. The majority only follows once it feels the "comfort" of others doing the same thing. And so the largest flow of funds into a new asset class like India will occur once it has become "mainstream" and every foreign media, broker, fund manager is talking about it. Prices are then driven by a flood of demand created by the desire to possess rather than any rational look at value.

And herein lies the paradox. The greatest opportunities of returns are in what are considered as the "worst" markets. The worst opportunities are in markets that are most talked about. It is not what a company is doing but what we are paying for it that's key.

Most market cycles are driven by booms because of heightened interest in a technology, a commodity, or in a country. Since 1850, we have had booms in autos, appliances, radio, movies and utilities, Japan, China, India, industrial commodities, and so on. A buy and hold strategy would not have worked. But following a strategy of latching on to the driver of the next boom would have worked just fine.

Markets typically don't focus on the long term. Immediate issues, such as margin calls, mood or sentiment, short term news events, etc. are what drive the market's behaviour.

A multibagger will start to stagnate at some point

No matter how great an advantage a stock has or its domination in the market, over a period of time the company's high profits or product profile draws competitors. Increasing competition ensures that the original innovator or company cannot generate higher returns than the other companies in the industry. As companies grow larger, they are unable to replicate the success they had at a smaller size. The compulsions of running large organizations makes these companies bound by bureaucracy and rules that restrict outperformance.

Invest when the market is not able to put a price on a stock

"In the stock market, value standards don't determine prices: prices determine value standards."

– Ben Graham

When a new business or investment theme originates, investors are unable to put a price on stocks in that industry. With interest high and everyone wanting a piece of the action, investors pour in excess money into such stocks especially when there are few listed companies in the industry to buy into. This creates multibaggers in short periods of time.

Stocks of companies in industries that have been around for long periods of time find it more difficult to rise exponentially except when there is a structural change in the business, like a change in the market cycle for a commodity.

Small changes create big multibaggers

A multibagger opportunity is rarely seen till the stock has already become a multibagger. Small, incremental changes in an industry or a company tend to create far reaching effects in the future changing the prospects of the stock. But you have to develop the ability to see these incremental changes and anticipate its eventual effect.

A personal experience may help you appreciate how a small change can change the prospects of the stock or the industry. I invested in a bank stock when a new CEO was appointed. The bank was on the verge of closing down. News reports were extremely negative. The founders were fighting with each other and the bank need immediate capitalization. Everything indicated the bank would be merged with another bank. I then saw a small news report that they had appointed a new CEO. The new CEO had been a founder of a very successful bank but had been forced out years ago from that bank. Almost no one knew the CEO's background but I was aware that he was capable of turning around the bank with his experience. In less than 3 months, the stock's price rose over 4 times as the CEO increased his interaction with institutional investors. This is the kind of small change you should look for to identify a multibagger.

Trial and error investing

"Starting with lots of alternatives and winnowing down to the most useful ones proves to be a robust process, even though it appears quite inefficient."
– Michael Mouboussin

Human evolution is all about trial and error. Before anything gets established in nature, thousands of combinations fail. You must look at hundreds of stocks to pick one that meets your criterion of a multibagger. Out of a dozen multibagger stocks you invest in, you must factor in that at least 70% to 80% will never turn out to be multibaggers. This will be an invaluable learning experience for you if you can document how you shortlisted the stocks to invest in, why you believe the stocks that did not turn into multibaggers failed and what you did right to pick the few multibaggers. Over a period of time both your investment process and methodology and your success ratio at finding multibaggers will improve significantly.

The market must eventually agree with your assessment

"Investors can't just consider innovation; they must assess how the market will consider innovation. Therein lies the potential opportunity."

– Michael Mouboussin

Will the market eventually agree with your assessment that a stock is a multibagger? Answering the question will eliminate many stocks that you incorrectly pick as multibaggers. If you don't believe the time is right for the market to be convinced about the potential of the stock, the stock's price may remain static for years.

For others to start getting into the stock, the stock has to go viral. You have to think of how quickly could people be "infected" with a desire to buy into the stock. That depends on the level of contagion. If everyone around you is talking about the stock or the market, then you will be infected very soon. If no one is, it will take a long time for your stock to become a multibagger.

Historical data is little guide to a stock's future price

"Sentiment is a critical determinant of performance. The mechanism that makes a company hot is the same as what causes investors to go back and forth from extreme optimism to extreme pessimism."

– Michael Mouboussin

Investors are hard wired to find simple cause and effect rationale to buy stocks they expect to be multibaggers. Using historical data caters to a human tendency for certainty and provides a point from which they can project the future. But this is a psychological fallacy and is not conducive to multibagger investing.

Buying multibaggers is by its nature uncertain and no amount of historical data can change that.

Change your views to fit the market's dynamics

"It is not the strongest of the species that survives, nor the most intelligent, but the one most responsive to change."
– Charles Darwin, *The Origin of Species*

Multibagger investing cannot be done in isolation. You have to change your view if the market's dynamics change from the time you invested. A stock that looks like a multibagger may turn either into a dud or deliver normal returns in a changed set of circumstances. Your thinking and process of identifying the multibagger opportunity may have right but circumstances changed and so did the stock's potential.

I have often wondered why I did not exit a stock even when I was sure the dynamics of the market were changing. Sometimes, the amount I invested may be too small but all too often it was plain inertia.

I strongly suggest that you consciously deal with this tendency to do nothing even when the market's dynamics have changed. Many potential multibaggers head back to where they started from in a changed market.

Look for loss of investor diversity

"The issue is not whether individuals are irrational (they are) but whether they are irrational in the same way at the same time."
– Michael Mouboussin

At most times, markets have investor diversity. Millions of buyers and sellers balance one another out and prices remain stable. But there are times where investors tilt to one side. Either an overwhelming majority starts to buy, or an overwhelming majority starts to sell. Such one-way flow of money starts to send stocks into the sky, or to the bottom of the ocean.

Multibaggers emerge when investor diversity reduces or disappears. When most investors start viewing a stock or the market as a continuing upward trend, the balance between buyers and sellers that keeps a stock price in a range breaks down and the stock starts to head up. The greater the breakdown in investor diversity, the more extreme can be the price rise.

Why future projections of earnings don't translate into multibaggers

The longer the projection, the more it is in the realm of nonsense. There are too many variables in the future and no one can project future earnings with any accuracy. This applies to company managements and owners, too.

Projections also have a funny way of always heading higher and higher. Nothing in life, let alone stocks, heads higher and higher. It just does not work this way.

Forecasts start with choosing a starting point based on today's condition. But investors tend to change their forecasts based on conditions that are continuously evolving. Their new forecasts have less to do with conditions on the ground and more to do with how optimistic or pessimistic investors feel about stocks at any given time. Because we never know how investors will feel in the future, using forecasts is useless for finding multibaggers.

Don't waste your time on projections. They are of no assistance in finding a multibagger.

You can rely only on yourself to find a multibagger

"Force means shifts in accumulated energy or momentum. Skilful warriors are able to allow the force of momentum to seize victory for them without exerting their strength."

– Sun Tzu

Have you ever seen or known anyone who comes to you and shares business secrets, or wants to tell you about making money. In fact, if anyone knows how to make money, he either keeps it to himself or makes every effort that you don't find out how it is done.

Don't expect people to behave differently with stocks. And that is why you cannot depend on promotion of stocks by people on financial media or brokers. They have their self interest and it may not be aligned to your interest or personality.

Many of us read Warren Buffett and almost believe we can replicate his returns by following his approach. But it's not so much what Warrant Buffett buys or sells that is important. It is his temperament, his personal reactions to market moves, etc., that are critical to his success.

Moreover, we must accept an unspoken, but not always pleasant rule: We are not all champions, certainly not at everything. In sports, this becomes particularly glaring and so our acceptance of this truth is also easier. If I am not Olympics material, I accept I cannot go to the Olympics. Just because I watch Wimbledon, it doesn't mean I can become a tennis champion.

Yet markets make us believe we can all do equally well. We may just not have the mental make-up to play like a Warren Buffett or a George Soros.

But it is in the acceptance of who we are, and where we stand, and in the desire to learn how to make up for our shortcomings that lies our biggest success. So, our focus has to be on whether we have done better than average given our real investing abilities, not on comparing our results with those of some big-time investor or trader.

Identify an illogical price and why it may correct

"When the speed of rushing water reaches the point where it can move boulders, this is the force of momentum."

– Sun Tzu

You must identify stocks where the price is illogical. Just because a stock has a low PE ratio or the book value is much higher than the stock's price, does not make the stock's price illogical. A stock's price may be illogical because a large institutional investor sold off its large holding in a hurry causing a big fall in the price, or a collapse in the entire market caused investors to sell the stock to put up margins for other stocks.

After identifying the illogical price, you have to think of when and how this illogical price could correct. This is a critical part of the multibagger investment process. If you are wrong about when and how the illogical price will correct, either the price is not illogical or you were not correct about when and how the price will correct.

You will find a multibagger in a company which has a good brand, long standing quality management whose stock which has been brought down either because of an exit of institutional investors or an economic scenario which has made it unable to deliver results. For example, a branded truck manufacturer who is reeling in heavy debt and poor sales in an economic downturn may deliver 3 to 5 times returns if things turn around.

Illogical prices can also occur owing to a drying up of liquidity. After every long term bull market, the market runs out of liquidity. Not only do investors run out of money, they don't even have money to pay margins. Mutual funds don't have money because investors want their money back. All this need for cash means that you have to dump stocks in a market with no buyers. Whenever this happens, stocks will go way below what their value is. And they will stay there only long enough for money to return. This is one of the best times to buy multibaggers.

How to protect your multibaggers

"In any market cycle, those who find themselves losing the game of musical chairs are bound to resist the inevitable. Denial, anger, desperation . . . these are just some of the stages that investors pass through before accepting defeat."

– Maggie Mahar, *Bull!*

Too many institutional investors are invested in popular or blue chip stocks. Ironically, stocks in which there are too many institutional investors are the most risky stocks to hold. If you have a multibagger at hand, you must protect your gains in stocks where there are too many institutional investors. Institutional investors tend to exit a stock at around the same time causing not just a very sharp fall in the stock's price but often creating a situation where you can't exit at any price.

The stock can collapse at any time because it is too crowded by institutional money.

The normal can change forever

"Victory in war is not repetitious, but adapts in form endlessly."

– Sun Tzu

A common mistake investors make is to buy a stock when it is down 90% to 95% from its highs, or from a price they are used to. Equally, they stay away from buying a stock if it is 100% up from a price they are used to. This type of investing assumes that a stock has some kind of normal price and we are getting a stock cheaper or more expensive than that normal price.

A stock has no normal price. A stock can go up a 100% — and then go up another 10-fold. A stock can do down 90% — and then continue to go down further. Think of a stock like an airplane on a runway. A plane takes off only when it gathers speed, not when it is slowing down. And a plane that is slowing down may come to a stop.

Multibaggers are like diamonds – what is the real value of a diamond?

"The only way investors can liquidate their equity position is by selling their shares to one another; everyone is at the mercy of everyone else's expectations and buying power."

– Peter Bernstein

A stock's price is as much driven by sentiment as it is by the stock's fundamentals. Value investors usually have an aversion to knowing what traders are up to in a stock. That is a blind spot that can be very costly. Multibagger investors must understand technical charts and keep an eye on the behaviour of traders, especially in futures and options. If traders are highly leveraged in a stock, it could indicate they know something about the stock; it may also indicate that a stock could take a sharp fall if there are margin calls on these traders.

You don't invest in stocks, you invest in risk

"Capital markets have always been volatile, because they trade nothing more than bets on the future, which is full of surprises."

– Peter Bernstein

Investors who focus on company data, financial information and other fundamentals may be on the wrong track. The only common measure among stocks is the risk. Multibagger investors must decide the stocks where they will get a 5 to 10 times return with the minimum risk. Thinking of stocks in this manner removes the ideological roadblocks to finding multibaggers. There is a myth that only value investors find multibaggers and a false sense of superiority in finding multibaggers through value buying. Multibaggers are about absolute returns and such myths and false sense of superiority can be dangerous impediments.

There is no right price in a discontinuous market

"When discontinuities threaten, it is perilous to base decisions on established trends that have always seemed to make perfect sense but suddenly do not."

– Peter Bernstein

A market may fall on its own weight or it may fall because of factors not directly related to the market. If stocks are falling because of a disruption in demand and supply in commodity markets, currency markets or some other phenomenon playing out in another part of the world, uncertainty sets in the market. When markets turn uncertain, managing risk becomes difficult.

Don't be tempted to buy when stock markets are unable to comprehend changes happening in other markets even when stock prices have dropped sharply. It is not necessary that prices may recover, or do so soon enough.

Look for multibaggers when rational investors have exhausted their patience

"The longer a market has been in an uptrend, the more likely a mania will follow, as the rising price trend becomes increasingly perceived to be permanent."

– Marc Faber in *Tomorrow's Gold*

A low risk point to invest in stocks is when a market has moved up to such heights where rational investors think they are overvalued. If rational investors sell out of a market, the market goes into the hands of uninformed investors. Uninformed investors, which is the vast majority of people in the market, have their own dynamics and rely on stories, narrative and greed to sell stocks to still other uninformed investors, creating a cycle where the market turns into a one-way buying spree.

You can then ride the wave and stay in till you see signs of panic or hesitancy on the part of uninformed investors.

Investment manias are like landslides. You can be sure that a landslide is certain. But when the rocks would come rolling down is anybody's guess. They may slide now, or the next day, or stay put for another year. Investment manias too can continue as long as people continue to support them.

In fact, in the current environment of 24-hour financial television, hordes of analysts and instant communication, the enthusiasm and interest of the public can be retained for longer than we can imagine.

Multibagger opportunities do not depend on the quality of a stock

"Only fools are dancing, but the bigger fools are watching."
– Japanese proverb on manias

When a stock market mania, or long term bull market persists, uninformed investors start to buy low price stocks and stocks of low quality. It is the easiest to drive up stocks with dubious managements and businesses in a long term bull market. Such stocks also have low floating stock and with few shares available and managements ready to feed the market's appetite, even small buying can push stocks up exponentially.

Conventional wisdom says we need do buy "safe" big stocks in a run away bull market. In fact, there is little risk buying these duds if we can make a reasonable call that the bull market cycle is likely to continue. That in itself is no rocket science. Just consider the mood in the market. If it is "stock passionate," then the bull rally may be far from ending.

Knowing that the rally is speculative may not necessarily be bad. There is no way to know how long the speculation may last or how high prices would move. If it seems like markets are speculative but investors are in a wild hurry to buy (and it has still not reached those far removed from anything to do with investments) you can be reasonably sure you have your best chance to make money. It is not how expensive the stock is. But how much more expensive that you anticipate it to get. This phenomenon is not just a stock market phenomenon. In fact, it plays out even more viciously in real estate and art. Speculators can hike up prices to any level way beyond what seems rational.

A good strategy in bull markets is to buy the stocks where we see the greatest potential of price appreciation. The gamble is, we will get out before the market falls. Call it the footboard mentality. It is like getting off a train in Mumbai before commuters try to enter the coach by being perched on the footboard and making an agile exit even as the train is coming to a stop.

Multibagger stocks are like rockets

"The great stock market bull seeks to condense the future into a few days, to discount the long march of history, and capture the present value of all the future."

– James Buchanan

The next phase starts only if the thrust in the previous stage is enough. Yet, we miss rallies as we keep anchoring the current level to the level of the market we got used to. When a market reaches a certain level, a new set of investors and traders enter bringing in liquidity needed for the market to head higher. A classic rally starts with individual stock pickers or traders, followed by mutual funds, followed by foreign investors and foreign exchange traded funds, who may then be followed by absolute return funds. The maximum liquidity comes in when institutional investors invest only because they are getting more funds to invest. Many institutional investors tailor their funds to be industry or country specific. A large flow of funds to such funds ensures the industry or market will continue to run up.

Even if you have to pay a higher price, wait for the move to begin

Stock prices may move up many times but they are usually false signals and the stock may head right back to where it began. Come up with a benchmark on when you will move into a stock. Wait for the stock to have gained 20% to 25% over a period of a month before investing. If the stock has gained 20% to 25% within just 2 to 3 trading sessions, the rise may not be sustainable.

Apply the same rule when a multibagger is heading down. Don't sell till the stock has lost 15% to 20% of its value over a month. A multibagger will make many false moves downward before continuing its uptrend. Only when a downward move becomes sustained, is it time to sell.

Averaging never works

"It is one of the great paradoxes of the stock market that when seems too high usually goes higher and what seems too low usually goes lower."

– Willaim O'Neil

Another common mistake is averaging the purchase price or buying more stock as it falls. If a stock continues to fall after you have invested in it, get out at a prefixed loss level. There may information you are not aware of that is driving the stock lower.

Investor always invest on incomplete information. The number of variables impacting a stock and the magnitude of their impact cannot be predicted with any accuracy. This is especially true when you pick multibaggers. You can only guess the overall potential of the stock. Think of it like driving a car. You can decide on a good car or a bad car by the way it looks or performs but you never know how many or which parts make that performance possible. When a stock does not do what you expect it to do, it is possible that there is some information that was not known to you or you under- or overestimated the magnitude of some information on the stock.

After a bubble, interest will shift to another investment class or group of stocks

Bubbles present two multibagger opportunities. Opportunities during a bubble and opportunities after the bubble. Opportunities during the bubble arise across the board in the sector which is the subject of the bubble. The sign of a bubble is that stocks start to rise 50% to 100% in a matter of days. Opportunities after the bubble arise in sectors that have not been a part of the bubble. A bubble sucks money from every other stock because investors can flip stocks at massive profits in a matter of days in bubble stocks. This leaves other stocks unwanted and extremely low priced setting the base for multibaggers.

Another common mistake is buying stocks after they have had a meteoric rise. But the reason the stock is falling is because investors have lost interest in it. And no amount of research or conviction about value in the stock will bring it back up without investor interest.

Sell out your investments if investors have lost interest in a sector or a stock. Look for the next theme for your stocks where you believe investors will pour in money.

Look for the mispriced bet

"It is not given to human beings to have such talent that they can just know everything about everything all the time. But it is given to human beings who look and sift the world for a mispriced bet that they can occasionally find one. They bet big when they have odds. And the rest of the time, they don't. It's just that simple."
– Charlie Munger

Stocks can get mispriced if too many sellers overwhelm buyers and send the stock to very low prices. Stocks also become mispriced when they stop being covered by brokerage firms, and when investors develop a disinterest for stocks in general or a particular sector. Look for mispriced bets. They are easier to find in a long term bear markets. You may find them in bull markets but it is a lot more difficult to find them in bull markets because a number of brokerage houses cover the stock and they are widely owned by investors.

A stock's price has so many variables and the psychology and opinions of so many individuals that no stock picking method can account for all. Instead of trying to figure out the potential of the stock, look for a stock where the odds are overwhelming for a 5- to 10-fold rise in its price. This will require you to pore over hundreds of stocks, think of multiple scenarios and, then, once in a while, you will hit upon a stock which has been mispriced and which will rise sooner or later.

How long has a bull or bear market been around?

"Whenever you find yourself on the side of the majority, it's time to pause and reflect."
– Mark Twain

Look for a bear market to have been around for a long time. Most people give up on a market when they see continued pain and sell at the sign of the slightest rise. When a vast majority of investors get used to low prices, it sets the base for multibaggers.

The duration of a bear market reduces the risk of investing in stocks and increases the prospects of the stock turning into a multibagger.

Predicting the length of a bear market is an art in itself. Longer term bear markets follow the economy. Shorter term bear markets may occur because of low liquidity or a rush out of stock or some shorter term reasons.

Multibagger buying secrets

"The doomsayers work by extrapolation; they take a trend and extend it, forgetting that the doom factor sooner or later generates a coping mechanism . . . you cannot extrapolate any series in which the human element intrudes; history, that is the human narrative, never follows and will always foil the scientific curve."

– Barton Biggs in *Hedge Hogging*

In bear markets — buy solid companies at ocean bottom after they have been at this bottom for years because of institutional disinterest. Buy only those stocks where institutional interest will return, but is currently minimal.

Buy value at bottom of bear market — and stocks will rise 5- to 10-fold from then. Buy index stocks first which are at ocean bottom, then buy stocks in futures, and then cash.

Use leverage by buying stocks in futures as downside risk is minimal when a stock is already at ocean bottom. Look for institutional stocks currently at very low institutional holding level. Such stocks shoot up.

Short term mood swings change the direction of longer term options and futures contracts, creating price inefficiencies that traders can use to make very high risk/reward ratio trades.

Watch for deception in the information you are relying on

Information available to the public is cloaked in public relation spins, deception and other coatings that help those who control the flow of information. The flow of information about a stock is controlled by owners, financial media and institutional investors. The individual investor is at the bottom of the pile in the quality of information he has access to.

If there is valuable information that can make money in the stock, it is available first to the owners and management, then to institutional investors and then to financial media. Be very sceptical about publicly available information. It is not meant to be given to you to make money. It is meant to be passed on to you to have someone pick up stocks, someone else wants to sell or have someone sell stock that someone else wants to buy.

That is why stocks bought on simplistic information, such as low PE ratios, excellent results, expansion plans, etc. do not lead to multibaggers.

Advantages of being a multibagger trader

Develop an expertise of finding trading multibaggers. This is a low risk way of finding stocks that can rise in multiples in short spans and it gives you the discipline of exiting stocks that don't move as you expect. Some of the advantages of using trading for finding multibaggers is:

- You stay in a stock only if it is going in the direction you expect, and you exit a stock at prefixed loss levels.
- You have no ideological investment in the stock unlike value investors who take it as a hit to their personal abilities when a stock does not go their way and continue to hold onto it even as it accumulates losses.
- Stocks are capable of very large moves on institutional selling or a change in market mood which value investors miss out. A trader can exit if he sees the market's mood change.
- If the stock rises as you expect, you can increase the size of your position. This requires practice as it is not a normal tendency among investors to increase the size of a position when the stock is moving higher.

Watch the flow of money to mutual funds

Mutual funds are a unique set of institutional investors. Their holding time of any stock is a slave to the money that they get or pay out from their funds. And mutual funds tend to get the largest amounts of money when stocks are at their peaks, and pay out the largest amounts when stocks are priced the lowest.

If mutual funds are a significant force, their activity can take stocks to multibagger levels especially when small cap and mid cap mutual funds become popular. With limited amount of stock available in small and mid cap arenas, and with their mandate to remain in small and mid cap space, they become the drivers of the stock's price.

Keep a track of the number of new small cap funds that mutual funds are introducing, or the interest of investors in small cap stocks. Small cap stocks stay at rock bottom prices for most of their lives but spring to life and head to multibagger status when mutual funds receive large amounts of money to invest in small cap stocks. Since mutual funds can only invest in stocks for which they get the money, they are forced to buy small cap stocks even if they consider them overvalued as long as they are getting more money.

Keep an eye on low float and low capitalization stocks

"John Law, who was also a land-bank projector, claimed that price was simply the result of the interaction of supply and demand. Applied to the stock market, Law's idea suggests that share prices are determined by liquidity rather than a reflection of inherent values."

– Edward Chancellor, *Devil take the Hindmost*

There are times where a vast majority of investors get into stocks with low market capitalisations or low floats. By taking fancy to these low priced, low volume stocks, every new wave of buyers drives the price of the stock higher. The stock's price in such situations takes on a life of its own which has nothing to do with business prospects.

You will find multibaggers in such stocks. The challenge is to get into these stocks early on and anticipate correctly that a vast mass of investors will try to enter the stock.

IPO stocks will rarely turn into multibaggers

An owner will do an IPO when the market is right for him to get the maximum price. An investment banker wins the bid to do an IPO because he offers the maximum possible price. If he cannot sell, he underwrites or has to pick up the stock. The dynamics of IPOs make sure there is little juice left for anyone outside the company. Don't get tempted by anchor investors or institutional investors who buy ahead of an IPO. They have cosy agreements to exit at a prefixed price even if the IPO does not do well. Why would the promoter or founder be party to such a thing?

Blue chip and index stocks are rarely multibaggers

Blue chip stocks get there because they have already been discovered. They have large institutional holdings and are market favourites. There is very little for a multibagger investor to find there.

Blue chip stocks tend to be crowded trades. They have too many institutional investors invested in them. And institutional investors are in the habit of getting out of a stock at the same time. This makes blue chip stocks some of the most risky stocks to be in.

The only time you may find multibagger stocks among index stocks is if the company has undergone a structural transformation because of the introduction of a new product, a fall in stock indices to very low levels, etc.

There can be no long term multibaggers without management integrity. You may get a trading multibagger if a dubious management is trying to pump up a stock but it almost always ends badly and investors rarely get to exit the stock.

Multibagger investing is context based

"The golden rule is that there are no golden rules."
– George Bernard Shaw

What works in bull markets does not work in bear markets. For example, following momentum in a bull market may make us very wealthy because once markets lose their connection with reality, it's anyone's guess how high stock prices will go. In such cases, it's best to buy stocks that show the maximum strength, namely those that are appreciating the fastest. Why even look at slow movers in such markets?

On the other hand, picking the cheapest stocks on the benchmark of value may be a great strategy in a bear market. Bear in mind, however, that in a bear market the perspective changes to a holding period of 3 to 5 years.

We don't know when the market will flip around again, and that would require us to sit on the stock.

Following technical chartists in a strong upmarket may be a great strategy.

Following logic in a bear market may get us the best returns when the markets turn around.

The market is simply too dynamic for any golden rule to apply all the time.

The market's cycles

Multibagger investing cannot be undertaken without keeping the stage of the market cycle in mind. Stock picking becomes a low risk, high return proposition when the market is in an upward cycle. A stock bought when the entire market is heading higher is much safer than a stock bought when only the particular sector or stock is heading up.

A distinction between cycles and trends is critical for buy and sell decisions. How do you read a cycle? Usually it lasts for years and is unrelenting in its up or down moves, as the case may be.

Investors make big mistakes when they try to invest in the early stages of new emerging areas, whether it be airlines or the Internet, or in new emerging economies. These mistakes have been made for centuries especially when there have been new discoveries, inventions and opening up of new lands, like the US or California within the US. In a way, India was in a similar situation at the dawn of the 21st century, in that it was opening up for foreigners. While investors are usually right about the prospects of the technology or country concerned, they are often wrong about the timing, and the companies that may make it and those that will not survive. Moreover, in their euphoria to catch the wave, they usually pay very high prices for anticipated returns. When returns don't match anticipation, mass selling follows.

Whenever a new asset class is identified, investors try to figure out what the new idea, country, or sector as the case may be, should be valued at. Some may call it speculation, but it is a process of discovering the correct pricing since there are no earlier benchmarks. In the process, the obvious euphoria of the new takes stocks way higher than their real delivery capability as investors factor in the future potential in their current prices. A key feature of such times is that demand is always overestimated and supply invariably underestimated.

This is a phenomenon that has repeated itself over the past three hundred years of market history, perhaps longer. From railroads to canals, to technology, to the opening up of the US, to Peru, to the Asian Tigers, to China and, then, India, the identification of a new asset class by investors, usually foreign investors, takes markets to ridiculous heights — and then they adjust severely. The up move, though, is usually unimaginably large before the severe correction.

Rational bubbles are also created when investors push up prices of the new era stocks, e.g. airlines or new technology stocks, such as the Internet. In these cases, the growth possibilities are enormous as investors try to figure out what a stock could really be worth. In such conditions, stocks could run up to crazy valuations, like Yahoo or ebay did — and then adjust equally severely. When the dust settles, some companies do change the way the world does business, except that their stocks regress back to delivering the same type of returns any other business would.

The listed stock fallacy

The universe of companies in a sector is not limited to listed companies but includes listed, unlisted and foreign companies. Stock valuations have to be compared to stocks in the unlisted space and global companies. There may be only a few listed companies in a sector but hundreds of unlisted companies. This can make it difficult for the stock to turn into a multibagger.

Most multibagger investors who invest on fundamentals end up comparing the stock's potential only to other listed companies and tend to disregard that the stock may have multiple competitors among private unlisted companies or foreign companies. This can cause wide difference in your perception about the potential of the company and the stock.

There are times when you should not think rationally

It is almost certain that traditional value investors will either sell out too early, or sit through a bull market, or, even worse, turn believers at the end of the bull market. Whatever be the case, these value investors can simply not match the returns of ignorant fools in such markets. Ignorance at such times is indeed bliss. Bull markets are more about anticipation of further returns and a highly optimistic mood. A value investor would look at traditional benchmarks and sell a stock because it now trades at a PE of 20 or 30. In a frenzied market, PEs become meaningless. In such markets, a mob psychology takes over and prices rise because the biggest mass of investors (and often with the least knowledge of the markets) start to enter at this point.

In bull markets, a strange phenomenon occurs when the crowds are right about the market's direction. When the market starts to get overvalued, smart investors who know enough about the market, start to go short thinking the stocks would correct. They may get badly trapped and speculators (even hedge funds and institutional investors) aided by the greed of the "crowd" continue to move stock prices. Fund managers too push the markets up as they get huge amount of funds in a bull market.

Wait for everyone to turn a believer before you sell or buy

"The fact that the bull market lasted so long presented problems even for the most skeptical reporters. 'You can only say that price/earnings ratios are too high so many times,' reflected a business writer at The New York Times. *'Eventually, you lose credibility'"*

– Maggie Mahar, *Bull!*

How do you know the markets have peaked? Financial TV will only have bullish voices. Anyone who thinks the market is overheated will not be called. Reporters who say the market is overdone will be sidelined. When financial media turns into a cheerleader and brokers and investment bankers are making it as fashion icons, wealth icons or popular figures, the rally is close to ending. Cash in your multibaggers.

The reverse is true when markets are at the bottom of a bear market. You will find it difficult to find a person or an expert or a broker who thinks things can improve. And this is precisely when you must buy your next set of multibaggers.

If you feel the excitement, it may not be time for multibaggers

"Focusing on the market's recent returns when they have been rosy will lead to a quite illogical and dangerous conclusion that equally marvellous results could be expected for common stocks in the future."
– Benjamin Graham

Excitement in the market is contagious. If you start to feel good about the economy, the markets or stocks, keep a sceptical outlook. If you believe a massive rally is building up, you can buy stocks that may become multibaggers. But excitement about markets comes towards the end of the rally because the market needs a vast majority of the investors to be uninformed before a rally ends. When buying stocks becomes the everyone's business, a rally is near its end.

Expectations of potential gains in a very short time outweigh any risk concerns we have. If you give me a big enough lollipop, i.e. incentive, you can lure me into the most preposterous proposition. And consensus makes such decision making easy.

Multibagger investing is akin to a leopard hunting

"The desire for constant action irrespective of underlying conditions is responsible for many losses in Wall Street even among the professionals, who feel that they must take home some money every day, as though they were working for regular wages."
– Edwin Lefèvre, *Reminiscences of a Stock Operator*

The way leopards hunt makes them perfect role models for multibagger investors. They wait for hours studying their prey, the surroundings and are paragons of patience. But when they make the sprint, there is little chance the prey can escape. You will need to have similar patience and discipline before you find multibaggers.

Don't stop listening to divergent views

Whenever you find yourself listening only to one particular view, whether a bull view or the bear view, and find yourself looking at news to confirm your view, immediately correct yourself. Divergent views are very important for multibagger investors. Look for views that test the bases for stocks that you are invested in or are investing in.

When markets turn unidirectional, especially when they get excessively bullish, dimwits and cheerleaders take over the role of experts, and those with deep market knowledge are either not interested in sharing what they really believe about the market, or are not given any space on media lest they spoil the party. This kind of skewed thinking attracts the largest mass of uninformed investors and lays the ground for the market to reverse.

Don't be influenced by your current investments in picking the next multibagger

"The hope of making the stock market pay your bill is one of the most prolific sources of loss in Wall Street. You will chip out all you have if you adhere to your determination."

– Edwin Lee'vre in *Reminiscences of a Stock Operator*

Think of flips of a coin. Once flip of the coin has nothing to do with the previous flip nor is it impacted by the previous flip giving you a heads or tails. Our natural tendency is to pick the next multibagger opportunity looking at our previous picks. For example, we are told not to concentrate our portfolio with stocks from a single industry, or that we should not have too much stock of a single company. None of this is necessary. As long as you can independently confirm that an investment may turn into a multibagger, your current portfolio or its composition should not matter.

Each multibagger investment must be independent of the other. Don't buy the next stock because you lost money on the previous one and now need to make good. The market has no obligation to make up your losses and if you buy stocks with this goal in mind, it will cloud your investment decision. You must make each multibagger investment independent of the previous one.

Multibagger opportunities abound at the start of a bull cycle

This is the best time to pick multibaggers. A bull cycle typically starts as follows: A large part of the industry is sitting with inventories and slow growth. And then, seemingly, out of nowhere, the markets begin to shoot up. Foreign money comes in and passes on to local investors, who take that money to buy cars, spend in hotels, buy houses, etc., thus generating incomes in these sectors. That kickstarts the economic engine and provides increasing fuel as more foreign money comes in. That brings in even more money, more white collar jobs — for example, in insurance, BPOs, etc. — which in turn adds more coal to the already roaring engine. Then, too, foreign investors make global media aware of India. As they write articles on India, global corporations and businesses became interested in India, driving up foreign direct investment (FDI) and economic growth.

A cheap stock may fall even further

"The securities might be unrelated, but the same investors own them, implicitly linking them in times of stress. And when armies of financial soldiers are involved in the same securities, borders shrink. The very concept of diversification would merit rethinking."

– Roger Lowenstein in *When Genius Failed*

What is cheap? It is a price much lower than the price you were used to? Can a stock be cheap even if the price is higher than a month earlier? Because there is no definition of cheap and we create our own definitions, an incorrect measure of cheap causes grave investment errors.

Cheap for most investors is a lower price than the price they have got used to seeing a stock trade at. But cheap for multibagger investors means a stock that has reached a point where acquirers would be paying a pittance of what it may take to set up the same business, or that a sell-off by institutional investors because of redemption has caused an unnecessary fall in the stock's price, or when a bank or other debtor has sold off the owner's pledged shares on a delay in loan repayments. Cheap then refers to a demand and supply imbalance, created either by a drying up of liquidity or a sudden sell-off of a large chunk of shares which the market could not suddenly absorb.

Why do stocks continue to rise when they seem expensive?

"Pardon me, but I think you have really no idea how the human bees will swarm to the beating of any old tin kettle; in that fact lies the whole manual of governing them. When they can be got to believe that the kettle is made of precious metals, in that power lies the whole power of men . . . ."

– Charles Dickens in *Little Dorrit*

There are two specific reasons why a stock may continue to rise when its valuations seem expensive. One is driven by the way institutional investors invest and the second is based on mass market psychology.

Institutional investors have specific rules about investing in stocks; they must have a certain market capitalization, trading volume or float (shares that are available with the public) among other restrictions. No matter how good an opportunity a stock presents, a fund manager cannot invest unless the stock reaches a certain market capitalization, achieves a certain trading volume, and has a certain float. Institutional investors also tend to get money when a market's rise captures the fancy of most investors. And institutional investors can only invest when they get money to invest. These peculiarities ensure that institutional investors, such as mutual funds, begin to buy stock not at the beginning of a rally but only when a large part of the market realizes that a rally is in full swing. That is also the time when institutional investors tend to get money. When they all rush to buy stocks at the same time, potential sellers, seeing the swift rise in stock prices, decide to hold back. The potent combination of too much money and shrinking stock for sale can cause a stock to rise many times.

Most fund managers and institutional investors are savvy about the market. Most know when markets are overheated. But the paradox they face is that they usually get the most money to invest when the markets are at their boiling point. And that drives overheated markets, sectors and stocks even higher, more by the sheer force of money rather than any rational reasons. That is one of the reasons that the fastest moves in popular sectors and stocks come exactly when the smartest investors think the stocks make no sense.

The next driver of a multibagger's price is the participation of the mass market typically comprising of the market novices. When people begin to invest only because they see others getting rich, you can be sure that a million others will enter the market and another tsunami of money will engulf available stocks. This will account for another round of multiple appreciation of stock prices.

Low priced stocks turn into multibaggers in mid- and small-cap rallies

Individual investors have a tendency to buy low priced stocks. It gives them some kind of psychological comfort to know that they paid for the stock in single or double digits. Such stocks have a low float and liquidity. In a mid cap or small cap rally such stocks can appreciate in multiples of their purchase price.

Investing in small cap and mid cap stocks requires a different set of skills and thought process. The perfect time to enter such stocks is at the bottom of bear markets when volumes are non-existent and the stock attracts no institutional interest. The only people trading in the stock then are those who are holding small lots. As a first step, prepare a list of such stocks. Then you have to figure out which ones are ripe to begin a rally or attract significant investor interest. Small cap and mid cap stocks can stay at very low prices for years. And if you enter them too early, you would stay with no returns for years too.

The time to enter these stocks is when the stock begins its initial move after months and years of staying in the dumps. Allow the stock to run up at least 5% to 10%. Since such stocks have many false starts and fall back to their lows, you will want to get a firm confirmation that the stock has started an up move. A good sign that the small- or mid-cap stock will continue its rise is a spurt in prices of large capitalization stocks in the same industry.

The bull market cycle

In a bull market, the sequence of events has been amazingly familiar for the past 300 years of market history:

- Stocks will reach a point where they have little to do with value.
- Then momentum kicks into overdrive.
- Those new to the markets are usually the last to turn believers — and they usually turn believers with a vengeance and in very large numbers. That provides the final push to the market and takes stocks to ridiculous

levels. In this phase, stocks are running only because people are ready to pay whatever the price to buy them.

- At the end of this euphoric phase, a massive blowout takes the stocks down very sharply.
- The hangover is equally severe and stocks lose as much as 90% of their value.
- Then the market looks for scapegoats to hang. One or more brokers are taken to the laundry by regulators and the markets settle into a period of stock apathy.

Blue chip, safe and popular stocks rarely make multibaggers

Blue chip stocks tend to have high institutional ownership, with millions of stocks being bought and sold every day, and thousands of traders trading them, and also buying futures or options in such stocks. Too many brokers cover these stocks. All this makes for very little opportunity for the stock to move significantly on the upside. The downside risk, on the other hand, is significant. Any selling by institutional investors can cause an imbalance in demand and supply, with supply outstripping demand and causing steep falls in price. Such stocks are unable to take negative news without causing havoc with their stock price.

Stocks that are popular have too many investors piled onto them. Their upside is limited because whoever wants to be in the stock is already there. Their downside, on the other hand, is unlimited. Any negative news or selling by investors can send the stock steeply down. Managements and owners of these popular stock have to continue dishing out positive news and keep negative news in the backburner unless forced by circumstances to present it.

Instead of considering too many investors piling into a stock as a risk, we find comfort in numbers. Take the example of ice skaters on a frozen river. Each skater feels confident that the ice will hold because of the presence of other skaters. In fact, the risk of the ice cracking is greater when the number of skaters increases. At the first sound of crack, each skater tries to rush out causing the ice to actually crack.

There is no absolute safety to stocks, irrespective of whether they are blue chip, mid cap, or small cap. Blue chip stocks may be liquid, popular and well covered but that does not make them any less risky than other stocks. Your goal is to identify stocks that can generate the best returns with the lowest possible risk. This depends on picking the right stock, at the right point in the market cycle, and before other investors make it a popular stock.

A frenzied bull market turns into a Ponzi scheme towards its end

"Whoever be the individuals that compose it, however like or unlike be their mode of life, their occupations, their character, or their intelligence, the fact that they have been transformed into a crowd puts them in possession of a sort of collective mind which makes them feel, think, and act in a manner quite different from that in which each individual of them would feel, think, and act were he in a state of isolation."

– Gustav LeBon

At what stage do you exit your multibaggers? When the market or the stock turns into a Ponzi scheme. You need to exit when a stock reaches a point where it is rising because there are others ready to pick it up from the current owners at whatever price is being quoted. By this time, the stock's price has little to do with the company's business, its fundamentals, or any measure of value. The only driver of the stock is the hope of buyers that they will be able to flip the stock to the next set of buyers at a higher price. It is no surprise, then, that the biggest rise in the markets comes when the least knowledgeable — and they constitute the largest number — rush in. A frenzied bull market is essentially a Ponzi scheme in its last stages. It rests on an ever growing group of fewer and fewer knowledgeable people getting into the market. It's the strength in numbers that makes people get into stocks at crazy prices. A mob mentality takes over.

What we don't know is the stage at which the pyramiding will totter. And when that happens, all those waiting to sell would rush to sell in a synchronized fashion. That usually coincides with a general disinterest to buy as buyers now expect prices to drop further.

There is no cheap and expensive stock because there is no mean or bell curve in a stock's price

"Successful investing is anticipating the anticipation of others."
– John Maynard Keynes

What is cheap for the buyer is expensive for the seller. That is why you are able to buy and sell stocks. This means that cheap and expensive are only an opinion, and no indication of the potential of the stock. Now imagine millions of investors making assumptions about a stock being cheap or expensive. Add to that millions of traders trying to figure out a trend. With so many investors and traders pulling at a stock who is to say if a stock is cheap or expensive. At most times, the amount of money pulling stocks higher or lower is evenly matched and that is why stock prices remain within a range for long periods of time.

At certain times this equilibrium between buyers and sellers of a stock breaks. Either a majority of buyers, or sellers, change their perception about the market. If this majority perceives stocks to be expensive, extensive selling will follow and stocks will collapse. But this collapse has not been caused by any change in a company's prospects but a change in perceptions. The best multibagger opportunities arise when an overwhelming majority of investors and traders sell stocks and there are not enough buyers to match that selling driving stocks to very low levels. Such low levels set the base for a multiple rise in stock prices as the perceptions of investors and traders turns for the positive over time.

You must look at a stock only from its potential to turn into a multibagger. Whether a stock will turn into a multibagger or not depends on the kind of price and volume momentum the stock shows, the state of the sector the stock is in, and the overall market's direction. Looking at stocks as cheap or expensive compared to some price that you are used to is fatal. A stock does not have a bell curve or a mean price. It can go up multiple times and, equally, drop to any level. It can also stay at the new price and never return to its older price.

Buying a stock because it is cheap or expensive compared to some price you are used to, is one of the most critical errors that multibagger investors run into.

Correlation between a business and its stock price

"Those who seek to relate stock movements to the current statistics of business, or who ignore the strongly imaginative taint of stock operations, or who overlook the technical bias of advances and declines, must meet with disaster, because their judgement is based upon the humdrum dimensions of fact and figure in a game which is actually played in a third dimension of the emotions and a fourth dimension of dreams."

– Barton Biggs

The extent of correlation between a business and its stock price is very similar to the correlation between a fault line and the chances of an earthquake because of the fault line. Just because there is a fault line does not mean there will be an earthquake. And if there is an earthquake, there is no way of knowing if it will be a minor or a major one.

Similarly, a good company does not give us an indication of what its stock price should be. That depends on the perception of the majority of its investors and traders, and how much money is entering or exiting the stock. Trying to link stock prices to low PE, zero debt, etc. is an exercise in futility because in bad times, investors and traders may avoid buying no matter what the business looks like; in good times, they may buy no matter how bad the business looks. The job of a multibagger investor is to focus on picking stocks where he expects the perception of investors and traders to turn overwhelmingly positive backed by a flood of money entering the stock.

Stock prices are driven by the optimism, imagination, hopes, fears and aspirations of investors and traders. There is a correlation between the underlying business and its stock price but the magnitude of the correlation can be tainted by the mood of investors and traders. The same stock could be trading at 2 time its PE, 10 times its PE, 100 times its PE, or any other multiple depending on how investors and traders perceive the stock and how the flow of money is driving the demand and supply for the stock.

You could be stuck with the stock for years. The first hurdle you confront is that the information you have access to about the business is second hand information, from financial media, management or other sources. The second hurdle is the unknown level of interest of other investors and traders in the stock.

How multibagger stocks emerge and sustain themselves

"The next man who has a large capacity for swindling will succeed as well. Pardon me, but I think you have really no idea how the human bees will swarm to the beating of any old tin kettle; in that fact lies the whole manual of governing them. When they can be got to believe that the kettle is made of precious metals, in that power lies the whole power of men like our late lamented."

– Charles Dickens, *Little Dorrit*

If your starting point is low PE, high book value to price, or any such conventional measure of value, you are not on track to find a multibagger. Multibaggers have little to do with these conventional measures and more to do with the context or stage you are investing in. The same conventional ratios may give you a stock whose price drops further, stays put, or rises, depending on the stage of the market. It is important to find the right time when a multibagger emerges. It is no different from agriculture. You have to plant a particular crop or vegetable in the right season and geography to get the right climate, moisture, soil, etc.

Multibaggers emerge at different times and at different places and this is not fixed. Nor is it based on any conventional value picking methods. A multibagger also sustains itself in certain environments and turns a dud in others. Think of how a crop may be bumper if it rains at the right time or may get ruined if it does not rain, or rains at the wrong time.

Investors generally deal with information at different speeds and make very different stock investing decisions based on the same information. At times, however, a vast majority of investors make similar investing decisions and drive the stock higher, or accelerate the speed at which the stock rises. Investors are also influenced by their recent experiences. If they are coming out of large losses, they may react abruptly to any drop in the stock price compared to someone who has had a streak of strong returns.

Why options work for finding multibaggers

Events that are not expected to occur for thousands of years statistically happen with unusual frequency in stock markets. Such events include a sudden rush out of stocks or bonds into cash, or the sudden collapse of a country's stock markets due to political or other developments. Options are an amazing tool to use for unexpected events. The multibagger nature is built into them. An option costs nothing close to the stock. You know the loss on the day you buy an option. But if an unexpected event happens, you could get many times the amount you put into buying it.

Markets go up and down in short bursts — and often gain or lose 50% of their value in these short bursts. The rest of the time, they just drift. You must be ready to take advantage of the rise or fall of the markets and one of the best ways to do it is with options. It is like a wager. Your cost is fixed but gains can be potentially unlimited.

The dawn of a new era or new asset class is ideal breeding ground for multibaggers

"The superior man in the world does not set his mind either for anything or against anything; what is right he will follow."

\- Confucius

Stock market bubbles are usually caused by the investors discovering a new technology, a new country's potential, or a new "asset class." Anything that creates a structural imbalance in an existing system like airlines, railroads, the Internet, China, etc. will cause a market bubble to build up as investors try to price the new asset class. In a sense, then stock market bubbles are almost a price discovery mechanism that provide a once in a life time opportunity to cash out big time at the peak of irrationality.

The euphoria is not so much plain greed or fear, which it may eventually turn into, but is the expectation that a new technology or country could result in such great profits in the future that even the current ridiculous valuations are justified.

During this process of trying to find the right price for a set of stocks based on a new idea, investors and traders tend to overvalue them. No one wants to miss the new wave and the horde of money that comes chasing the new dream can drive stock prices up in multiples. Such opportunities are rare, and for an investor who gets such an opportunity, it is the chance of a life time.

The vast majority of investors miss such opportunities. Shocked by the stunning rise in price, investors tend to avoid the sector and buy what they consider "cheaper" stocks in some other sector. Only when prices in this new wave rise to spectacular heights do investors get the feeling of being left out, and then they get in at peak prices, preparing the grounds for spectacular losses at some point.

Multibagger investors should prepare themselves for such an opportunity. This is the safest time to get multibaggers. Stocks may rise not just 5- to 10-fold times but even 50- to 100-fold. This is also the time to keep your personal ideology, concepts of value investing, and all other such mind blockers on the side and go all out to invest.

Small in size does not mean small in returns

The larger its market capitalization, the more difficult it becomes for the stock to go any higher. And the larger the market capitalization, the higher the risk that the stock could take a hit. But a stock with a small market capitalization has a lot of ground to cover and since the worst that can happen is that it can go to zero, there is not much of a fall to worry about. Think about a larger market cap stock as being on the 12th step of a 15-step stairway and a small cap stock to be on a 2nd step of a 15-step stairway.

Smaller stocks typically provide much bigger multibagger opportunities. Concentrate on stocks which are small in size; they are the ones likely to give you large returns.

The challenge is the large number of smaller cap stocks that you have to go through to find a single good one. That challenge can be overcome by creating and refining your own stock selection process.

The easiest time to find multibaggers

"Follow the course opposite to custom and you will almost always do well."

– J. J. Rousseau

Markets will often get excited about individual stock stories or sectors. Money will flow into such stocks and sectors because that is where the returns are the highest and quickest and it will stop flowing to stocks with very significant differences between the stock's intrinsic value and price. Riding such waves will produce easy multibaggers but you must use this investment method only after you have gained 3 to 5 years of experience.

You must invest against the existing theme and instead focus on an emerging theme. It takes time for a new theme to take hold, and the stronger the scepticism about the theme accompanied by rising stock prices, the higher the chances of stocks turning into multibaggers. Take advantage of the lag time between the emergence of a new investment theme and the market's ability to find the right price.

Being contrarian works only at market extremes and not when markets still have a long way to go either up or down. For a multibagger investor understanding how to read market extremes becomes critical.

Stocks can fall way lower than you think

"Market values are evanescent, ephemeral and extravagant, as much a reflection of passing fashion as female modes of attire. A fashionable style, like a speculative movement, is subject to a popular consensus and follows a trend until it reaches a point of extravagance from which it can only retreat."

– Edward Chancellor

Stocks can drop way beyond what investors can imagine. Take the example of the Philippines stock market to keep in perspective what can happen to stocks and how a down and out market creates multibaggers:

- The Philippines stock index was down 75% in US dollar terms in just 5 years (from 1980 to 1985). The Mining Index had declined by 94% and the Oil Index by 97%.
- The combined market capitalization of the six largest companies had fallen to only US$340 million and the entire Philippines stock market amounted to less than US$ 500 million.
- By 2000, even after the 1997 crisis, the market capitalization of the Philippines stock market was about US $25 billion.

8

~

Multibagger Investing Rules

"As frogs to wells and tanks repair, and water birds to ample lakes,
So fortune, helpless as it were, its home in men of diligence makes."
– Hitopdesa

Stay invested in a winning stock

Staying invested in a winning position is more difficult than it looks. The temptation of getting out of a stock when it has appreciated 2- to 3-fold is overwhelming. And if you manage to hold on to the stock, the pressure to take the profits off the table when the stock drops 20% to 30% after a 2- to 3-fold rise is immense. It takes years of discipline, and a mastery of technical charts to know whether a stock's out of steam, or is just taking a breather.

The risk you take when you make the investment can be made minimal. If a stock drops 10% from your purchase price, you must exit. But as the stock piles on profit, you have much greater bandwidth to stay with the stock when it drops. You can come up with your own thresholds but you can also use the following markers to stay with a stock which is on an upward trajectory:

- Be ready to take a 20% loss from the high if the stock has appreciated 2- to 3-fold.
- Be ready to take a 25% loss from the high if the stock has appreciated 5- to 10-fold.

But don't hold on to a stock that loses more than 25% from the high at any point of time. A 25% loss stock may indicate that the supply of stock or the sellers of the stock are ready to flood the market.

Opportunities arise when investors are focused elsewhere

". . . much of the stock market 'action' occurs in very brief periods and at times when investors are most likely to be captives of a conventional consensus."
– Chares Ellis

It is easy to be caught up in an existing trend or mood of the market. The longer a trend or cycle has been around in the economy or the market, the larger the number of people who start believing that the ongoing conditions are permanent. But it is precisely at these points, where a very large majority of investors and traders expect existing conditions to persist, that markets reverse.

Opportunities arise in other sectors when investors are focusing on one or two sectors alone. Money flows into sectors where investors find quick returns and divert money from other sectors. Even mutual funds are forced to invest in sectors holding investor interest, driving money out of other stocks and sectors. When stocks fall only because investors are moving then money to another sector for quick profits, long term multibagger opportunities arise in these neglected sectors. It is not because anything is wrong with these stocks, but simply that the flow of money is moving to only those stocks or sectors that deliver quick profits.

Limit your losses

"Mathematics is ordinarily considered as producing precise and dependable results: but in the stock market the more elaborate and abstruse the mathematics the more uncertain and speculative are the conclusions we draw from them. Calculus . . . [gives] speculation the deceptive guise of investment."
– Benjamin Graham

If you picked a wrong stock, sell it before it moves down significantly. You can develop your own system, but you can start with the following rules if you picked the wrong stock:

- If you buy a stock and it falls 10% from your purchase price instead of rising, sell it. You can always buy it again at a lower price.

- If you buy a stock and it appreciates 50% from your purchase price, sell it if it then loses 50% of the gains.
- If you buy a stock and it appreciates 100% from its purchase price, sell only if it comes back to the purchase price.
- If you buy a stock and it appreciates more than 100%, don't sell it. This is the stage where your investment methodology and experience will tell you when to sell.

These rules may not fit your current mindset. At first glance, it looks as though you are giving away your entire gains if you follow these rules. But that's the price you have to pay to get a multibagger. Let me explain the rationale. A stock that falls after you have bought it indicates you may have missed something that the market knows and it is thus best to stay out of the stock. A stock that appreciates 50% indicates there are chances it may appreciate more but may also indicate low float or a large order pushing up the price as a one-time event. In such a scenario, it is best to lock in 50% of your profit. However, if a stock gains 100%, there may be a longer term move building up and unless it loses its entire gain, there is no reason to sell out. If a stock moves more than 100%, it indicates a revaluing of the stock's price. Hold on to that stock.

Mastery of technical charts is a must

"Those who seek to relate stock movements to the current statistics of business, or who ignore the strongly imaginative taint of stock operations, or who overlook the technical basis of advances and declines, must meet with disaster, because their judgment is based upon the humdrum dimensions of fact and figures in a game which is actually played in a third dimension of emotions and a fourth dimension of dreams."

– Barton Biggs in *Hedge Hogging*

~

"One reason why many types of technical analyses don't work too well is because such methods are often applied indiscriminately. Trading the market without knowing what stage it is in is like

selling life insurance to twenty-year-olds and eighty-year-olds at the same premium."
– Victor Sperandeo

Value investors have an aversion to charts or technical analysis. For some reason there is some intellectual superiority attached to investing on fundamentals. It's a mistake to pooh-pooh charts, technical analysis, or the role of the market's psychology on the stock's price. Stock charts give you the context you need to make your multibagger decisions in.

If you have picked a stock as a multibagger opportunity, what harm would it do you to find out how the stock has moved in the past 5 to 10 years. What if you find that the stock never goes out of a price range for years? This could well make you reconsider your rationale for being in the stock. If the charts show that the stock is not moving out of a price range; or that it tends to fluctuate wildly, there may be something you have missed in your analysis. Stock charts are the best way to check your investment process in the context of the stock's price movements.

One of the most crucial decisions investors face is when to invest and when to exit. You may find a stock with price way below its intrinsic value but what technicals do for you is to give you the most appropriate point to enter and exit the stock.

Technical charts have to be read in context. The context depends on the strength of the stock's rally in terms of increasing price, volumes and the time that has elapsed since the rally began. We have to also see if the stock's rallying along with the entire sector, or whether it is rallying by itself.

Technicals tell you when the stock is getting ready to move and when the stock is starting to sputter. It gives you a proven way of anticipating demand for the stock. Without technicals, you could be stuck with the same stock for years.

Go over thousands of intermediate term, short term and long term charts. Look at charts of hundreds of stocks. Then study the stock price's move along with the increase or fall in volumes. At the next level, check a chart after a major news announcement. The stock price's reaction along with the move in volumes will tell you if the market has already factored in the news or if it has been surprised by the news.

It tells you if the market is beginning to align itself to your thinking about a stock or, conversely, if the market knows something that you may not know.

No matter what your view is about "value" in a stock or your beliefs in picking a multibagger, entering one without reading a stock's chart is fatal. A technical chart is a must when you invest, for anticipating the mood of other investors, and for knowing when to exit the stock.

If you have decided to invest in a stock because of its undervaluation, the charts would show low volume and a stagnant price over a period of time. If a stock shows high trading volumes and a declining trend over the short term, it may indicate that the stock may be heading even lower. You can hold off your investing decision till the chart indicates the stock has turned stagnant in terms of price, and volume is declining indicating, waning interest.

Over a period of time, other investors need to get interested in the stock to make it a multibagger. A chart showing you an uptrend in price, along with an increase in volume, may indicate an increase in interest in the stock.

Check the charts before you decide to sell. If a stock indicates increasing volumes and a rise in stock price, there is no need to sell. Wait for the stock to start stagnating, or start to dropping after a long term uptrend before you sell.

You must be liquid when you expect multibagger opportunities

There are times when multibagger opportunities will scream at you. But these are precisely the times when investors are bleeding heavily and don't have extra liquidity.

Multibagger investors must always maintain a cash cushion of 25% at all times to leverage such opportunities. In times of a market collapse or wide-spread selling because of margin payments or a liquidity freeze, remain 50% liquid in order to buy stocks when a liquidity scarcity event is coming your way.

If you are convinced, your investment must be of a significant size

A small amount invested in a potential multibagger stock remains a small amount even if the stock delivers multibagger returns. When you are convinced about the potential of a stock, go after it with a big amount. You can come up with your rules on how much you want to be invested in a stock which you are convinced will turn into a multibagger but listed below is a benchmark you can follow till you set your own rules:

- At the time of entry into the stock, invest a minimum of 5% of your capital.
- If the stock rises 50% and the technical charts confirm rising prices on rising volumes, invest another 5% in the stock.
- If the stock rises 100% and the technical charts show an increasing momentum in the stock and in volumes, and it is backed by a strong rise in stocks in the sector or a bull market, invest another 5%.

Avoid investing more than 15% of your capital in any single stock, no matter how strongly you feel about its potential.

Wait for the easy kills

The market will provide you enough opportunities to pick multibaggers. Such an opportunity could arise when investors move to cash from stocks, there is a panic sell-off driven by liquidity, or some other short term factors.

You don't have to attempt a hit every time. Only when the big swing comes, should you bat. Big swings come once in a while and you must not get out too early out of such big swings.

This is also called "fish in the barrel investing." You can try and shoot fish in the sea or a lake, or spread your net and catch them and put them in a barrel and shoot them. Spend most of your time spreading your net and keeping a list of stocks that will become multibagger opportunities in certain circumstances. And when those circumstances present themselves, go for the easy kill.

How to invest at the lowest risk

"When a switch in a major investment theme is about to occur, there is a strong disbelief and enormous scepticism in the minds of investors as to the merits of the new theme."

–Marc Faber, *Tomorrow's Gold,*

It is difficult psychologically to be one of the first to invest in a stock. Few people are in the stock and most are sceptical about your choice. No one in the media is talking about the stock and there is no way to confirm if you have done the right thing.

Being a contrarian alone is not enough to find multibaggers. But being ahead of the crowd when a new investment theme is emerging is a low risk strategy to find multibaggers. How do you know a new investment theme is emerging? Over the years, your experience will show you how and when investment themes emerge. You can also use the following benchmarks.

- An investment theme starts to emerge when we are at the threshold of a supply and demand imbalance which will take a few years to correct. For example, rising demand for hotel rooms but limited availability of hotel rooms, or a limited production of automobiles accompanied by a rising demand.
- An investment theme starts to emerge when investors begin to feel extremely optimistic about a market. For example, if foreigners get excited about your market, the entire market may turn into multibagger returns. From time to time, several Asian markets have risen 5- to 10-fold in a span of 2 to 3 years.
- An investment theme starts to emerge when investors start to pour in capital blindly in the hope of an instant gain. For example, when Exchange Traded Funds (ETFs) investing in a country, a sector, or a commodity start to receive billions of dollars, stocks in that country, sector, commodity will rise multiple times by the sheer force of money.
- An investment theme starts to emerge when a few powerful or influential people in the stock markets decide they want to make something an investment theme.
- An investment theme starts to emerge when a sector or stock starved for demand and facing extreme investor disinterest starts to find interest. Even small flows of money into the stock spring the stock to life.

Exit when everyone notices a problem with a stock's price

Stocks don't necessarily fall because something has changed in the business or in the fundamentals of the stock. Large and permanent drops in a stock's price happen when a majority of investors and traders recalibrate their opinions about the prospects of the stock. Such recalibration causes stocks to lose value suddenly and permanently as a change in opinion or interest takes times to return to an out of favour stock or sector.

Even "blue chips" or the "safest" stocks can see a collapse in price if institutional investors decide to exit or a large number of investors don't want to be in the stock. The timing of selling a multibagger must correspond to the long term end of price rise. Stocks rarely go back to where they were when investors exit *en masse*. At least they won't do so anytime soon.

There is safety when the entire market moves

Picking multibaggers when the whole market is moving up is much easier and safer than going against the market. If an entire market is moving up, there is enough interest and money chasing stocks. At such times even if you are wrong, your stock picks may not show a loss even if they don't turn into multibaggers.

There will be times when an entire sector will find investor interest. While institutional investors may stick to picking larger capitalization stocks in the sector, the biggest rise may come in the sector's small cap stocks. Individual investors tend to buy low priced stocks with low liquidity rather than large capitalization high priced stocks. A combination of a large number of individual investors and low liquidity in small cap stock drives many stocks up multiple times when a sector's stocks are in demand.

Don't confuse multibagger investing with value investing

Multibagger investing requires a whole different skill set than traditional value investing. When picking a potential multibagger stock, the threshold is so high that ordinary value investment principles become ineffective. The starting point for multibagger investing is a return of 5 to 10 times your purchase price. How does one beat a stock market index, institutional investors and millions of other investors and traders to achieve such spectacular returns?

Finding stocks that return 5 to 10 times in a market which stays in a range for the most part is a challenge. However, you can achieve this with discipline and a proprietary stock picking style.

Here is a roadmap you can follow towards picking multibagger stocks:

- Pick a stock only if you are convinced it is going to rise 5 to 10 times from its current price.
- Invest using an investment method. Make frequent corrections in your method as you make mistakes and gain experience.
- Learn to read technical charts and see if the direction of the market favours your beliefs.
- Repeat the process for hundreds of stocks till you get perfect in your investment method.
- Don't allow a stock to go deep into losses. If a stock is not doing what you expect it to do, exit it.

Pick stocks that turn into multibaggers in the shortest time

"All businesses, all industries are cyclical. There has never been a scenario where the tree grows to the sky."

– Lee Ainslie in *Hedge Hunters*

Investing is often associated with waiting a few years to see a stock give great returns. Investing, however, is not like planting a tree that you have to wait for years to see a sapling grow into a tree.

The longer you are waiting for a stock to turn into a multibagger, the higher the chances that you picked the wrong stock, or that you entered the stock too early. Timing your entry is even more important than identifying the multibagger opportunity.

Timing your entry into a multibagger opportunity depends on whether the flow of money is moving in or out of the stock, and what is driving the flow. If the flow is driven for reasons that have nothing to do with the stock or its business but because investors need cash or are deserting stocks, that's when you will get multibagger opportunities.

In bull markets, or markets focused on investment themes, your focus should be on identifying stocks that can turn into multibaggers in the shortest possible time. It is in such times that your mastery of technical charts comes into use. When the flow of money starts to dominate investing considerations, stocks with low floating stock and large inflows of money start to appreciate the fastest.

Dealing with the wealth created by multibaggers

Multibagger investing throws up money in multiples of what you invested. It also tends to make you feel like you have some special skill and that you can repeat the performance again and again. Think of each multibagger investment as different from another multibagger investment. Getting it right in one stock is no guarantee of getting it right in another stock. Growing overconfident, we may also be tempted to invest in other stocks at a phase in market which is not conducive multibagger opportunities.

Every time you sell a multibagger, take out 50% of your profits from that stock. The lure of stocks is so great that if you don't take profits out of every multibagger investment, you will end up losing all your profits and your capital.

There will be phases where it will be difficult to find multibagger stocks. The temptation for doing something will make you pick stocks that have only a long shot at becoming multibaggers. When you have losses, you will be tempted to hold on just a little bit longer than the limit you set for yourself to exit a stock. These are human follies that even the smartest, biggest and most successful investors suffer from. Only the discipline of taking out 50% of your profits, never letting losses cross limits you have set, and never buying stocks where the odds of a 5- to 10-fold return does not exist will help you emerge a multibagger winner.

Stocks near their lows don't become multibaggers

"Do not be desirous to have things done quickly; do not look at small advantages. Desire to have things done quickly prevents their being done thoroughly. Looking at small advantages prevents great affairs from being accomplished."

– Confucius

Don't confuse a stock that is down 90% or 95% from its highs with a potential multibagger. Stocks neither need to nor tend to go back to any "average" price. A stock that is up a 100% may rise another 200% in a few weeks or months. A stock that is down 90% from its peak can drop to 99% below.

A stock that has dropped significantly may indicate a multibagger opportunity but this is not a blanket rule. The reasons for the fall are critical to determine whether a stock that has fallen 90% to 95% from its peak is a multibagger opportunity. There are times when a stock's price fall has nothing to do with the stock. It may have large institutional investor holdings and redemption pressure on mutual funds could drive the stock price down. If a stock has dropped significantly for reasons not related to the stock but due to investor considerations, then there may be a multibagger in the making.

When stocks trade at their lows, there is no way to know how long they will continue to be at that level — and whether they will fall further. Stocks can stay at their lows for years. Such stocks should not even make it to your shortlist of stocks to pick.

Don't look for reasons when a stock begins to stall

If a stock is heading up, no elaborate explanations are required for why it is going up. More money is entering the stock than is leaving it. If it continues to rise with some minor corrections, stay invested in the stock. But be extremely wary if a stock's upward move begins to slow down, or starts to fall with a few small rallies. It is then clear that the stock's direction has changed. You don't need to look for reasons for this change in direction. Just get out of the stock.

There are usually very good reasons why a stock is heading lower and those reasons are always known to a few people, including the company's owners, management, etc. And they have no obligation to let you in on this information. In fact, in such situations individual investors are often misled into believing that the stock is now "cheap," and that it is a good time to buy it.

Don't fall for this trap. If the price has changed direction, it is your best cue to exit the stock no matter what you hear about its prospects or potential in financial media or anywhere else.

How do you make money being right only 10% to 20% of the time

Only 10% to 20% of your picks will turn into multibaggers. 80% to 90% of your stocks will deliver losses. You have to make enough to have a 5- to 10–fold times return on your investment after taking losses in 80% to 90% of your stock picks.

The only way you can achieve this is to limit your loss to 5% on any stock. For those stocks that are turning out to be multibaggers, you must not sell-out just because the stock has already risen 2- or 3-fold. Let the stock run as far as it can before you exit.

A combination of limiting your losses and letting your profits run will get you multibagger returns even if you are right only 10% to 20% of the time.

Staying in the proper frame of mind

Try and not use stock picking strategies you have used in the past, nor the results generated from these strategies, from interfering with picking new multibagger candidates. A strategy may give you a multibagger in one phase of the market but end up as a dud in another phase. Keeping your mind focused on the investment in context of the market phase, and not being influenced by outside chatter or past experience, is essential. Think of it as flipping coins. The result of one flip of a coin is independent from the next. Multibagger investing has to be looked at similarly.

Your frame of mind at the time of making the investment is the most critical element in multibagger investing. If you have made 7 or 8 wrong stock picks and you are in an agitated state of mind, take a break and don't pick stocks for a few weeks or months. When your mind is agitated because of losses in the market, or owing to any other issues unrelated to the market, you will lose your objectivity which is essential to pick multibaggers.

There are no multibaggers to be found in stagnant markets

"Buffett understood that everything depends on the price you pay when you get in. In that sense, any value investor is a market timer; at the end of a cycle when prices are highest, he stops buying."
– Maggie Mahar, *Bull!*

For the most part, markets either stay stagnant or move within a range. This can happen for years at a stretch. There are no multibaggers to be found in stagnant markets or sectors. Wait for the overall market or a sector to stir. See how sharply the market or sector has bounced. Let the market, the sector, or the stock appreciate 5% to 10% from the lows. This will confirm an upmove, wherefrom you can begin to monitor and pick stocks.

Whenever demand for a stock picks up, it is not going to be isolated. It will show a continued increase in price and trading volumes over a period of weeks or months. This is the only kind of sustained move in which a multibagger may materialize.

Multibagger investing rules

Never average

Investors tend to average, namely buy more of a stock when it is falling. This would be a sound strategy if you had all the information at your command in order to know that the stock's going to reverse course at some time. More often, though, the stock is falling because investors don't know what is ailing the stock. And there are hundreds of variables unknown to you because of which the stock may be moving lower.

Since multibagger investing requires that you never let your losses go out of hand, you cannot average a falling stock under any circumstances.

There may be times when you buy a stock and it is heading higher and the information you have on the stock's potential becomes clearer. In such times you can think of adding more stock to your current holdings. So if you have to average, you can do it on the way up but never on the way down.

If your pick is not heading the way you expected, leave the battlefield. There will be another day to fight.

Made a mistake? Wrap it up

"The true investor welcomes volatility . . . a wildly fluctuating market means that irrationally low prices will periodically be attached to solid businesses."

– Warren Buffett

If you are losing, set the threshold and then wrap it up. You are not going to get every multibagger right. And those we get wrong should not become our noose.

Wrapping up is going to be much tougher than you may think. Our psychological makeup does not allow us to give up, especially when we have made a mistake. But you will get good at wrapping up if you keep reminding yourself that you cannot let your losses go beyond 5 or 10 percent of your purchase price.

9

~

Types of Multibaggers

Multibagger types

Multibaggers should be looked at their potential from the context of market conditions, developing conditions for the stock, imbalances between buyers and sellers, etc.:

- Long term multibaggers.
- Stocks that have been at the bottom for years because of a bear market.
- Stocks which are ripe for acquisition or are being acquired.
- Low volume stocks that hit a freeze every day.
- Multibaggers are produced for various reasons — liquidity, capital raising, acquisitions, etc. and are not always driven by fundamentals.
- Institutional buying of low volume stock.
- Stock market bubbles.
- Small cap multibaggers.
- Retail investing driven multibaggers.

Supply lag time multibaggers

In certain industries, additional supply takes times to build up. In those phases when demand continues to grow but supply will come in only over the next few years, stock prices could rise by several multiples. A good example are hotel stocks. If hotels are running at 100% occupancy in a certain city or country, it will be years before new room supply can come on board and in the period before supply catches up with the demand, hotel stocks can rise many times.

Multibaggers from a structural shift in demand caused by regulations, lowering of price points, etc.

A structural shift in demand or supply can cause a stock to turn into a multibagger. This is a phenomenon observed in commodity stocks. Take, for example, a government regulation banning diesel cars. It will create sudden demand for petrol vehicles.

A company with a brand that has pricing power

There are several companies globally that demonstrate pricing power despite being in commodity type businesses. Take Starbucks or GAP, for example. Companies that build a brand enjoy pricing power and can scale up to unprecedented levels providing multibagger opportunities.

Risk free multibaggers

"Intelligence is all about making a guess that discovers some new underlying order."

– Michael Mouboussin

If you see small and mid-cap funds being flooded with money by investors, your odds of finding a multibagger among them are close to 100%. Small and mid-cap stocks don't have liquidity, they have large promoter holdings, and react sharply to any new flow of money. Mutual funds which restrict themselves to buying small and mid-cap stocks have no choice but to buy these low float, low liquidity stocks, driving up their prices in multiples in very short intervals of time. Watch the interest level of individual investors and whether they are converting it by giving mutual funds increasing amounts of money to invest. You will have to fight with a natural hesitancy to buy stocks that have already moved up 2- to 3-fold from when you started to observe them. But the price when you started to observe the stock, or its current price, is irrelevant as long as you are sure investors will pour increasing amounts of money into small and mid-cap stocks.

Foreign buying into a local market

Foreign buyers like the comfort of the herd. When they enter a local market, it will be in droves. When billions of dollars enter a local market, stock prices spike up in multiples. Foreign investors usually stick to bigger and large capitalization stocks. If the market is being driven by such flows, the odds of finding a multibagger among the top 100 or 200 stocks are very high.

If foreigners or institutions withdraw money, stocks will fall steeply, sometimes by over 90%. This is not the right time to buy a stock. With no local buyers to support or absorb such large scale selling, it could be years before a stock begins to move up again. In such markets, even if a stock has fallen over 90%, it is not a cheap stock.

Multibaggers based on the "mass psychology of a large number of ignorant individuals"

"I have always tended to underestimate the ignorance and greed of the investing public and the heights to which speculation can push up prices."

– Marc Faber in *Tomorrow's Gold*

In bull markets, most investors have their antennae up and start tuning in to profit making opportunities. According to Keynes, since most of us have no way of knowing the future with any degree of certainty, stock prices ultimately depend on the confidence of investors which, itself, is the outcome of the "mass psychology of a large number of ignorant individuals." Stock prices can rise multiple times towards the peak of a bull market. Those who own the stock continue to hold it in anticipation of higher prices. Those who don't have the stock, buy at whatever price it is available at. Low availability of stock and too much money entering the stock creates the multibagger.

As a multibagger investor, you must learn to anticipate the thinking of others in the market, and whether they will tilt the balance in favour of buying a particular stock. If the supply is low and demand is increasing, a multibagger may be in the making.

Forced selling opportunity

When the large majority is forced to sell because they are leveraged, or trading on margin, or because of redemptions from mutual funds, or panic, multibagger opportunities arise. The price at which you buy is so out of sync with the intrinsic value of the stock that sooner or later the stock will move up in multiples. But forced sellers are not always present in the market and you must be ready with the money when this happens.

Dodo multibaggers

These are multibaggers that God gifts you. You just happened to pick the right stock and it shoots up. It is very dangerous to extrapolate this multibagger experience to picking other stocks since such multibaggers qualify as a flukc. Fluke multibaggers give a false sense of confidence and eventually end up sending you on the path of picking losing stocks.

Wave or bubble multibaggers

This is the kind of multibagger you get in a dotcom sort of mad frenzy of 2000, where a stock could be up 10 times and rise still another 10-fold. Bubble multibaggers occur only a few times in one's life.

Bubbles are one of the best times to get multibagger returns. And it happens in the shortest periods of time. Most experienced investors become extremely averse to stocks in bubbles. They find valuations to be very expensive. But during bubbles, stocks don't move on valuations; they move on a tsunami of money chasing stocks. In such scenarios, stocks that have a low float (ownership is concentrated) or are facing an ever increasing flow of investor money will move up in multiples in a matter of days or months. Bubbles build up in particular industries or new emerging industries and can take stocks in that industry up exponentially.

Scarcity premium multibaggers

When a sector that is becoming popular does not have many listed stocks, the one or two stocks that are listed may go up by 10-fold or even 100-fold.

What makes a sector popular? Influential story tellers, which includes influential brokers or market gurus for one. An industry's popularity or stock price rise can also be driven by the low availability of stock either because stocks in the industry have a low float or because there are only a few listed stocks in the space. This happens in emerging industries, and regulated industries such as banks which may require licenses, etc. Whenever there is an overwhelming imbalance between the amount of money being invested in a stock or an industry and the amount of stock available, multibagger opportunities spring up.

Trading multibaggers

Multibagger investing is usually associated with value investing. But multibagger investing is any type of investing or trading that can generate exponential returns. Trading is usually not associated with multibagger investing but trading could generate exponential returns, especially when it uses leverage. Futures trading is one such opportunity where you could magnify your gains with very low capital, if you get the trade right.

Futures and options trading enables you to put up very little money and gain significantly on your investment. The flip side is that such multibagger picking is a very advanced stage of multibagger investing. If you are not adept at trading futures and options, you could end up losing significant money.

Conventional multibaggers

Conventional multibaggers include multibaggers that we get investing in traditional ways, such as value investing, investing on fundamentals, etc.

This is the most common way of multibagger investing but it requires long periods of waiting for stocks to turn into multibaggers. This is what investors believe is the right way to have a multibagger. For some reason, the longer the period of time that elapses, the more it gives legitimacy and credibility to the investor and his investing process. When people make money quickly, they somehow feel they did not work for it, or that it was not based on some well thought out intellectual process.

Valuation multibaggers

Valuation multibaggers originate when you can find significant undervaluation in a stock. Now, what is significant undervaluation? How does one know the stock is undervalued, let alone significantly? There is no single definition of undervaluation. You can start with a few pointers but will have to build your own definition of when you consider a stock undervalued. Undervaluation must not be looked at in isolation but in the context of the stage of market rally, the business cycle, growth prospects, etc.

Some of the situations that create undervaluation include:

- The stock may be undervalued if the market has not noticed a sector or the stock for various reasons, including insufficient research coverage, etc.
- The promoter's pledged shares are sold off by creditors either because of the promoter's inability to pay off the margin or pay back the debt. In such cases, the stock's fall could be extreme driven by the creditors seeking to recover dues, irrespective of the price. Such falls may lead to a price way below what the stock is worth.

Commodity multibaggers

Finding a commodity multibagger is like waiting to pluck an orange off the tree when it is ripe. Commodity stocks are among the safest ways to ensure multibagger returns if you enter at the bottom of a commodity cycle. Commodity cycles run for years and prices rise exponentially, not just in the underlying commodity but also in stocks related to the commodity.

Commodity stocks move in cycles and provide the most consistent multibaggers when a commodity is an up cycle. Each commodity will have its own cycle, and the lengths of cycles vary among commodities.

The trick here is to identify a cyclical upmove in a commodity. The rise in the commodity's price tends to become both quicker and larger as we approach the last leg of the cycle. And, in this phase, lies the commodity multibagger.

Penny stock multibaggers

"Men, it has been well said, think in herds; it will be seen that they go mad in herds, while they only recover their senses slowly, and one by one."

– Charles Mackay, *Extraordinary Popular Delusions and the Madness of Crowds (1841)*

As preposterous as it may sound, low priced unknown shares are the ones that do the best in the last phase of a bull rally — and the worst in a bear market. This smacks at the face of conventional wisdom that says we need do buy safe, big stocks in a runaway bull market. In fact, there is little risk buying duds if we can make a reasonable call that the bull market cycle is likely to continue. And to do that is no rocket science. Just consider the mood in the market. If it is stock passionate, then the bull rally may be far from ending.

That the rally is speculative may not necessarily be bad. There is no way of knowing how long the speculation may last, nor how high prices will move. If it seems like markets are speculative but investors are in a wild hurry to buy, and the excitement has still not reached those people usually far removed from anything to do with investments, you can be reasonably sure you have your best chance of making money. It is not how expensive the stock is that is important, but how much more expensive that you anticipate it to get. This phenomenon is not just a stock market phenomenon. In fact, it plays out even more viciously in real estate and art. Speculators can hike up prices to any level, way beyond what seems rational.

A good strategy is to buy those stocks in which we see the greatest potential of price appreciation in bull markets. The condition is that we will get out before the market falls.

The mania multibaggers

"Note how the financial news viewer ratings skyrocket in bull markets and during market plunges. Those are the times viewers most feel a need to figure out what to do with their money. They are either missing opportunities or losing money. Latching onto

technical and fundamental analysis is their way of searching for answers and gaining control."
- Victor Neiderhoffer

Why manias happen is a long story but, essentially, when everyone wants to participate in a stock or a group of stocks, chances are that they will climb to crazy valuations.

Are manias bad? Well, if you get in at the start of a mania, stocks can multiply a number of times. Manias appear from time to time and could infect any sector, especially sectors that may need massive amounts of money and look new age, fashionable, or those that catch investor fancy.

Manias are like virus. They spread with speed and velocity that are beyond imagination. If there is too much money chasing the same stocks — a "rational bubble" since everyone thinks they can flip those stocks around — the prices of such stocks will rise and rise till there is a flood of IPOs.

"New era" or "new asset class" multibaggers

Stock market bubbles are usually caused by the discovery of a new technology, a new country's potential, or a new asset class. Essentially, then, by anything that creates a structural imbalance in an existing system, for example airlines, railroads, the Internet, China, etc. cause a market bubble to build up as investors try to correctly price the new asset class. In a sense, then stock market bubbles are almost a price discovery mechanism that provide a once in a lifetime opportunity to cash out big time at the peak of irrationality.

The kind of frenzy we saw as the technology bubble burst in 2000 was such one once in a lifetime phenomenon in the market. Whenever a new technology, discovery or country promises to "change the face of the world," or impact it severely, the markets try and adjust to this new reality. For example, railroads, the Internet, and recently China and India all promised to change the face of the world. Investors rushed in to get a piece of the action. It is that rush that takes prices to stratospheric levels. Most investors get in late and at very high prices.

In most cases, though, the market overshoots and then corrects itself. Once in every decade or two it runs into a euphoria. The euphoria is not so much plain greed or fear, which it may well eventually turn into. Rather, it is the expectation that a new technology or country could result in such great profits in the future that the current, ridiculously high valuations are justified.

The crash multibagger

From time to time a panic, an investigation, or just plain selling driven by an inability to pay margins, drive stocks down very sharply. In such a situation, the stock falls without any reference to its real value.

Let's assume a promoter has given 50% of his shareholding as pledge for a loan. Let's further assume that there is an investigation launched against the company and this makes the stock fall. The bank now tells the promoter that since the stock has fallen the existing collateral or security is not enough and the promoter must pay more. If the promoter says he can't give any more security, the bank goes ahead and sells the shares it holds in the market, no matter what the price. Such forced selling, combined with a lack of interest in the stock — the retail and institutional investors may themselves be trying to sell off — causes the stock to fall significantly below its value.

This may be the time to buy the share. Since you are willing to sit out the current forced sale negativity, the stock will head back up once sanity prevails. And some time, in the next 2 to 3 years, the stock or the entire sector will come back in favour, providing a multibagger.

The liquidity squeeze multibagger

"It (the market) looks just a little more mathematical and regular than it is; its exactitude is obvious, but its inexactitude is hidden; its wildness lies in wait."

– Adapted from a quote by G. K. Chesterton

To demonstrate how a liquidity squeeze drives down the value of every investment, here is what happened in the month of October 2008:

- Gold lost 17%, the biggest percentage monthly loss in 25 years.
- Copper lost 34%.
- Silver lost 21%.
- The Dow lost around 15%, making it the biggest decline in October since 1987. It also logged the most down days since August 1973.
- Crude oil futures lost 32% on the NYMEX, its biggest monthly fall in 15 years.
- The dollar gained 14% against the euro, 22% against the Canadian dollar, and 32% against the Australian dollar.

- The MSCI Emerging Markets Index dropped 30% during the month, its biggest fall since August 1998.
- The Japanese Nikkei 225 hit its 26-year low.
- Iceland's stocks fell 80%.
- Argentina's markets fell 37%, and Brazil's markets lost 25%.

So, was this the time to find a multibagger? Not yet! This was just the start of the collapse.

The panic and despondency actually hit a low in March 2009 and that was the time to buy stocks that turned into multibaggers in the next 12 to 24 months flat.

In over 200 years of financial history, there were more than enough precedents to see that a banking crisis was going to create waves of panic selling driven by the massive falls of October 2008. In fact, it was not as much panic selling as it was the selling of pledged shares by collateral holders.

So what happened next? There was a severe compression of prices in all asset classes. Not just stocks but commodities, including oil, and real estate bore the pain since all investors are linked, and price compression in one asset class will bring about a price compression in other asset classes.

Neither foreign institutional investors nor promoters have extra cash to buy at such times. Even if they did, they were concerned that an economic compression was going to bring even more pain.

To pick multibaggers at such times, you need to study the various investment themes and the liquidity picture to see how things would pan out:

- A fall in all asset classes, i.e. equities, real estate and commodities was creating a serious dent in the wealth effect. And this effect can smother most economic stimulus.
- Some of the biggest drivers of the preceding boom, whether it was in equities, real estate or commodities, were Middle Eastern investors, including their sovereign funds, or other sovereign funds of the sort Singapore and China have.
- All asset classes, including equities, real estate, debt, art were affected. This was not about safe haven investing, but credit requirements or the search for liquidity.
- Selling first started with the most liquid assets, usually stocks and commodities, moving on to real estate and art, irrespective of the value. Ironically, that meant many stocks sold off for no reason except that they were quality stocks and so would be readily sold. Stocks in the next tier did not find buyers even at rock bottom prices. Multibaggers were now available by the hundreds.

- The lack of liquidity among buyers was also why real estate prices did not fall that much in the beginning of the crisis. As there were no buyers whatsoever, there were no trades to reflect the extent of the downturn. But when the markets opened, they did so with a gap, i.e. the prices had corrected significantly as soon as liquidity returned.
- It was a cash and carry market. No money was available for long gestation projects like roads, airports, ports, power, refineries, etc., and that is where the best potential multibaggers lurked.

Can trading give multibaggers?

"It's very difficult to be different from the rest of the crowd the majority of the time, which by definition is what you're doing if you're a successful trader."

– Bill Lipschutz

The power of trading on margin gives you the instant multibaggers but this is the riskiest method and one that can also cause instant losses. If you don't have the stomach to take large losses, you can skip this method.

Futures and options allow you to take large positions with little money down, and if things go your way, you could quickly be sitting with a multibagger.

Unless you are trading or investing for a living, you should stay away from trading futures and options, let alone trying to look for multibagger returns here. Futures and option trading are full time occupations and require your undivided attention. They also require a very composed psychological framework.

Futures or options trading for multibaggers is a very evolved stage of multibagger investing. The level of expertise required to do this will not be possible before you have been trading and investing for 3 to 5 years. It's not so much about your trading or investing skills alone. It is more about your psychological make-up. To get to the level of self control and mental make-up, you have to go through at least a 3 to 5-year market exposure, and experience a full bull and bear market cycle.

Asset class multibaggers

"In our own stock market experience and observation, extending over 50 years, we have not known a single person who has consistently or lastingly made money by 'following the market'."

- Benjamin Graham in *The Intelligent Investor*

When markets move to adjust to any tectonic shifts in the world economic balance, it is a time of great excitement that may need to be tempered with cool calculation.

As Marc Faber says in *Tomorrow's Gold:* ". . . . When a shift in major investment themes is about to occur, there is a strong disbelief and enormous skepticism in the minds of investors as to the merits of the new theme."

Charles MacKay, in *Extraordinary Popular Delusion & the Madness of Crowds* written in 1852, sums it up beautifully: "Each age has its peculiar folly, some scheme, project or phantasy into which it is plunged, spurred on either by the love of gain, the necessity of excitement, or the meagre force of imitation . . . . Money has often been the cause of the delusion of multitudes. Sober nations have all at once become desperate gamblers and risked almost their existence upon the turn of a piece of paper . . . . Men, it has been well said, think in herds; it will be seen that they go mad in herds, while they only recover their senses slowly and one by one."

The low float multibagger

Low float stocks bode well for getting multibagger returns, especially after a bear market. Take, for example, a stock where the government owns 80% of the shares, while another 10% is held by a government owned insurance company. That means that 90% of the company's shares are not even in the market. If there is a surge in interest in the sector or the stock, any large institutional order can drive the price up. Now imagine a couple of institutions getting interested in the stock in stages and you have the making of a multibagger.

Low volume / low float stocks in a changing economic trend

Let's take the example of company in the poultry business. Let's assume big format stores start to maintain entire refrigerated sections, a key requirement for putting poultry on the shelves. That changes the nature of the business from selling poultry to selling finished food products. This would be enough ground to see a multibagger poultry company.

For this kind of multibagger, you need the following:

- Low volumes and low float;
- Very few or no research reports;
- Little market interest in the stock;
- A structural shift in the business, in this case the availability of packaged meats in supermarkets, and large scale refrigeration along with the growth of non-vegetarian fast food chains, like Pizza Hut and McDonalds; and
- A position of industry leadership and the scale to deliver.

The "boys club" multibagger

A stock may have been grabbed by a big individual investor and that could have dried the public float completely. In fact, big individual investors usually make money this way — though their explanations on how they did it tend to be more of a demonstration of their "genius." It may be part intelligence but for the most part it's money power. If you suck out all the availability, then you are the only seller and if you don't sell, even small orders you place can drive the price higher. You can get a multibagger by piggybacking such rides.

Multibaggers in down and out stocks in a consolidating industry / M&A

Stocks in complex industries and sectors often get little coverage from brokerage houses. Even when they have coverage from brokerage houses, investors keep away from such stocks because they don't understand the business. Such stocks come into attention when they sell parts of their business to investors or global companies for multiples of their total market capitalization, thus taking the stock prices up multiple times in a short period of time.

A stock may be lying dormant. Such stocks almost never show up on a chart. Their rise depends on a change in ownership, or on M&A activity. I had a stock which stayed around the same price for almost 3 years. And then a competitor made an open offer to buy it out and the stock went up 5-fold in less than a month.

Stocks that will never become multibaggers

- Stocks on the index are past their prime. The reason they made it to the index is that they are already in everyone's portfolio and there is enough liquidity in the stock to absorb any buying.
- Another group of stocks that will find it very hard to become multibaggers are large capitalization stocks, or what are referred to as blue chips. If they already have significant capitalization, its going to take very large buying to budge them. Becoming a multibagger is a far cry.
- Government owned companies.
- Companies with very high institutional holdings.

10
~
Strategies for Multibagger Investing

Puts for M&As

Be ready to lose the option amount in an M&A situation. Don't put stop losses as the volatility in the options price is high. Take cheap short term options. Initial euphoria about a deal is what gets the stock to head up sharply. Eventually, M&As are never that easy. Keep the position large enough so that you make some significant gains. The size of the position should only be limited by the amount you are ready to lose.

You cannot win unless you learn to lose. Keep aside 10% to lose on puts on stocks, indices, currencies that you find euphoric and mispriced. Falls can be sudden. Also, buy puts for the occurrence of extreme events that happen more frequently than statistics indicate.

You have to look out for scenarios, and over a period of time build scenarios in which multibagger opportunities arise and as you gain more experience you have to find stocks where the odds that it is a multibagger increase.

A few scenarios that throw up multibaggers include:

- Economic turnarounds which increase operating cash flows and reduce debt. In certain economic scenarios, companies see operational benefits that set them on the path of a revaluation of their stock price by institutional and other investors. Such revaluations can take the stock up by several multiples.
- Delisting of a foreign subsidiary. Several global companies don't feel the need to be listed as local markets grow in size. Many such stocks shoot up in multiples when a foreign parent starts the process to delist a local subsidiary.
- High book value to price. This principle cannot be applied across the board but may be very effective in large capital intensive businesses, like steel, cement, etc. An economic slowdown sends many of these stocks

down 80% to 90%. As soon as the economic cycle picks up, the stocks are primed to rise in multiples. Look for a stock where the price is 10% to 20% of book value in a capital intensive industry, and where the business cycle is beginning to turn.

- Tomorrow's gold: Look for businesses that have not been noticed by investors but which you believe have a very significant potential of scaling up. For example, BPOs were a small part of the Philippines stock market before the stocks rose in multiples as BPOs grew mainstream.
- Stock buying and selling should adjust to market phases. Don't buy when a market begins its fall after a bull run, no matter how tempting or cheap stocks look. When investors lose confidence or significant money in a market or a stock, there is no telling how long it will take them to return, or whether they will return at all, no matter how much a stock has fallen. And without investors or interest, no stock is cheap at any price.
- Stocks rise 5 to 10 times in a manic phase. When it looks like only fools will invest at crazy prices — something that will happen at the height of bull markets — stocks will often rise a further 5- to 10-fold. If investors want to buy stocks at any price, then they will have to pay higher and higher prices. For you to find a multibagger in this phase, you will need to deal with a mental block which will stop you to buy at a crazy price. The buying price should not concern you, however, as long as you are certain the price will rise further because of the buying frenzy.
- No risk in buying in "phase zero." Multibagger investors usually follow this conventional approach. They buy stocks when stocks have slipped to multiyear lows and are down 90% to 95% from their highs and the management or the business looking poised to grow. This is a prudent and safe strategy. You must have patience to implement this multibagger strategy because it may be years before the stock begins its fresh upward move. Use technicals to determine when this is happening. Watch out for the other common mistake multibagger investors make when using this strategy. They sell out too early. Just as stocks take years to begin an upmove, an upmove may continue for years and deliver returns many times in excess of the purchase price. You must stick around for the ride.
- Stocks may build a base for several years, and then when there is no supply and immediate demand, prices can rise 5- to 10-fold very quickly.
- Invest in speculative markets for quick multibaggers.

You can find immediate term, short term and long term multibaggers. Each has a different strategy and approach and you must choose one that fits your personality. It is rare to find someone who is successful at picking multibaggers over all kinds of time spans.

Check the level of pledging

Promoters and company owners often use their stock to either borrow or to guarantee the borrowings of their companies. If the lender decides to sell the stock because of a default in payments, a stock could lose more than 90% of its value. Pledging is common among small cap and mid cap companies, usually owned by entrepreneurs and their families. The price of the stock falls because the lender has sold off the stock held as security or collateral. Now, the company's default or delay in payments may be because of short term reasons. You will find multibagger opportunity in these stocks. Look for companies with quality management, a product with healthy demand, and a short term financial issue that has caused the lenders to sell off. Over a period of time, such stocks will gain back their momentum and give you multibagger returns. Avoid companies that are habitual defaulters and have no desire to return loans. Such stocks never recover after the lender sells off. Look for stocks where the promoter or company founders are pledged to the hilt (over 80%). This indicates that they have little space to put up more security if they fall back on payments.

Multibaggers in long term commodity cycles

Commodity stocks provide an excellent opportunity for multibaggers and, as long as you are in a long term cycle in a commodity, the risk in buying commodity stocks is low as compared to their multibagger potential.

Investing in commodity stocks requires a deep knowledge of the concerned commodity and its cycles. Commodity stocks can turn into multibaggers and continue their rise for years if your timing is correct. Investing in commodity stocks is a very long term game and if you time it wrong, the stock may not move for years.

Multibaggers are found in the extremes

"Buffett once said that the great thing about being an investor is that you're like a batter in a baseball game in which there are no called strikes. They have to keep pitching and you don't have to swing. So if you're patient, the odds are with you. You might not swing for six months; you might not swing for two years, but the odds of hitting it out of the park are a lot better when the pitch is fat. You must be patient!"

– Barton Biggs in *Hedge Hogging*

Infrequent events occur more frequently than statistically possible both in the universe and in the markets. Extreme and unexpected market events create multibagger opportunities.

Global, local, economic, currency and other types of volatility creates multibagger opportunities. It is only when a large mass of people panic or decide they need to enter or exit a market or stock that stocks turn into multibaggers. But volatility has to be extreme. It could be foreigners exiting a country so fast that its foreign currency reserves are depleted and the currency crashes, accompanied by a market crash. When foreigners get concerned about an impending devaluation, they may all try to leave at the same time, creating significant value in stocks which are not impacted by currency volatility.

Sell as the plane takes off

"Never try to sell at the top. It isn't wise. Sell after a reaction if there is no rally."

– Edwin Lee'vre in *Reminiscences of a Stock Operator*

You must squeeze as much returns you can get out of the stock. Just like an orange, you will not be able to squeeze as much returns as possible if you exit the stock too soon. Don't set any price target for selling the stock. How much a stock can move up from your purchase price is not related to your purchase price.

Develop an expertise in reading charts and technical analysis. Charts are one of the best ways to know when a stock is getting tired and may begin to head down.

Selling is an art more in need for mastering than buying. Just like a plane, a stock gets off its parking, taxies up to the runway, runs on the runway — and then takes off. You don't sell the stock any time till the stock has taken off and completed its ascent.

The greatest returns lie in the worst markets

"This is the strange reality of financial bubbles. When one really gets going, the people who – correctly – warn that it won't go on can be wrong year after year after year. Meanwhile, the overenthusiastic, ill-informed sorts who cast such worries to the wind can get seriously rich."

– Justin Fox in *Fortune*

Major investment themes like technology, China, India, or commodities, etc. become obvious to most investors somewhere in the middle, or at the peak of the respective cycle. The majority only follows once it feels the comfort of others doing the same thing. And so the largest flow of funds into a fancied asset class occurs only when it has become mainstream and every foreign media, broker, fund manager is talking about it. Prices are then driven by the flood of demand, fuelled by the desire of the ever-surging numbers of investors to possess the asset concerned, rather than by any rational look at value.

And herein lies the paradox. The greatest opportunities of returns are in what are considered as the worst markets. The worst opportunities are in markets that are most talked about. It is not what a company is doing but what we are paying for it that's key.

Multibaggers in a liquidity squeeze and a bubble

"A panic seized upon the public, such as had never been witnessed before; everybody begging for money – but money was hardly on any condition to be had. It was not the character of the security that was considered; but the impossibility of producing money at all."

– Charles Kindleberger on the Banking panic of 1825 in *Manias, Panics & Crashes*

A liquidity squeeze usually leads to gross underpricing, or mispricing, of assets and asset classes like equities, real estate, etc. because of a mismatch of sellers and buyers. There is too little money but too many assets available. There are usually no buyers at any price. Consequently, such markets throw up unbelievable opportunities to buy stocks at prices which are way off from their real value.

In liquidity squeeze situations, you also find the owners of a stock getting decoupled from the sellers of stock. From promoters to investors, many use stock as collateral to borrow. Once we end up in a situation of tight liquidity, the guys selling the stock is probably the collateral holder and not necessarily the owner of the shares — and the collateral holder does not care one bit whether the selling price is right or wrong. He is a lender and an investor. His sole aim is to get back the money he lent. Consequently he sells at prices which no owner in his right mind would. This is what compounds the market's fall in times of tight liquidity.

In markets affected by liquidity seizures, the chances that shares will be mispriced downwards is great. Liquidity forces institutions and investors to sell things in their portfolio that otherwise make perfect sense to hold except that the bidders need the money. Which is why this kind of selling throws up unbelievable opportunities. However, it is important that the portfolio be limited to 10 to 15 stocks, otherwise diversification takes returns closer to the index.

In a bubble, we see an extreme condition of overvaluation. As we saw in the dotcom boom, all bubbles are caused by pure greed and delusion and neither central banks nor governments care if they go under. That's way the recovery from the bursting of a bubble is usually long-drawn and very painful.

A market fall due to a credit squeeze or a credit seize is different than the fall after a bubble, whether it be the dotcom boom, the Asian financial crisis, the railroad crisis in the UK, or the famous Tulip bubble. All others were asset class bubbles. During a credit squeeze, there is a loss of confidence and a freezing up of credit which impacts the real economy in ways that the creation and bursting of an asset class bubble cannot. On the other, after credit seized liquidity comes back sooner rather than later.

Excessive leverage is the real cause of market falls

"Liquidity is a straw man. Whenever markets plunge, investors are stunned to find that there are not enough buyers to go around. As Keynes observed, there cannot be liquidity for the community as a whole. The mistake is in thinking that markets have a duty to stay liquid or that buyers will always be present to accommodate sellers."

– Roger Lowenstein in *When Genius Failed*

If you were a freshly minted 26-year old analyst, you would have been stunned by the brutality of the fall in icons like AIG and Lehman in 2008, especially if you were one of the thousands of freshly minted MBAs in Finance who marched out of a business school only to be feasted and fattened by ever expanding brokerage firms.

But for most serious investors there was nothing endemic to the fall of AIG, Lehman, etc. For that matter, there was nothing new either. Such Black Swan events have happened in the past with amazing regularity. Such events cause a contagion panic but usually the markets spring back over a few months as central banks intervene.

The real cause of market collapses is not fraud, lack of intelligent people, lack of systems or a lack of regulations, but too much leverage. And too much leverage has been a bane of society for as long as humans have been around, and of the financial markets for as long as they have been operational. When leverage seeps into every pore, investors in multibaggers get out and keep their powder dry. They wait for this leverage to turn on its face and make investors sell not because they did not pick the right stock but because they have no option but to return the amounts they have borrowed. When this turns into a snowball, keep yourself dry to pick up any amount of multibaggers to your wallet's content.

Multibaggers for a living

"When victory and defeat are already determined before movement and uprising, you do not become confused in your actions and do not wear yourself out rising up."

– Sun Tzu

If you plan to pursue multibagger investing for a living and get it right, you will be able to fulfil all your dreams of a blissful life. You can spend your time at the beach or on the mountains, or anywhere else you wish to be. The nature of multibaggers is such that opportunities come occasionally and most of your time is spent on reflection, reading and keeping a diary of your experiences in multibagger investing. This is your best chance of enjoying your life and making more money than you ever imagined pursuing a highly intellectual activity.

Your investment approach for picking multibaggers will incorporate some changes to ensure that it does not alter your lifestyle or create any disturbance in leading a pleasant life. The first thing you must do is to make significant money in one or two multibaggers before leaving your normal pursuit of work or business. It has to be significant enough to give you enough money to invest in multibaggers in the future, and also have patience to wait for the next opportunity. After you start on multibagger investing to sustain yourself, you must put way 30% to 50% of all profits out of the market no matter what the temptation to invest more. You cannot afford to let market pressure affect your personal life.

Here are some of the investment approaches that can be used for multibagger investing for a living:

Market timing

You don't have the luxury to buy stocks at the wrong time and see them do nothing for years. Your entry and exit points become critical in sustaining you. Spend time mastering technical charts and pore over hundreds of charts. After some time, the activity in price and trading volume will jump out at you and give you indications on the potential of the stock.

Stock selection

This is another approach you can use for finding stocks that indicate a very large upside. I have discussed several approaches to finding such stocks in this book.

Weeding and changing the portfolio strategy

You must constantly weed out stocks that are not doing what you expected at the prefixed loss levels and be flexible in changing a strategy when it does not deliver returns to justify the investment.

Developing and implementing a superior investment philosophy

This requires 3 to 5 years of investing, following the discipline I have talked about in this book, and also learning from your experience by keeping a diary of the reasons for your decisions, the results, and why you think the results were or were not in line with your expectations.

Selecting blue chip stocks or safe stocks is neither here nor there if you plan to sustain yourself on investing. An alternate strategy is to leave 80% of your money in debt mutual funds, or something else that gives you a steady return with no risk to capital. The other 20% you can put in quick multibaggers, including using futures, options and trading. The margin can either sink you or get you a big multibagger. Either way, the maximum loss you can suffer is to lose the 20% in these leveraged investments. This also harbours you from any sudden shocks in the markets or stock, like a liquidity freeze, etc.

If you cannot comprehend it, skip it

"When you have assessed the opponent and sees the opponent's formation, then you can tell who will win. If the opponent is inscrutable and formless, then you cannot presume victory."
– Sun Tzu

If you don't understand the business, you won't find the multibagger. That does not mean you have to get into the nitty gritty of the business, but understanding its cycles or its ups and downs helps you comprehend when the multibagger opportunity is beginning to emerge.

Some industries have too many coatings to understand the real business. Some industries create terminology of their own as a cover up for lack of basics, like profits. Still other businesses are too complex for everyone to understand. Don't invest in any stock where you cannot comprehend how things work, or what impacts the industry and stocks in the sector.

Multibagger investors should also keep away from regulated stock unless you are betting on a change in regulations which could benefit stocks in the regulated industry significantly. In emerging markets, several industries are at the whims and fancies of governments and regulations can change overnight to kill a business, or create a brand new one.

Why you should not buy in a falling market

"Do not be impatient. Do not see only petty gains. If you are impatient, you will not reach your goal. If you see only petty gains, the great tasks will not be accomplished."
– Confucius

Falling markets may indicate a change in investor and trader psychology and changes in psychology have longer term consequences. As stocks fall, it is likely investors turn pessimistic and traders go short on a market pushing it down further.

It takes years of experience before you can make out the difference between a market falling because of change in investor or trader psychology, and a market falling because of other causes. In the meantime, just assume that a falling market has a high risk of falling further and is not a good time to look for multibagger opportunities.

If a person in ICU seems to have better variables on some day, it does not mean he will survive. There will be days in a falling market where it will seem things are fine but that is only temporary. A person in ICU, or a market in a severe fall, is in no condition to take shocks and any further fall and a new collapse will begin.

In a bear market, buy penny stocks

"Never count on making a good sale. Have the purchase price be so attractive that even a mediocre sale gives good results."
– Warren Buffett

Many stocks turn into penny stocks in bear markets. Prices of several stocks may be so cheap that you don't have to worry about the price you may later sell it at. The sales price will be way higher than the current price when the market turns.

Stocks can turn penny because there is almost no interest in them. When there is no interest in a stock, a stock does not have a market determined price. When a stock does not have a market determined price, and nobody is looking at it, or has an interest in holding the stock, prices have no relationship to the company's potential.

Prices in such circumstances are so low that even the downside is limited. This type of multibagger investing is one of the lowest risk investing strategies.

This strategy will work if you don't mind losing a little money in the worst scenario and making money in multiples if the bear market ends.

Supply Squeeze

"Look at market fluctuations as your friend rather than your enemy; profit from folly rather than participate in it."
– Warren Buffett

A supply squeeze comes about whenever there is an imbalance between the buyers of a stock and the sellers. This can happen in stocks with high promoter or founder holdings. In fact, it can happen in any stock where there is very low floating stock. Any extra demand is not met with supply as the holders of the stock have no mandate or reason to sell.

A supply squeeze may also happen when stocks have large institutional holdings and one institution has to buy from another. Since institutions trade in large chunks of stock, any institution who is buying additional quantities has to buy from smaller investors. A large bulk order from the buyer and a few sell orders from individual investors with small holdings creates a significant spike in stock prices.

In bull markets, index stocks become scarce. Sellers stop selling and buyers buy. As more money comes in stocks that have large capitalization and low floats, like government owned banks and companies, go into a supply squeeze and their prices can rise vertically.

Multibagger investment styles

"Great players consider their next move without playing it. You should never play the first good move that comes into your head. Put that move in your list, and then ask yourself if there's an even better move"

– Michael Mouboussin

Life insurance style

20-year olds and 80-year olds pay different premiums for their life insurance. Investors must pay different prices for stocks with different speeds. Paying for stocks based on value is like saying you will pay the same life insurance premium for 20-year olds and 80-year olds.

Extreme event investing

Invest in a market or stocks on the possibility of extreme events. For example, if you expect an extreme shortage of hotel rooms that may take 3 to 4 years to be made up by new supply, invest in hotel stocks.

Structural imbalance investing / liquidity

From time to time, money flows to 2 or 3 sectors at the cost of the rest of the market. When investors start to buy stocks only because it generates instant gains on flipping, they pull money out of quality stocks in other sectors not showing the same pace of rise. This creates a structural imbalance in sectors that are starved of money. Such imbalances last for short periods of time and provide an excellent price and opportunity to pick up future multibaggers.

Deleveraging investing

Significant opportunities can arise when an industry begins to deleverage, namely bring down its debt. In the initial phases of this deleveraging, companies experience extreme pain and stocks head to the bottom. But that pain is the harbinger of better times and sows the seeds for multibaggers.

Trade money, not markets

If your personal outlook can allow it, multibaggers can be obtained by keeping your focus on absolute returns and having the ability to lose the entire principal. A major roadblock is that we don't like to lose what we put up. But some multibaggers require you to cultivate that ability:

- Put a trade risking 1% to 2% of your capital if you believe there is a 50:50 odds that you will get a return of 4 to 5 times your investment if you get it right, but you will lose your entire principal if you get it wrong. For these kinds of odds, options provide you the best opportunity, especially around a turn in market cycles. Options are priced based on how the market's been moving in the past. When the market's been bearish, options will be expensive for those who are bearish, but cheap for those who take a bullish view.
- Buy puts (repeated) on heavily institutional owned stocks at the peak of a bull market, or in a sector where they are so heavily invested that there is no margin of error.
- Make repeated trades in long term direction of the stock (or call/put options). Cut losses at a 1% loss.
- Develop an idea from a very low risk standpoint. Pursue it with a call/put option, until proven wrong, or until there's a change in your viewpoint.
- When stocks start hitting peaks, sell puts.
- The Russian strategy: Wait till stocks hit their peak or when they hit their bottom, then go with puts and call or futures for very significant returns. Similar to the Russian strategy for Napoleon.
- Play deep out of the money puts or calls on stocks that are ripe for a rise or fall, respectively.
- Play futures ripe for rise.
- Buy long term stocks at ocean bottoms with a risk reward ratio of 1:5.

Start with options — because of leverage and the odds of exponential gains.

Special situation investing strategy

"Although markets are generally good at estimating the magnitude of a contingent liability, they are often poor at evaluating outcomes probabilistically."

– Jamie Mai

Special situations arise when the market factors in a certain risk in a stock or the sector, and starts to discount the stock's price for that risk or uncertainty. But, sometimes, the market has discounted the stock's price way beyond what the risk entails. This creates a situation where the stock is going cheap.

Special situations are events that occur once in a while and there is no reason for them to repeat again. For example, a Tsunami in Japan may cause a drop in Nickel prices because Japanese high grade steel plants have temporarily ceased production, or consumption of a company's products has collapsed because of negative news about its health effects. Multibagger investor must use such opportunities to pick stocks that seem to have been hammered out of shape for temporary conditions that are not likely to last.

Don't buy falling stocks

"I won't buy a stock when it's dropping even if I like the fundamentals. I have to see some stability in the price action before I buy the stock."

– Richard Driehaus

Don't be in a rush to strike. Wait for the easy picks where the returns are exceptional but the risks are exceptionally small. You will get such opportunities. And when they come, close your ears to opinions and go for the jugular. But buy only up to the level where you are able to take the market's temporary swings that go against you. Most investors get taken out by the temporary swings against them even when they are spot on about the long term direction of the investment.

Coming up with a value investing formula requires 5 to 10 years of dedication and specialization. Some of the key elements of that developing an edge include:

- Defining the specific instances in which value that delivers exceptional returns is created. Is it created when liquidity dries up, or when institutional interest is high, etc.?
- Define and keep records of your experience and returns when you have invested in a specific situation and if things did not go your way. Why did that happen? Improve your value investing model to include the things you missed or overlooked that impacted your returns.
- As you perfect your value investing model, reduce the number of stocks you pick, and increase your position in each stock.
- Invest only in those opportunities where value is so obvious that it is only a question of time for you to get significant returns.

Stocks waiting to become multibaggers

Buy pledged shares when they are sold by the creditor. The stock could collapse by 90% to 95% in such circumstances. But the real value of the stock is not reflected in forced sale by a creditor trying to collect his debts. For example, a company with 7-star hotels went down 95% when the creditor sold shares he held as collateral. This made the market capitalization of the company 3% to 5% of the net value of its assets. This kind of stock can turn into a multibagger once the one-time sale of the big chunk of shares is absorbed by the market.

Multibaggers through options

An option is an all out bet — or should be used as such. If you are wrong, you lose a small amount. So find those options that have a low cost but offer a high risk/reward ratio.

Buy put options on stocks that are on record highs, or on a market that is at record high, or on stocks that have high institutional holdings. If the market or the stock does not head your way, you lose the amount you put up to buy the option. But if it does head your way, you could have gains that are in multiples of what you stand to lose.

Buy very cheap options that are "deep out of the money" — for example, on a stock that is at ₹ 2,000, buy a 1,600 strike option to sell/put. The option will be cheap since no one expects the stock to head there. But if for some reason it does, your gains are in multiples, while your loss is capped to the price you paid for the option. It is possible you will lose the option amount twice or thrice before you get it right because when a market will stop running, or what will trigger a fall, is never clear. But bubble-like situations always implode.

Options are like buying car insurance. You pay a premium and if there is an accident you can claim the value of your car. If you don't bang your car, you lose the premium. But options come with an even more amazing feature. If you are wrong, you lose the premium you paid to buy the option. But if you are right, and an extreme event does happen, you get returns in multiples of the premium.

Using options for multibagger returns works best for extreme events. It does not work for normal markets which is what markets are most of the time. When you expect extreme disequilibrium in prices because of a major event or want or have a strong view on a major event one way or the other, options are the best way to protect your downside and play for the chance of multibagger returns.

Buy an option when are convinced about a stock's short term move. If it does not move you lose the option premium. But if it does move, you could end up making in a month or two 5 to 10 times the capital you put up in.

Do nothing if the market is directionless. You will not find multibaggers in dull markets.

Do nothing if the market is plunging down. There is a reason everyone is getting out. Don't subsidize their exit by paying a high price for the stock.

Cheap is not what you think it is

A cheap stock is stock whose price has not factored in the potential of a future rise. There are a number of reasons why the current price may not be the correct price for the stock:

- A future rise could come because there are only 2 or 3 stocks in a listed space where foreigners have become very interested, or it could occur because the stock or the sector is going to see institutional buying.
- A cheap stock could be a pharmaceutical stock which may be near to receiving a large milestone payment. Pharmaceutical stocks that have drugs in various clinical trials may sell a drug for hundreds of millions of dollars driving the stock up in multiples.
- Stocks with low institutional interest and low liquidity may also be cheap. When institutional interest in a stock increases, its price will shoot up as a large amount of institutional money will chase retail sellers who take

longer to sell small quantities when the demand is for large quantities, driving prices higher in very short spans of time. But you have to buy stocks which are globally known to have institutional interest. A stock which has very low market capitalization or very small volumes, and has never had institutional interest, will find it very difficult to rise. Usually, an entire sector catches institutional fancy and most large stocks in that sector rise.

- Penny stocks that have drifted to penny status because of an exit of institutional investors, or because there is temporary a lack of interest in a sector are well placed to become multibaggers when the sector, again attracts interest. Cyclical sectors like cement or sugar tend to have such stocks. When global prices of sugar go below cost, sugar stocks trade in pennies. But that is the best time to buy because farmers will grow less cane the next season (the cost is more than the revenue) and once the existing sugar stocks are used up, prices will shoot right up.
- Stocks that have the potential to attract retail interest may also be cheap at current price levels. When retail investors get euphoric you can find multibaggers in hundreds of stocks. Retail investors pour money both through mutual funds and directly, driving up prices of low liquidity, low volume small cap stocks.

When multibaggers are available

After a bubble bursts, or a long term bull market gets over, the market takes a very steep fall. Stocks may fall by 50%. The market then makes a bounce back and may make up another 25% to 50% of the fall. That's because you have the usual value buyers. But when the market fails to go higher, it starts a long, painful wait at the bottom of the ocean. This wait may last from 3 to 5 years. The reason why you should wait 3 to 5 years is that investors get used to any price that has been around for a long time. So if stocks have been at historic lows for many years, it is difficult for investors to expect or imagine that stock prices will rise 5- to 10-fold. This is when you should buy. Let a stock rise about 10% to 20% from its 5-year lows. You have a multibagger here.

Commodity multibaggers are available when a commodity cycle turns. Commodity cycles take a long time to turn because the previous bull rally creates so much capacity and leaves so many mines mid-way that the incremental cost of increasing production is not much.

What not to do

- Relying on financial media or market experts is downright dangerous. The really smart traders don't speak to the media, and those who do usually don't know what they are talking about; so the information is worthless.
- Don't look for the typical cheap stocks — stocks that have low PE ratios, pay dividends, etc. are cheap for a reason. You will not find multibaggers here.
- Don't look where everyone else is looking. If you are buying popular stocks, everyone's already there, which means that there is little to drive the price higher.
- Don't attempt to buy on the way down after a long term bull rally. You should wait till you know how deep the well or the ocean is, or when the stock has touched its bottom. Stocks can fall over 90% to 95% after a long term bull rally.

Managing risk

Managing risk entails ensuring your losses are never out of hand, and are limited. You can do that by buying options where the downside is automatically limited or by practicing the discipline of getting out stocks at a certain preset limit:

- High and low risk multibaggers do not depend on the stock but on the circumstances. A high risk stock may be a low risk multibagger in certain markets, while a blue chip stock may be a high risk multibagger in certain markets.
- Don't buy stocks that are heading down. We are programmed to think a price lower than what is on a label or has been told to us, is a deal or a bargain. But unlike groceries or consumer products, you don't hold a stock till its expiry date. You have to sell it some day. And you have to think if the sale price of the stock will be lower than what you are paying for.
- Buy stocks that have time and price momentum. A rise in a stock's price that is not confirmed by rising volumes and has not happened over a stretch of time may not continue. Multibagger investors must avoid picking stocks where there is no increase in volume of trading, even when the price is rising.

Penny stock multibagger strategy

Penny stocks can be tricky. Most are down to pennies because of good reason and will never get out of the penny cycle. From time to time, good stocks may turn penny. Their penny price may not be a reflection of their value. This could happen when managements are either not good at communicating with financial media, or don't want to communicate, brokerage houses don't cover the stock, a very significant part of the stock is with the founders, etc. In such circumstances, multibagger opportunities get missed. But beyond identifying such stocks, you have to think if there is something about the stock which will make financial media, brokerage houses or institutional investors provide it the big push. One good way of making sure they will get that push is to ensure that you get someone with significant influence in the markets, financial media, brokerage houses or institutional investors to put the stock on the radar of people who can bring investor attention to the stock, or bring significant money to turn the stock into a multibagger.

Such multibagger opportunities may arise under the following conditions:

- Stocks sold out in a pledge.
- Penny stock investing is a winner's game.
- Can rise 5- to 10-fold in the next 2 to 3 years.
- In sectors where a turnaround is imminent.
- Produce something that is accepted in difficult market, like Japan, such as chemicals, and when the global manufacturing base is shrinking.
- Operators pull out the supply when there is demand in a penny stock. That creates a rush to buy and there are no sellers. Selling quantities are released in small lots to keep up the interest and let buyers feel thankful. Then larger quantities are released. By now buyers are so desperate to buy, they pay whatever the selling price. When the frenzy reaches the peak, the operator releases large lots which finally causes the distribution.
- You have an edge if you have figured out why the stock may rise — most investors in penny stocks are "informationless" and just "noise." Don't buy penny stocks either because others are getting in or leave because they are getting out.
- Stocks that turn penny because of management fraud or because their debt levels are just too high to ever pay back with operating cash flows almost never recover and penny stocks remain penny stocks.
- Keep 50% of penny earnings for testing other penny stocks.

- Once the stock goes into strong hands you can see appreciation of 100% to-200% in a few days and the stock may be in a freeze for several days.
- The reasons why the stock has become penny are critical:
  - Is it a temporary or structural problem?
  - Is the management capable of execution and raising capital?
  - Are the reasons short term — exit of institutional investors, pledge, working capital?
  - Does the company have a brand?
  - Did the management run the company down because of mismanagement or was it the overall economic environment?
  - Will the company be able to come back again?

Bull market momentum buying

Such buying is for economies that are in the process of liberalization or a structural change. For those who like to stay in a stock for the long term, it is important to identify stocks, industries and countries where there is a structural shift. Such investment themes provide multibagger opportunities before they become mainstream. They also require investors to stay with the stock for a couple of years and provide some of the most significant multibagger opportunities.

A few good stocks is all you need

You have to choose between having a top quality multibagger opportunity process which will end up giving you only a few stocks that meet your criterion, or a low quality process that will make you pick too many stocks that don't deliver returns.

Buying too many stocks delivers average returns and close to what you can get by investing in a stock market index. It also shows that you have not refined your investment process to a level where only the best opportunities make it.

If you go about picking ten stocks at a time, forget about finding a multibagger. Stocks require tending and deep study. That is not possible without limiting the number of stocks and following them closely.

Opportunities in crappy stocks

"There is a misperception that value investing is cigar-butt investing – buying the moribund leftovers of the market."
– Christopher Browne, Tweedy, Brown Company

Certain stocks become castaways when investors decide that there is no price at which the stock is worth a buy. Investors can brand a stock a "no go" zone because of regulatory changes, management mistakes, etc. Research coverage and institutional investors leave and no one believes anything the company is saying. Look for multibagger opportunities here. You will get obvious clues of a change in the stock's fortunes but because of pre-existing bias investors will keep out of the stock till the new story in the stock becomes so big that no one can avoid it.

These stocks may have been written off by the world. But, like dormant volcanos, when they burst you get multiples of their prices. But their moves are rare. Largely they stay dormant.

Who will buy from you?

"I bought sugar and it went limit up . . . then I bought copper and it went limit up, so I bought some more. Then it went limit down. I called my broker and told him to sell and he said to whom?"
– Angell

Let's take the example of a stock that rises 10-fold in 6 months. The founders hold 45% and institutional investors have built up their holdings to another 45%. If the stock continues to move up, stay out of it. A point is reached where the stock cannot move any higher and the holding is highly concentrated with either the owners or institutional investors. At this point buy puts which will be very cheap because of the unidirectional nature of the stock's recent move. Buy put options repeatedly because it is a question of time before the stock will collapse. If institutional investors try to sell a stock with such concentrated holdings, the market has no capacity to absorb it.

My multibagger picking style

"Don't invest in new or 'interesting' investment. They are all too often designed to be sold to investors, not to be owned by investors."

– Charles Ellis

I avoid investment themes that are popular and where too much money is flowing in. I also avoid themes where retail investors are pumping in money directly, or through mutual funds.

I try to think of which stocks and industry themes will be so compelling in the next few months that they will get institutional and retail investors to put money into them.

I never hold a stock if its price falls 5% below my purchase price. If I have a very strong conviction about the stock, backed by facts, I either wait for the stock to drift some more but never allow more than a 10% fall below my purchase price. My thinking is that if a stock falls 10% from my purchase price, either my assumptions about the stock's potential are wrong, or the information that I have analysed itself is incorrect, or that there are things at play in the stock that I don't understand.

Stock of a company in the multiplex operation business

I picked this stock when it was at ₹ 50. I thought of India's consumer class, the ability to see a movie in a neat and clean environment, and leveraged my experience of multiplexes in the US. At that time, the company had at a market cap of a very small cap stock, US$10 million. My thought was that while they did not have scale, they knew how the business worked and when money came into the sector, they would be an acquisition target. That's what happened. When big money came in, the stock went up to ₹ 1,500, an appreciation of over 3,000%, or 30 times.

Penny stock of a pharmaceutical company

The market cap of this company was around US$ 2 million. I met one of the founders and realized that his ambition was king size and he was committed to growing the business and the market cap of the company's stock. The stock went from ₹ 10 to ₹ 300 in a matter of 2 to 3 years.

The same stock can also provide you a multibagger opportunity on its upward move. If you see institutional investors building up their holdings and the float (or share available in the market) dropping, only small holdings are available and for any institution to buy small lots will require higher and higher prices turning the stock into a multibagger.

Be sceptical of management claims

"Never, ever, follow conventional wisdom in the market. You have to learn to go counter to the markets. You have to learn how to think for yourself; to be able to see that the emperor has no clothes."

– James Rogers

Management will always overestimate their prospects and underestimate risk until they can hide no further. Their stock is their currency. They use their stock to borrow and to issue more stock. A higher price ensures that they don't need to pledge too much stock and that they have to issue less stock to raise more money. Moreover, most debt taken on using the company stock as collateral requires the company to put up more stock if the price of the stock falls.

It is therefore clearly in the management's interest to give you an optimistic picture. Even when the company starts to tell you that things are not good, be sceptical. The founders may know things are turning around, or they may have some arrangement to sell the stock to institutional investors and may want to acquire the stock cheap before they sell it, or before the stock's price appreciates.

Multibagger vs multibagger

"You want the fastest horse, even if your first horse is still trotting in the right direction."

– Jack Schwager

When you develop an expertise in picking multibaggers, scale up your stock picking criteria by picking stocks that will turn into multibaggers in the shortest periods of time. The shorter the time, the higher the annualised return. If your stock goes up 10-fold in 10 years, the stock was not a multibagger.

Cashing out your investment in shorter periods of time allows you to put your money to work on other potential multibagger opportunities.

There is nothing special about a stock that takes a longer time to turn into a multibagger. If you have limited capital, choose a stock that will run the fastest. In bull markets, most stocks move up. You have to find the stocks that move up the fastest.

Playing the increase in capitalization

You have an unbelievable advantage over institutional investors. Institutional investors like mutual funds cannot buy stocks that don't move even if they have great value. Their need to report their performance every 3 months ensures that they buy trending stocks and not value stocks no matter what they say. If they buy stocks that don't move, they won't be top performing funds and won't get more capital (or may face redemptions). And to pay for redemptions they will not be able to hold value stocks. Institutional investor decision making is thus, a captive of fund flows. But you have no such constraint. You can buy stocks that don't move in the next 6 or 12 months but which you know may deliver returns in multiples in a matter of months when the rally starts.

Cause and effect don't work for multibaggers

There are hundreds of causes and hundreds of effects as to why a stock's price is going up and down. And no one knows how much of an effect a major or minor event, news, change can have on a stock's price. Because so many causes are driving stock prices, and their magnitude or impact on the stock's price is not known, using simple cause and effect relationships, such as "The stock will move up because consumption is growing," or "Automobile stocks will do well because a young population has to buy cars" can be fatal to your investment results.

There is an inflection point in the business that the market rarely notices without a lag time. This lag time gives you the opportunity to enter the stock ahead of the market. Your returns will be in multiples if you can beat institutional investors into the stock. The biggest rise in stocks comes when institutional investors enter the stock — and they enter the stock when it has gained momentum.

Don't overrate your ability to comprehend the markets

"Avarice, I bow to you
You make men do things, they ought not have done
And wander in places, where they ought not have gone."
– Panchtantra

The real reason for picking a stock is in the subconscious and it is the need to make money out of the stock — some call it greed but that's an extreme take on our natural instinct to be right about what we do. So when by a fluke we get our investment right, we tend to believe that we have some superior insight into investing. Such misconceived thoughts about our understanding of stocks and markets can and will lead to fatal investment mistakes.

Even the best investors in the world realize that what they know about the market is the tip of an iceberg, and that the market is like a vast unexplored ocean with dangerous beasts and icebergs and coral reefs that can wreck you anytime. That realization is the first step towards achieving multibagger returns and tuning out of investments the minute you realize you were wrong.

It is human for us to consider that we do a better job in figuring our investments than others do. We overrate our ability to make profits and underrate the chances of losses. This can cause a wide difference between your expectations out of a stock and what it can really deliver.

Making a living with multibaggers

"All men's miseries come from their inability to sit quiet and alone."
– Anonymous

You can make a living out of investing in multibaggers. If you decide to take this course to make a living, you will need to make some adjustments to your methodology, style and psychology. When you depend on multibagger investing to provide for your day to day living, you have to have much higher risk standards and make few fewer mistakes in picking stocks than someone who is just investing.

It will take at least 3 to 5 years before you reach the level of competency to live on money made from multibaggers. In those 3 to 5 years, you will need to gain knowledge, develop a style, gather the psychological make-up that you will need.

One of the most important things you must work on is to have a zero threshold for losses if you pick the wrong stock. You must exit such stocks at a pre-specified loss percentage. Don't allow losses to go out of hand at any point no matter what you believe. If you make exceptions, you are messing around with a disciplined approach critical for multibagger investing and exposing yourself to a mental and emotional imbalance which is a direct result of excessive losses. This can cause so much disorientation that it will impact your ability to pick the right stocks or may dishearten you to the extent that you stop investing.

Most of your time will be spent preparing to find the opportunity. Multibagger investing is not a regular, daily pursuit but years of preparation for short phases that throw up opportunities for large gains.

Set a goal on how much money you will need for the next 3 years. Invest enough to generate that kind of money. The amount you invest must be at least 20% of what you expect in returns. Make sure you have the cushion to take losses and you have enough capital to put up if you lose 10% or 20% of capital.

Chances of finding multibaggers increase exponentially for those who have been in the markets for over a decade, or have seen a complete boom and bust cycle. If you have, you can leverage that experience into learning and picking multibaggers.

Remember, the market does not owe you a living. You have to extract a living out of the market but it does not owe you one. You cannot blame others for your mistakes, don't get angry at the market and continuously improve your approach if the stock you pick heads down.

A good way to begin is to start picking multibaggers while you are still pursuing another profession. Since multibagger opportunities don't occur daily, you don't have to spare too much time in finding one. Develop a written criteria for picking multibaggers and put up some money to see if your process works. Repeat the process multiple times after refining it using your previous investing experience till you have a method in place to pick multibaggers.

If you are on the right track, you should have accumulated significant gains over 2 to 3 years to begin multibagger investing full time. If you do not have significant gains, your process is not working and you may want to spend some more time refining your process before you leave your full time professional pursuits.

The market phase determines your multibagger investing strategy

"Investment themes only become obvious to most investors long after they have emerged – only once the bowl has been leaning and overflowing to one side for quite some time and created a bull market in a particular sector. Not surprisingly, we find that the largest flow of money into an asset class such as stocks, bonds, real estate or commodities will occur when just about everybody has fully understood the theme – which will inevitably coincide with that sector's peak in popularity and prices."

– Marc Faber in *Tomorrow's Gold*

It is commonsense that when no one is interested in stocks, they will be at their lowest price, and when every Tom, Dick and Harry is in stocks, they would be overpriced. Yet, what is it that makes people stay out of stocks at points they know the stocks are selling at prices where multibagger returns are almost certain? It has largely to do with psychology. We don't like to do things different from the herd. It is easier to invest when stocks are at highs and be wrong along with everyone else than be wrong when others are right.

But this hard wiring of investors and traders gives you "fish in the barrel" opportunities to buy multibaggers. When others are out of stocks, you bet your house on them and when the world is in them, take your multibagger returns.

You can find multibaggers in three different phases of the market but stocks and rules that apply to one phase don't apply to another. To find multibaggers, it is critical that we follow the rules of each phase.

When stocks break the link between rationality and expectations, they can drift anywhere. It is like a boat that has broken anchor in a stormy sea. Where the boat will drift is anyone's guess. This is a good situation to be in to find multibaggers.

When to exit a multibagger

"While enthusiasm may be necessary for great accomplishments elsewhere, on Wall Street it almost invariably leads to disaster."

– Benjamin Graham

There are times when irrespective of your belief in a stock, you must exit. Much of this has to do with a change of the market's mood or investor perceptions about the market. In emerging markets, for example, if foreigners reduce their demand for the stock, or actually start selling it, the market deflates and all stocks, irrespective of their potential, take a hit.

A stock may rise on its own steam but the price rarely sustains if the overall market takes a big hit. You must be careful if the multibagger you are invested in has large institutional holdings. Selling by institutional investors causes stocks to show very sharp losses.

Stocks can also drop significantly if a stock falls out of favour or there are sudden change in regulations or the direction of a commodity cycle reverses.

Don't count forever on a winning strategy

"Determine changes as appropriate, do not repeat past strategies to gain victory."

– Sun Tzu

There is no normal stock price. As technology, consumers and production techniques change, the blue chips of yesterday turn into the penny stocks of today and new entrants find their place on major market indices. The challenge in multibagger investing is to figure out how changes will impact a stock in a specific period of time. I emphasize a specific period of time because things can go exactly the opposite way in the short term before they head the way you expect.

If a multibagger strategy has worked a couple of times, don't count on it working again. Markets are constantly in flux and rules of the game continually change. No single multibagger strategy works in all markets and for all stocks. That is one of the reasons "get rich quick" books giving you standard formulas for investing almost never work.

Multibaggers in manipulated stocks

"The element of manipulation need not discourage anyone. Manipulators are giant traders, with deep pockets. Little traders are at liberty to tiptoe wherever the food trail leads, but they must be careful that the giants do not turn quickly on them."
– Richard Wyckoff in *The Day Trader's Bible*

If someone is creating the price and volume action on which you can ride, you may find a multibagger. The only risk with stocks that are manipulated, or artificially pumped up is that you will not know when the pumping ends, or when manipulators withdraw support.

There will be pockets of manipulation, sometimes across an industry, when stocks will run up multiple times. Think of this multibagger investing like a school of fish swimming with a shark. As long as you swim with the shark in synchronized fashion, you may get a multibagger.

The risk of loss because of the chance that you will not be able to exit the stock is very high in such stocks. This type of investing is not for someone who is new to the markets, and certainly not for someone who is not a master trader.

How to pick a multibagger

Read, Invest, Fail, Record
Read, Invest, Fail, Record
Read, Invest, Fail, Record

Look for signs of an overwhelming disinterest in the market. These are not too difficult to find. Here are some:

- Financial media tells you to look elsewhere as the markets are dead.
- Brokers and gurus predict a multi-year bear market.
- Foreigners sell out and no one is investing in equity mutual funds.

A market always starts rising when it reaches a point of maximum pessimism, and that point is reached when no one wants to invest in stocks. Without a roaring stock market, even institutional investors don't get any more money to invest in stocks.

When a market reaches such low levels, there are several stocks where the cash with the company is more than the market capitalization, or prices are so low that potential buyers may rather acquire a business than set up a new one, or market capitalisations of even blue chips are so low that they don't meet the entry thresholds of institutional investors. This indicates the bottom for a market.

Start by picking 10 stocks based on your anticipation of which sectors will attract the money. At this stage, the best stocks in the sector get the first flush of money.

The first flush of money will come from smart retail money. These are investors, like yourself, who have figured out that any investment at this stage will turn into a multibagger. It is only a matter of time. Don't expect prices to move much at this stage. Stock prices would have been low for so long that any buying will be absorbed by the selling of those who have waited for years to see some sign of a rise in the market. These sellers are usually the heart broken investors who bought at the peak of the earlier bull phase.

Any further buying will cause two things to happen:

- Sellers will stop selling as they start to believe that they may get a much higher price.
- The number of buyers will increase as financial media, brokers, etc. try to push stocks to retail buyers.

This is the phase when you will see stocks double or triple as the supply is limited and demand starts to pick up. Stocks would then have reached market capitalisations where institutional investors can also begin to invest. Retail investors, too, would begin to return to equity mutual funds giving fund managers money to buy more stock.

Then comes the most explosive phase for the stock's price. Fund managers will begin to buy stocks but since institutional holding is very low at this stage, any large order for stock must be catered to by a large number of individual investors. This pushes up prices in spikes. Stock prices may double or triple again in this phase. Mutual funds and other institutional investors will end up reporting stellar returns, driven partly by their own buying activity. This will bring a flood of foreign and local money into the market.

The last phase of the market can again drive the stock prices up in multiples. There will be excess money chasing existing stocks and each new flow of money will cause stocks to shoot up. This is the phase when you must begin to sell your multibagger.

Scarcity premium provides one of the best multibagger opportunities

Scarcity premium works for the stock markets of a country as a whole, for stocks in a particular sector, and / or for individual stocks.

When foreigners get interested in a market, their sudden rush to buy its top 10 to 50 stocks creates a mismatch between the demand and supply of such stocks. Such demand / supply imbalances don't last long as many new stocks get listed due to the mismatch. But the period of the mismatch creates 10 to 100 times gains for the stocks in demand.

The same happens to sectors. Let us say aviation becomes a popular sector and there is only one aviation stock listed. For the period of time when everyone rushes to buy that single aviation stock to play the sector, the stock's rise could be meteoric. Those who get in early enough, and then get out once additional aviation stocks list, have multibaggers in their hands.

There are a few market basics that you must keep in perspective when investing:

- Greed and fear are the two guiding factors of all markets and will always remain so. As long as they do, history will repeat itself. The objects of passion and speculation change, the countries in fashion change, the year, decade and century look different, but greed and fear remain intact.
- Emotional temperament is key to taking action on the structural shifts the markets may be undergoing. It takes courage to follow one's own beliefs and analysis because at the point of making these investment calls ahead of the market, the crowd is usually betting the other way.
- Instead of being a suitor running after a damsel (stocks) and seeing your infatuation increase as she (read, rising stocks) spurns you, treat stocks like products. Buy when they get cheaper or seem like value for money, or buy them ahead of their becoming the pursued, and sell them when they become the crowd's favourites. Multibaggers happen when we can also hold such stocks till they become the favourites of the most ignorant among the crowd.
- Knowing what everyone knows is no competitive advantage. Knowing what to do with what you know is the advantage.
- You don't need any investment gurus to guide you. Unlike other arts, investment mastery is a proprietary art.
- Human behaviour is the underpinning of all market action. Despite all the technological advancements in the financial markets, the explosion of financial news and the financial understanding of investors, there is no

empirical evidence to show that investors today can generate any better returns than investors did a hundred or two hundred years ago.

- Identifying the right theme ahead of the crowd is critical, — but only just ahead of the crowd. If the crowd has no desire to follow you, then while you might have bought a stock for all the right reasons, it will not move unless a large number of investors also buy it. The typical investor psychology is to buy with the crowd and also sell with the crowd. People find comfort in crowds and it takes singular conviction to act independently — but that's where all rewards in life, including multibaggers, lie. It is similar to buying real estate. If you can guess the direction in which a town will move, you could buy land very cheap. Buy ahead of the crowds and sell ahead of the crowds — again, remember, just ahead, but not going against the flow.
- All you need is a few stocks. Contrary to popular belief, it is a statistical fact that the more you diversify, the more your returns will look like the index's returns. The investor looks at only a few stocks. It is not possible to understand and keep tabs on numerous stocks and companies.
- Some stocks require a deeper understanding of the industry and its cycles. Commodity stocks fall in this category. For example, let us take coffee. Coffee is usually of two types, Arabica and Robusta. Arabica is the expensive, exclusive coffee grown in smaller quantities in countries like Ethiopia, Cuba and Brazil. The cheaper and more abundantly available coffee is Robusta. In Vietnam, it became a cottage industry creating a long term glut situation. The coffee you get at a fancy global coffee chain is usually 100% Arabica, or so they claim, and thus expensive. The coffee you get in the bottle of instant coffee you buy at your grocer is a blend of Arabica and Robusta — the instant coffee companies increase the Robusta proportion when they want to cut costs. For decades the Arabica and Robusta coffee markets remain severely depressed. Then, suddenly, they shoot up in multiples.
- There is no substitute for experience. Every mistake is a learning experience and adds to your mastery of the art of investing.
- Learn to recognize the dawn of a new era or new asset class.
- Destroy and throw out ideology, construct stock picking discipline, instead.
- There are opportunities at all times, and in all markets.
- Go over your holdings again and again and ask yourself if you would be willing to buy them at the current price. If the answer is no, sell them.
- Stay away from stocks with large institutional holdings. You are betting against informed people. The institutions may not be always right but you will really have to be ahead of the curve to be more right than them.

- Don't waste your time placing 10 or 100 share orders or playing for pennies. It is not worth your time. When you place a trade, have conviction, pick up 1,000 shares or 10,000 shares and exit if it is not going your way. This way if the share goes up you make decent money. If it does not go up, you take a small loss.
- Identify the next big investment theme.
- Liquidity scarcity causes structural imbalances in prices. Market dynamics are suspended if everyone needs to get out to get cash. Prices will get more depressed than justified by their underlying fundamentals giving rise to fortune making events for those with liquidity.

Speculative markets are required to turn stocks into multibaggers

"If the facts change, I change my mind, sir. What would you do, sir?"

– John Maynard Keynes

If value itself is ephemeral and can shift depending on the level of influence of those who enter the stock, a stock's price can change significantly depending on who is entering or who is leaving it. All investors may have money but few have sufficient influence to drive a stock up. And investors tend to follow influential pied pipers into a stock in droves. That drives stock prices up. And when large numbers of people start entering a stock, usually in a speculative phase, stocks can rise exponentially.

If stocks are not moving, the trading volume is low, the number of investors and traders is small and if the public is disinterested in the markets, stocks will not turn into multibaggers. For that, you need a speculative market where people are trading on margin, futures and options activity is strong, and the public suddenly finds markets to be the place to invest.

Look for sectors that investors are treating like a step child

Investors rarely allocate capital among stocks in a very rational fashion. Capital tends to flow into popular sectors and stocks rather than into stocks that provide the best opportunities for returns. Since most investors enter stocks that are popular, it ensures that they will make low returns, or even losses. The market then is rigged in favour of a few and programmed to lose money for the majority of investors. This is what throws up excellent opportunities for the multibagger investor who allocates his capital in the least loved sectors, and waits for them to move up the popularity charts.

From time to time, money will flow too easily into a sector investors have taken a fancy to, making it expensive or difficult for other sectors to raise money. It is in such a sector that you will find the next multibaggers.

11

~

The Multibagger Quiz

Test Your Multibagger Expertise

1. The way we think and perceive information, news and other data about stocks needs to be counter-intuitive to human nature if we want to pick multibaggers. T/F?
2. Chartered accountants, MBAs in finance and those good in math, such as engineers have a distinct advantage in picking multibaggers. T/F?
3. To pick multibaggers, we must rely on financial data, read or watch financial media, and listen to market gurus. T/F?
4. Much of what an individual investor hears about markets and stocks are carefully cultivated myths and sales pitches to entice you into investing. T/F?
5. What you know about markets from financial TV and literature will make you money. T/F?
6. The market's mood and direction is not an important factor in picking multibaggers. T/F?
7. An edge built on an individual stock picking style that is different from the crowd is essential for multibagger investing. T/F?
8. Anyone can build a multibagger investing edge in a short period of time. T/F?
9. Trial and error making losses is essential to master multibagger investing. T/F?
10. Almost everything you are told, know or learn about stocks or investing does not work in multibagger investing. T/F?
11. Understanding human psychology is more important than logic and facts for investing. T/F?
12. To find multibaggers, investors must focus on which stocks money will flow to rather than the stock's fundamentals. T/F?

13. Investors are more emotional than rational and anticipating their mood helps you anticipate the stocks where money will flow. T/F?
14. For multibagging, you must necessarily buy stocks at low PE ratios or high dividend yields rather than stocks with high PE ratios. T/F?
15. Mood and perceptions of the future are not important for investing in stocks. T/F?
16. Multibagger investing is a lonely pursuit. T/F?
17. An individual investor is better placed than institutional investors to pick multibaggers. T/F?
18. Markets never rise (or fall) forever — The Law of Means catches up. T/F?
19. The timing of your entry and exit is not important for consistent multibagger investing. T/F?
20. Even 2 multibaggers obtained from great timing more than make up for losses in 8 wrong calls. T/F?
21. When the mood in the markets shifts, liquidity dries up and without liquidity even the best stocks languish. T/F?
22. If investors feel positive about the markets, there is no saying how high they could run up a stock or a market. T/F?
23. Investing risk increases in a market or sector which is consistently running north. T/F?
24. If a stock's got the momentum, we don't need to know the reasons for the momentum; we only need to ride it. T/F?
25. Cutting stocks with losses is as critical to maintain high returns on the entire portfolio. T/F?
26. Fundamentals can be picked up through public media or publicly available information. T/F?
27. There are going to be many times when you think a company's growth will show up in the price and it does not. T/F?
28. Stock prices may drop, rise or rise exponentially on the same "fundamentals." T/F?
29. The balance of buyers of the stock has to overwhelm the sellers of the stock for a stock to turn into a multibagger. T/F?
30. The right way we buy "value" stocks is to buy them when they are trading at low PEs. T/F?
31. Investing in low PE stocks may get you stuck with a dud for a very long time. T/F?

32. A stock can be priced as low as possible but without others ready to put money into it, there will be no multibagger. T/F?
33. Multibaggers cannot be found in short spurts of market mania. T/F?
34. There is no difference between impulsiveness, recklessness and risk in stock investing. T/F?
35. The timing of your entry before money flows in and exit before money flows out of the stock is the edge that will stand you out. T/F?
36. Money, fashion and opinion can be far greater definers or redefiners of value than any conventional measure of value. T/F?
37. If your portfolio is diversified or has more than 10 stocks, your returns will start to gravitate to the mean or towards the returns of the index. T/F?
38. A great way to develop an edge is to keep a diary and make notes on your investments and what you need to do to improve your performance. T/F?
39. Positive economic growth drives up individual stock prices. T/F?
40. Extrapolation of economic growth on stocks will result in multibaggers. T/F?
41. A stock that is losing ground does not indicate a loss of confidence in the company or management, or a loss of interest or a withdrawal of money. T/F?
42. Multibaggers emerge in brief periods and in various market conditions and most of us during such periods seem to be struck with disbelief or frozen not to act. T/F?
43. Investing because you like the "story" means you are relying on someone's construction of the real events. T/F?
44. Listening to promoters, experts, financial media, etc. is the right way to pick multibaggers. T/F?
45. You are better off taking several small losses early in your multibagger investing period. T/F?
46. "Value" in the company transfers to "value" in the stock. T/F?
47. A stock's performance is directly linked to the financial performance of the company. T/F?
48. If stocks are not moving, trading volume is low, number of investors and traders is small and the public is disinterested in the markets, stocks will not turn into multibaggers. T/F?

49. From time to time, money will flow too easily to a sector or business investors have taken a fancy to making it expensive or difficult for other sectors to raise money. T/F?
50. Our bias to base our decisions on our most recent memory rather than our most rewarding or painful memories sets the tone for most investing mistakes. T/F?
51. When a large part of the market's rise is funded by leverage, margin, borrowing or hedge fund money, it is the most reliable indicator of the end of a boom. T/F?
52. Supply and demand imbalances may take years, or even decades to reverse in stock, commodities and real estate markets. T/F?
53. Stock prices may remain depressed for years and may then gain exponentially in just 1 or 2 years. T/F?
54. Markets were not perfectly liquid and investors are not perfectly rational. T/F?
55. Superior returns are only temporary. T/F?
56. Option prices are primarily determined by models that assume that large price movements are unlikely. T/F?
57. The more the risk, the higher the return. T/F?
58. You can get exponential returns by taking minimal risk. T/F?
59. Being too early and right is the same as being wrong as investors have repeatedly discovered. T/F?
60. You must exit a stock whose price is falling at a prespecified loss percentage. T/F?
61. Multibagger investing is a regular, daily pursuit. T/F?
62. Chances of finding multibaggers increase exponentially for those who have been in the markets for over a decade, or have seen a complete boom and bust cycle. T/F?
63. Losses can cause disorientation that it will impact your ability to pick the right stocks or may dishearten you to the extent that you stop investing. T/F?
64. You should not time the market. T/F?
65. Stocks are not like products. You must buy them when they are at a discount. T/F?
66. For those who are in the markets for superior returns, a popular stock may not equate with a "high return" stock. T/F?
67. One of the most common investing errors is assuming that you have a multibagger at hand just because the "intrinsic" value is low. T/F?

68. In bull markets, "cognitive dissonance" takes over. We want to hear what makes us feel good about stocks not how things really are. T/F?
69. Stock prices are based on expectations and expectations are fickle. T/F?
70. When a stock's price has risen considerably, investors should stay away as the stock is "overvalued". T/F?
71. What gets treated as "fundamentals" by most investors is nothing but a sales pitch or information that has been structured or presented in a manner to meet the goals of the presenter. T/F?
72. Infectious enthusiasm ensures a stock's price rise will be swift and steep or not at all. T/F?
73. Access to increased information and technology has improved our emotional stability or temperament. T/F?
74. What is important news is not necessarily what is important in making investment decisions. T/F?
75. Financial TV magnifies the ups and downs of the market — usually the ups. T/F?
76. We remember events that are the most recent, and not necessarily the ones that are the most important or powerful. T/F?
77. If prices have not risen for years and then do so suddenly, small investors sell off. T/F?
78. Bull markets are more about anticipation of further returns and a highly optimistic mood. T/F?
79. In a frenzied market, PEs become meaningless. T/F?
80. We can predict what will happen to a stock price on which we have no control in 3-5 years. T/F?
81. You must give a stock 3-5 years is not going to turn it into a multibagger. T/F?
82. The best returns are always made in short spurts. T/F?
83. The timing of your entry and exit from a stock is a prerequisite to multibagger investing. T/F?
84. You can buy and hold just as long as the technical charts indicate that the stock has price and volume momentum or the price is backed by an increasing in volume over a period of time. T/F?
85. If volumes drop and the stock price stagnates, it may indicate a loss of interest and buy and hold will not work. T/F?
86. The maximum rewards are also reserved for those who take least risk. T/F?
87. The correlation between risk and reward in stocks is not clear. T/F?

88. Buying at the bottom of bear markets could deliver exponential rewards far in excess of the risk. T/F?
89. At the peak of bull markets, the reward may be small compared to the risk. T/F?
90. Mood and liquidity are of no consequence on the future outlook of stocks. T/F?
91. Exponential economic growth is always good for stocks. T/F?
92. Low PE stocks turn into multibaggers. T/F?
93. Low PE may indicate a problem that you may not be aware of. T/F?
94. Buying low PE stocks is a good strategy when investors have been forced to sell shares because of liquidity issues. T/F?
95. Buy high and sell higher is a good multibagger strategy. T/F?
96. A falling stock may reflect a lack of confidence or a problem with the stock. T/F?
97. When investors lose confidence in a stock, it usually takes a long time for that confidence or investors to return to that stock. T/F?
98. Relying on financial media for picking stocks is a sound multibagger strategy. T/F?
99. Access to increased information and technology has improved our emotional stability or temperament. T/F?
100. If we mistime purchases, it could be years before there are any returns. T/F?
101. Stock prices are driven by perceptions of economic growth, confidence, etc. T/F?
102. Fundamental analysis tells you about when money will flow into the stock or how the stock's price will rise. T/F?
103. Low PE stocks are cheap and indicate low risk. T/F?
104. "Cheap" for most investors is a lower price than the price they have gotten used to seeing a stock trade. T/F?
105. Averaging our purchase price by purchasing more stock at lower price is a sound multibagger strategy. T/F?
106. An understanding of cycles can indicate that the rise in a stock price is over and it is time to cut losses and book profits at the earliest. T/F?
107. Markets work in cycles. A cycle lasts for years. Within cycles, there are trends. T/F?
108. You can find multibaggers in different phases of the market but stocks and rules that apply to one phase don't apply to another. T/F?

109. When stocks break the link between rationality and expectations, they can drift anywhere. This is a good situation to be in to find multibaggers. T/F?
110. Multibagger investing should be based on fundamentals / value, and not timing your purchases. T/F?
111. Commodity stocks move in cycles and provide the most consistent multibaggers when a commodity is an upcycle. T/F?
112. Low priced, unknown shares are the ones that do the best in the last phase of a bull rally — and the worst in a bear market. T/F?
113. It is not how expensive the stock is that is important, but how much more expensive that you anticipate it to get. T/F?
114. Speculators can hike up prices to any level, way beyond what seems rational. T/F?
115. Mid- and small-caps need to wait for a significant rally in large caps before they rise. T/F?
116. You may get a multibagger by going by your intuition but just as soon, you will lose the money in other stocks you pick. T/F?
117. Humans have a natural tendency to find a cause for an effect. They see patterns where there are none. T/F?
118. There may be things that you don't know or are just beyond your comprehension driving the stock's price and they may not be in consonance with the assumptions you based your investment on. T/F?
119. There is a lag between economic cycles and the pace and time investors take to change or form a perception about economic cycles. T/F?
120. Multibagger investors must exit the market or the sector or the stock when the sector's cycle has come to an end. T/F?
121. The more you diversify, the more your returns will look like the index's returns. T/F?
122. Unless others agree with you that the stock you picked is undervalued, it is not going to move. T/F?
123. The trick is to be have the same view as the rest of the investors but way ahead of them and at a price much lower than they decide to enter. T/F?
124. Before you pick a stock, determine if the sector the stock belongs to or the entire market is a long, mid or short term bull or bear cycle. T/F?
125. The risk increases and the frequency decreases of finding multibaggers as you try to invest in a mid or short term cycle as it can reverse anytime. T/F?

126. Select a stock based on an "undervalued theme" and exit when the theme becomes a "popular theme" to take the maximum out of a multibagger. T/F?
127. You must invest an amount material enough to give you a significant amount when a stock turns into a multibagger. T/F?
128. A liquidity freeze results in losses across the market and no stock no matter how precisely it has been picked can last a market meltdown. T/F?
129. If you have money when others don't you are bound to get bargains and if you can wait it out till markets find equilibrium again, you will exit at multiples of your purchase price. T/F?
130. Winning streaks make you continue on the same course of picking stocks without any method and eventually result in losing whatever you have made. T/F?
131. Technical charts have to be read in the context of increasing price, volumes and the time that has elapsed since the stock began its rise. T/F?
132. The speed at which the stock moves and the direction it takes depends on the majority of those putting up the money. T/F?
133. Disregarding the role of other players in the stock can lead to miscalculations on where the stock could head and what it could produce in returns. T/F?
134. A stock can turn into a multibagger in a few weeks or a few months or in a year. T/F?
135. Take advantage of the lag time between a new investment theme and the market's ability to find the right price. T/F?
136. Irrespective of your belief in the stock, you must exit when the market's mood or investor perceptions about the stock have changed. T/F?
137. A stock may rise on its own steam but it rarely sustains its price if the overall market takes a big hit. T/F?
138. The only relevant point for an investor is to pick stocks which the most potential to rise from the point of their purchase. T/F?
139. Because of the tendency to look for "cheaper" or "low priced stocks" or stocks that have not risen as much, most investors lose out on bull market opportunities. T/F?
140. Being a "value investor" is better than being a trader or a chartist or a speculator. T/F?
141. The sense of fallibility, even paranoia about failure, is a key ingredient in the success of great investors and traders. T/F?

142. At the end of this euphoric phase, a massive blowout takes the stocks down very sharply. T/F?
143. Too many investors piling on a stock makes a stock safer. T/F?
144. The biggest rise in the markets comes when the least knowledgeable — and they constitute the largest number — rush in. T/F?
145. Losing streaks are not damaging to your psychology. T/F?
146. A stock has a "bell curve" or a "mean" price. It can't go up multiple times and drop to any level. T/F?
147. A stock can stay at the new price and never return to its older price. T/F?
148. The same stock can't be trading at one time its PE or 10 times its PE or 100 times its PE or any multiple depending simply on how investors and traders perceive the stock and how the flow of money is driving the demand and supply for the stock. T/F?
149. A great business means a great stock for multibagger investing. T/F?
150. As the stock's price rises, the market capitalization of the stock rises bringing in institutional investors. T/F?
151. Investors make similar stock investing decisions based on the same information. T/F?
152. Investors are not influenced by their recent experiences. T/F?
153. Investors who have suffered large losses may react abruptly to any drop in a stock's price. T/F?
154. The point of your exit is when people stop listening to anything that contradicts their thought process. T/F?
155. Investors find it easy to consider alternate views on why a stock may or may not rise. T/F?
156. Investors look for a rationale to justify the rise in a stock's price. But "cause and effect" plays an important role in a stock's rise. T/F?
157. Stock prices are driven by multiple factors and depend on the psychology of thousands and millions of investors. T/F?
158. A stock pick is low risk when you are convinced that there is undervaluation based on conventional stock picking methods like low PE, etc. T/F?
159. A stock is high risk when investors believe the stock is overvalued. T/F?
160. If the stock has a high institutional shareholding, it indicates there is plenty of upside left in the stock's price. T/F?
161. Understanding the behaviour of crowds is a key skill for picking multibaggers. T/F?

162. The reasoning of crowds is always inferior but it is enough to drive prices to extreme levels. T/F?
163. The imagination of crowds can be a driving factor for stocks to multibagger levels. T/F?
164. The largest number of investors enter the market when it is at its peak. T/F?
165. If an investment theme is still being discussed at a conceptual level or scientific manner, it is the time to get into a stock. T/F?
166. It will take time before an investment theme is planted in the minds of the public. T/F?
167. A good sign for a multibagger investor to get out is when the crowds are right and sophisticated investors are flummoxed by the market's rise. T/F?
168. The public is not driven by anticipation of easy money. T/F?
169. Crowds can change their opinions very quickly causing stock prices to rise or collapse in short spans of time. T/F?
170. We remember events that are the most recent and not necessarily the ones that are the most important or powerful. T/F?
171. Risk requires us to invest in stocks where the odds of gains are high. T/F?
172. Inherent in investing is the ability to take a loss. T/F?
173. The way we manage risk is to limit our losses to a certain percentage of our purchase price. T/F?
174. When stocks fall only because investors are moving money to a sector for quick profits, long term multibagger opportunities arise in neglected sectors. T/F?
175. A stock that falls after you have bought it indicates you may have missed something that the market knows and it is best to stay in the stock. T/F?
176. If a stock shows high trading volumes but a declining trend over the short term, it may indicate the stock may be heading even lower. T/F?
177. A chart showing you an uptrend in price along with an increase in volume may indicate an increase in interest in the stock. T/F?
178. Big swings come once in a while and you must get out early of big swings. T/F?
179. Being a contrarian alone is enough to find multibaggers. T/F?
180. Being ahead of the crowd when a new investment theme is emerging is a high risk strategy to find multibaggers. T/F?

181. An investment theme falters when investors begin to feel extremely optimistic about a market. T/F?
182. An investment theme starts to emerge when a sector or stock facing extreme disinterest from investors starts to find interest. T/F?
183. Picking multibaggers when the whole market is moving up is much easier and safer than going against the market. T/F?
184. A combination of a large amount of individual investors and low liquidity in small cap stock drives many stocks up multiple times when a sector's stocks are in demand. T/F?
185. When the flow of money starts to dominate investing considerations, stocks with low floating stock and large inflows of money appreciate the slowest. T/F?
186. The cyclicality of markets makes it imperative that the entry and exit must never be timed. T/F?
187. A wrong entry point delays your gains and a wrong exit point either compounds your losses or does not let you extract the full profit potential of the stock. T/F?
188. A large market capitalization is a guarantee for a stock's safety. T/F?
189. The trait you need to work on is the ability to take losses naturally and without impacting your peace of mind. T/F?
190. Stocks can't stay at their lows for years. T/F?
191. Stock market bubbles are usually caused by the discovery of a new technology or a new country's potential or a new "asset class" and provide a once in a life time opportunity to cash out big time at the peak of irrationality. T/F?
192. During this process of trying to find the right price for a new set of stocks based on a new idea, investors and traders tend to undervalue stocks. T/F?
193. When there is a stunning rise in price in a sector investors should avoid the sector and buy cheaper stocks in some other sector. T/F?
194. Multibagger investors should buy low PE stocks in a bull market. T/F
195. A low PE could indicate that the owners or institutional investors know something about the company's financial health that has not been made public or known to the public. T/F?
196. A combination of limiting your losses and letting your profits run won't get you multibagger returns if you are right only 10% to 20% of the time. T/F?
197. Markets for the most part stay stagnant or move within a range. T/F?

198. If no one wants stocks and there is bad news all around, it is possible that investors have slammed the stocks way below their true worth. T/F?
199. If foreign investors have losses in other market or face redemption, they sell out of all markets to get into cash. T/F?
200. The stocks may change, the investors may change but the motivations of investors to be in stocks remain the same. T/F?
201. This constant pruning of your portfolio does not help you build a multibagger portfolio. T/F?
202. Holding losing stocks colour your outlook on picking multibaggers in the future. T/F?
203. You should be willing to pay higher prices for a company which has great prospects or is growing. T/F?
204. This excess flow of money into a stock does not make it more expensive. T/F?
205. The financial media presents news that is important to make investment decision. T/F?
206. We can improve our returns almost immediately if we paid a more attention to when we exit a stock. T/F?
207. When a bear market has lasted several years, investors either develop a disinterest in stocks or start to believe that the prevailing price is the normal price for the stock. T/F?
208. If a majority of investors are ready to pay any price for the stock, it will not have much upside left. T/F?
209. A multibagger investor has to find a stock whose price has been "discovered" by a majority of the investors. T/F?
210. Penny stocks are an easy way to pick multibaggers. T/F?
211. If investor interest vaporizes, even quality stocks may turn into penny stocks. T/F?
212. The usual reaction of investors to new market trends is to price stocks in this new interest at extremely low levels. T/F?
213. When overleveraged markets / top of bull markets explode, the need to pay margins, draws down stock way below their intrinsic value. T/F?
214. If the ownership of stock is largely with promoters and institutions start to increase their stake, stocks will double or triple very quickly. T/F?
215. You will find multibaggers using the same conventional measures like low PE ratios in all kinds of markets. T/F?
216. At the peak of a bull market or when the market becomes dominated by uninformed investors, a stock can go into a free fall. T/F?

217. Markets typically don't focus on the long term. Immediate issues, such as margin calls, mood or sentiment, short term news events, etc. are what drive the market's behaviour. T/F?
218. No matter how great an advantage a stock has or its domination in the market, over a period of time, the company's high profits or product profile draws competitors. T/F?
219. When most investors start viewing a stock or the market as a continuing upward trend, the balance between buyers and sellers that keeps a stock price in a range breaks down and the stock starts to head up. T/F?
220. Stock investing and stock markets are conducive to cause and effect thinking. T/F?
221. A low PE ratio or the book value is much higher than the stock's price makes a stock a value buy. T/F?
222. Illogical prices can also be created by a drying up of liquidity. T/F?
223. Stocks in which there are too many institutional investors are not be risky stocks to invest in. T/F?
224. Institutional investors tend to exit a stock at around the same time causing not just very sharp fall in the stock's price but often creating a situation where there is no exit at any price. T/F?
225. A stock can collapse anytime because it is too "crowded" by institutional money. T/F?
226. A stock's price is driven by fundamentals and not sentiment. T/F?
227. Value investors usually have an aversion to knowing what traders are up to in a stock. That is the right approach to investing. T/F?
228. A key expertise for value investors it to master chart reading so that they are not too early to exit a stock. T/F?
229. To determine if a stock is building up the momentum to rise look at its price and volume rise on technical charts. T/F?
230. Investors must focus on company data, financial information and other "fundamentals" to find multibaggers. T/F?
231. If you can look at stocks as the risk you are taking compared to their potential to turn multibaggers, you will have a standardized measure of picking stocks. T/F?
232. A market may fall on its own weight or it may fall because of factors not directly related to the market. T/F?
233. When markets turn uncertain, managing risk becomes difficult. T/F?
234. If a multibagger strategy has worked a couple of times, you can count on it working again. T/F?

235. Markets are constantly in flux and the rules of the game continually changes. T/F?
236. Get rich quick books give you standard formulas for investing that work. T/F?
237. A low risk point to invest in stocks is when a market has moved up to such heights where rational investors think they are overvalued. T/F?
238. Informed investors rely on stories and narrative to sell stocks to still other informed investors creating a cycle where the market turns into a one way buying spree. T/F?
239. As a stock market mania or long term bull market persists, investors stop buying low priced stocks and stocks of low quality. T/F?
240. It is the easiest to drive up stocks with dubious managements and businesses in a long term bull market. T/F?
241. It is the low priced, unknown shares that do the best in the last phase of a bull rally. T/F?
242. Low priced shares do the worst in a bear market. T/F?
243. You must purchase more stock if it falls to bring down your purchase price. T/F?
244. If a stock continues to fall after you have invested in it, get out at a prefixed loss level. T/F?
245. You must invest based on fundamental and ignore the technicals. T/F?
246. Value investing is based on fact and figures in a game. T/F?
247. Multibagger investors should keep away from market emotions. T/F?
248. When central banks and governments flood the economy with easy money, excess liquidity tends to flow into stocks taking most stocks up. T/F?
249. A stock's price has so many variables and the psychology and opinions of so many individuals that no stock picking method can account for all. T/F?
250. Look for a bear market to have been around for a long time to buy multibaggers. T/F?
251. When a vast majority of investors get used to low prices, it sets the base for multibaggers. T/F?
252. The duration of a bear market does not reduce the risk of investing in stocks. T/F?
253. Buy stocks where institutional interest will return but is minimal currently. T/F?

254. Information available to the public is cloaked in public relation spins, deception and other coatings that help those who control the flow of information. T/F?
255. Stay in a stock even if it is not going in the direction you expect and prefixed loss levels to exit the stock. T/F?
256. Stocks don't make very large moves on institutional selling or a change in market mood. T/F?
257. Look for "low float" stocks that are generating institutional interest. T/F?
258. The amount of "float" or stock that is available is not an important factor for finding multibaggers. T/F?
259. An owner will do an IPO when the market is right for him to get the maximum price. T/F?
260. Buying into an IPO because it has "anchor investors" or institutional investors ahead of the IPO is a good strategy. T/F?
261. Value investing in a bear market may get us the best returns when the markets turn around. T/F?
262. Rush to buy stocks when the market changes direction after a bull market. T/F?
263. The longer the bull market has lasted, the shorter it will take time for stocks to recover. T/F?
264. The stage of the market cycle irrelevant to multibagger investing. T/F?
265. A stock bought when the entire market is heading higher is much safer than a stock bought when only the sector or stock is heading up. T/F?
266. A distinction between cycles and trends is critical for buy and sell decisions. T/F?
267. Investors do the right thing when they try to invest in early stages new emerging areas or in new emerging economies. T/F?
268. Stocks that are well researched will make it easy for you to find something that the bigger investors have missed. T/F?
269. Stocks that have stopped being researched may have multibagger potential. T/F?
270. Always be wary of stocks that have been falling continually. T/F?
271. A low priced stock may also attract institutional interest if the stock moves from being a small cap stock to a mid cap stocks. T/F?
272. Institutional interest indicates that someone with superior knowledge has looked at the stock. T/F?

273. Multibagger investors should focus on stock splits, increased dividends, news announcements and brokerage firm or advisory recommendations. T/F?
274. Bottom fishing is one of the best ways to pick multibaggers. T/F?
275. Multibagger investors should stay invested irrespective of market cycles. T/F?
276. If you are convinced about the stock's potential to become a multibagger and the price falls, buy more at lower prices. T/F?
277. An understanding of market cycles can help you decide whether the stock will or will not become a multibagger. T/F?
278. "Bull markets" are more about anticipation of further returns and a highly optimistic mood. T/F?
279. Expectations of potential gains in a very short time outweigh any risk concerns investors have. T/F?
280. Whenever you find yourself listening to one particular view, a bull view or the bear view and find yourself looking at news to confirm your view, you're on the right track. T/F?
281. Divergent views are very important for multibagger investors. T/F?
282. Look for views that agree with the basis for stocks that you are invested in or investing in. T/F?
283. Multibagger investors must exit all investment if their losses exceed their preset loss limit. T/F?
284. If a stock is drifting lower after you have invested, it is possible you have missed something that others know. T/F?
285. Human beings are programmed to become risk averse to anything in which they have taken a hit. T/F?
286. A winning strategy need not be tested and improved rather than being accepted with one or two lucky multibagger picks. T/F?
287. Each multibagger investment must be independent of the other. T/F?
288. Don't buy the next stock because you lost money on the previous stock. T/F?
289. Value investors tend to turn the most bearish during investment manias. T/F?
290. Just when it looks like a stock is "overpriced" it rises because of buying from those caught on the wrong side of the fence in a "short squeeze". T/F?
291. Look for signs of a overwhelming disinterest in the market to buy. T/F?

292. Keep away from stocks when financial media tells you to look at other investments as the markets are not going to turn around soon, brokers and gurus predict a multi-year bear market, foreigners sell out and no one is investing in equity mutual funds. T/F?
293. You need investment gurus to guide you. T/F?
294. There is evidence to show that investors today can generate any better returns than investors did a hundred or two hundred years ago. T/F?
295. People find comfort in crowds and it takes singular conviction to act independently but that's where all rewards in life, including multibaggers lie. T/F?
296. The more you diversify, the more your returns will look like the index's returns. T/F?
297. Destroy and throw out ideology, construct stock picking discipline. T/F?
298. Go over your holdings again and again and ask if you would be willing to buy them at the current price. If the answer is no, sell them. T/F?
299. Stay away from stocks with large institutional holdings. The institutions may not be always right but you will really have to be ahead of the curve to be more right than them. T/F?
300. Don't waste your time placing 10/100 share orders or playing for pennies. When you place a trade, have conviction, pick up 10,000 shares and exit if it is not going your way. T/F?
301. Buy when a market begins its fall after a bull run as the stocks are cheap them. T/F?
302. When it looks like only fools will invest at crazy prices at the height of bull markets, stocks will rise 5- to 10-fold. T/F?
303. Just as stocks take years to begin an upmove, an upmove may continue for years and deliver returns many times in excess of the purchase price. T/F?
304. Do not invest in speculative markets for multibaggers. T/F?
305. You cannot find multibaggers in the immediate term and short term. T/F?
306. Commodity stocks can turn into multibaggers and continue their rise for year if your timing is correct. T/F?
307. Investing in commodity stocks is a very long term game and if your timing is wrong, the stock may not move for years. T/F?
308. Major investment themes become obvious to most investors somewhere in the middle or peak of the respective cycle. T/F?

309. The best multibagger opportunities may be in markets that are most talked about. T/F?
310. In markets affected by liquidity seizures, the chances that shares will be mispriced downwards is low. T/F?
311. The nature of multibaggers is such that opportunities come occasionally and most of your time is spent on reflection, reading and keeping a diary of your experiences in multibagger investing. T/F?
312. Investing in "blue chip" stocks or "safe" stocks is a safe strategy. T/F?
313. For your entire portfolio to be multibaggers, you must remove anything that does not deliver. T/F?
314. The amount you should invest in multibaggers must be big enough to make a real change in your wealth when the stock turns into a multibagger. T/F?
315. Market fluctuations are not good for investing. T/F?
316. A good time to find the next set of multibaggers is at the peak of an investment mania in stocks of a particular sector or industry. T/F?
317. When an investment mania ends, money flows to stocks in another sector or industry. T/F?
318. Look for stocks that have dropped only because investors have withdrawn money to invest in the mania. T/F?
319. Don't invest in a market or stocks on the possibility of extreme events. T/F?
320. Investing risk is high when an industry begins to deleverage or bring down their debt. T/F?
321. Buy puts (repeated) on heavily institutional owned stocks at the peak of a bull market, or in a sector where they are so heavily invested that there is no margin of error. T/F?
322. When stocks start hitting peaks, buy puts repeatedly. T/F?
323. Buy a stock when it's dropping if you like the fundamentals. T/F?
324. Most investors get taken out by the temporary swings against them even when they are spot on the long term direction of the investment. T/F?
325. A cheap stock is stock whose price has factored in the potential of a future rise. T/F?
326. A future rise could come because there are only 2 or 3 stocks in a listed space where foreigners have become very interested or it could come because the stock or the sector is going to see institutional buying. T/F?
327. When institutional investors get interested in a stock, prices will go up over a long of time. T/F?

328. Penny stocks that have drifted to penny status because of an exit of institutional investors or because there is no interest in a sector are well placed to become multibaggers. T/F?
329. Retail investors pour money through mutual funds and directly driving up prices of low liquidity, low volume small cap stocks. T/F?
330. Commodity multibaggers are not available when a commodity cycle turns. T/F?
331. Buy stocks on the way down after a long term bull rally. T/F?
332. Stocks on the index will deliver the best returns in a flat market. T/F?
333. Large capitalization stocks find it easy to become multibaggers. T/F?
334. Stocks that have been at the bottom for years because of a bear market will not turn into multibaggers. T/F?
335. Multibaggers are "produced" for various reasons — liquidity, capital raising, acquisitions, etc. and are always driven by fundamentals. T/F?
336. Institutional buying of low volume stock can turn it into a multibagger. T/F?
337. Stock market bubbles do not produce multibaggers. T/F?
338. Following technical chartists in a strong upmarket may be a great strategy. Following logic in a bear market may get us the best returns when the markets turn around. T/F?
339. Even if you manage to pick the bottom, the market can end up sitting there for years and tying up your capital. T/F?
340. Wait until the move is already under way before you get into the market. T/F?
341. Smaller capitalization stocks typically provide much bigger multibagger opportunities. T/F?
342. Even when the company starts to tell you things are not good, be sceptical. T/F?
343. Successful investors talk about their strategies on TV. T/F?
344. A wildly fluctuating market means that irrationally low prices will never be attached to solid businesses. T/F?
345. Follow conventional wisdom in the market. You have to learn to flow with the markets. T/F?
346. Leverage or buying on margin can't give you multibaggers in a few days. T/F?
347. The number of times we'll lose or make a mistake is drastically reduced if we analyse our failures. And the number of times we can get superior returns has multiplied just by knowing how things work. T/F?

348. Every successful investor (including great traders) are convinced they are fallible (not invincible) and that they can be wiped out anytime. T/F?
349. The sense of fallibility (even paranoia) is a key ingredient in the success of great investors and traders. T/F?
350. Value investing is not a game for the lone ranger. If you like to follow your own road, make your own decisions and have faith in your own convictions you will not do well. T/F?
351. A value investor does not need any expertise in trading techniques and charts. T/F?
352. There is an inflection point in a business that the market notices without a lag time. This lag time gives you the opportunity to enter the stock ahead of the market. T/F?
353. Your returns will be in multiples if you can beat institutional investors into the stock. T/F?
354. The biggest rise in stocks comes when institutional investors enter the stock and they enter the stock when it has gained momentum. T/F?
355. We overrate our ability to make profits and underrate the chances of losses. This can cause a wide difference between your expectations out of a stock and what it can really deliver. T/F?
356. A structural shift in demand or supply can cause a stock to turn into a multibagger. T/F?
357. Companies that build a brand that can set prices and scale up to unprecedented levels providing multibagger opportunities. T/F?
358. Mutual funds who restrict themselves to buying small and mid cap stocks have no choice but to buy these low float, low liquidity stocks driving up prices in multiples in very short intervals of time. T/F?
359. A stock has fallen over 90%, is a "cheap" stock. T/F?
360. Stock prices ultimately depend on the confidence of investors which itself is the outcome of mass psychology of a large number of individuals. T/F?
361. Stock prices can rise multiple times towards the peak of a bull market. T/F?
362. Low availability of stock and too much money entering the stock creates the multibagger. T/F?
363. You must think about the thinking of others in the market and if they will tilt the balance in favour of buying a particular stocks. T/F?

364. Industries in which it takes time to build up capacity when demand increases provide an excellent multibagger opportunity. T/F?
365. Most investors are afraid to buy a stock that is beginning to go into new high ground, pricewise. This is the right approach to multibagger investing. T/F?
366. Personal feelings and opinions are far more accurate than the markets. You should stick to buying stocks based on your own analysis. T/F?
367. Multibagger investors should focus on stock splits, increased dividends, news announcements and brokerage firm or advisory recommendations. T/F?
368. Bottom fishing is one of the best ways to pick multibaggers. T/F?
369. Multibagger investors should stay invested irrespective of market cycles. T/F?
370. If you are convinced about the stock's potential to become a multibagger and the price falls, buy more at lower prices. T/F?
371. An understanding of market cycles can help you decide whether the stock will or will not become a multibagger. T/F?

Answers to the Multibagger Quiz

~

1. T	20. T	39. F	58. T	77. T
2. F	21. T	40. F	59. T	78. T
3. F	22. T	41. F	60. T	79. T
4. T	23. F	42. T	61. F	80. F
5. F	24. T	43. T	62. T	81. F
6. F	25. T	44. T	63. T	82. T
7. T	26. T	45. T	64. F	83. T
8. F	27. T	46. F	65. F	84. T
9. T	28. T	47. F	66. T	85. T
10. T	29. T	48. T	67. T	86. T
11. T	30. F	49. T	68. T	87. T
12. F	31. T	50. T	69. T	88. T
13. T	32. T	51. T	70. F	89. T
14. F	33. F	52. T	71. T	90. F
15. F	34. F	53. T	72. T	91. F
16. T	35. T	54. T	73. F	92. F
17. T	36. T	55. T	74. T	93. T
18. T	37. T	56. T	75. T	94. T
19. T	38. T	57. F	76. T	95. T

96. T	121. T	146. F	171. T	196. F
97. T	122. T	147. T	172. T	197. T
98. F	123. T	148. F	173. T	198. T
99. F	124. T	149. F	174. T	199. T
100. T	125. T	150. T	175. F	200. T
101. T	126. T	151. F	176. F	201. F
102. F	127. T	152. F	177. T	202. T
103. F	128. T	153. T	178. F	203. F
104. T	129. T	154. T	179. F	204. F
105. F	130. T	155. F	180. F	205. F
106. T	131. T	156. F	181. F	206. T
107. T	132. T	157. T	182. T	207. T
108. T	133. T	158. F	183. T	208. F
109. T	134. T	159. F	184. T	209. F
110. F	135. T	160. F	185. F	210. F
111. T	136. T	161. T	186. F	211. T
112. T	137. T	162. T	187. T	212. F
113. T	138. T	163. T	188. F	213. T
114. T	139. T	164. T	189. T	214. T
115. T	140. F	165. T	190. F	215. F
116. T	141. T	166. T	191. T	216. F
117. T	142. T	167. T	192. F	217. T
118. T	143. F	168. F	193. F	218. T
119. T	144. T	169. T	194. F	219. T
120. T	145. F	170. F	195. T	220. F

221. F	246. F	271. T	296. T	321. T
222. T	247. F	272. T	297. T	322. F
223. F	248. T	273. F	298. T	323. F
224. T	249. T	274. F	299. T	324. T
225. T	250. T	275. F	300. T	325. F
226. F	251. T	276. F	301. F	326. T
227. F	252. F	277. T	302. T	327. F
228. T	253. T	278. T	303. T	328. T
229. T	254. T	279. T	304. F	329. T
230. F	255. F	280. F	305. F	330. F
231. T	256. F	281. T	306. T	331. F
232. T	257. F	282. F	307. T	332. F
233. T	258. F	283. T	308. T	333. F
234. F	259. T	284. T	309. F	334. F
235. T	260. F	285. T	310. F	335. F
236. F	261. T	286. F	311. T	336. T
237. T	262. F	287. T	312. F	337. F
238. F	263. F	288. T	313. T	338. T
239. T	264. F	289. T	314. T	339. T
240. T	265. T	290. T	315. F	340. T
241. T	266. T	291. T	316. F	341. T
242. F	267. F	292. F	317. T	342. T
243. F	268. F	293. F	318. T	343. F
244. T	269. T	294. F	319. F	344. F
245. F	270. T	295. T	320. F	345. F

346. F	352. T	358. T	364. T	370. F
347. T	353. T	359. F	365. F	371. T
348. T	354. T	360. T	366. F	
349. T	355. T	361. T	367. F	
350. F	356. T	362. T	368. F	
351. F	357. T	363. T	369. F	